OUR WILD CALLING

ALSO BY RICHARD LOUV

Vitamin N

The Nature Principle

Last Child in the Woods

Fly-Fishing for Sharks

The Web of Life

FatherLove

101 Things You Can Do for Our Children's Future

Childhood's Future

America II

Our Wild Calling

How Connecting with Animals Can Transform Our Lives— and Save Theirs

RICHARD LOUV

ALGONQUIN BOOKS OF CHAPEL HILL 2019

Published by
ALGONQUIN BOOKS OF CHAPEL HILL
Post Office Box 2225
Chapel Hill, North Carolina 27515-2225

a division of
WORKMAN PUBLISHING
225 Varick Street
New York, New York 10014

Library of Congress Cataloging-in-Publication Data

Names: Louv, Richard, author.
Title: Our wild calling : how connecting with animals can
transform our lives—and save theirs / by Richard Louv.
Description: Chapel Hill : Algonquin Books of Chapel Hill, 2019. | Includes
bibliographical references and index. | Summary: "The author shows how cultivating
the powerful, mysterious, and fragile bond between humans and other animals
can improve our mental, physical, and spiritual health, protect our planet,
and serve as an antidote to the loneliness of our species"—Provided by publisher.
Identifiers: LCCN 2019019787 | ISBN 9781616205607 (hardcover)
Subjects: LCSH: Human-animal relationships. | Animals—
Therapeutic use. | Human-animal communication.
Classification: LCC QL85 .L68 2019 | DDC 615.8/5158—dc23
LC record available at https://lccn.loc.gov/2019019787

10 9 8 7 6 5 4 3 2 1
First Edition

To Kathy, Matthew, Jason, Mike, and all my other relations

With their parallel lives, animals offer man a companionship different from any offered by human exchange. Different because it is a companionship offered to the loneliness of man as a species.

—JOHN BERGER, *About Looking*

I looked about me once again, and suddenly the dancing horses without number changed into animals of every kind and into all the fowls that are, and these fled back to the four quarters of the world from whence the horses came, and vanished.

—BLACK ELK in *Black Elk Speaks*

CONTENTS

A Mystery

A few years ago, at an isolated camp on Alaska's Kodiak Island, I walked up a path through the woods at the edge of a still lake. I was heading to the main lodge to meet my son, who worked there during his college summers. The light was fading. Usually when I walked this path, I was watchful. On this island, massive brown bears often followed the shoreline, sometimes wandering into the camp. But on this evening, my eyes were down as I thumbed through the contents of my wallet.

When I glanced up, I was startled by two piercing eyes. They shone like stars.

A black fox stood three feet in front of me. The foxes on Kodiak are among the largest in the world. This one was the size of a coyote. Its gaze was disconcerting, and it wasn't budging. We stared at each other for what seemed like minutes but was probably only seconds. In those eyes I felt a distant kinship or perhaps only the suns of a parallel universe. The fox held perfectly still. Was it was anticipating food? Not likely. The lodge's policy was not to feed wild animals. Or was it rabid?

I stepped forward. The fox moved aside and continued to watch. I lifted my hand and said, "I'm going to the lodge. Would you like to come with me?"

Earlier that year, I had noticed how aquatic iguanas and sea lions basked within inches of each other on the volcanic ledges of the Galápagos Islands. When I asked a naturalist how each species perceived the other, he said, "To the iguana, the sea lion is just another part of the landscape. That's all." To the fox, then, was I just another part of the landscape?

The British writer, painter, and art critic John Berger, in his famous 1977 essay, "Why Look at Animals?," describes how a wild creature's gaze unnerves us by forcing us to see ourselves across an abyss through an unfamiliar lens. The fox followed me toward the building. Several yards from the door, it veered off and dissolved into high grass.

Today I recall few significant details about most of the people I met that summer in that Alaskan camp. But the black fox's eyes are still watching.

I often wonder about the quality and mystery of that encounter. Like many people, I had experienced similar moments, particularly as a boy, but had never really paused to think about their deeper nature.

During the following years, I have asked friends, colleagues, and strangers of different ages and cultures and professions—including scientists, psychologists, theologians, trackers, teachers, physicians, traditional healers, and one polar explorer—to describe their brief encounters and longer-term relationships with other animals, wild or domestic. Everyone had a story to tell: the glance of a kestrel on a fence or a pigeon on a sidewalk never forgotten; a cat who curled on a chest, warmed the heart, and somehow provided deliverance from depression; a dog who parented a child; a sounding porpoise; a whale's eye; a stalking bear; a cougar at once there and not there. Even a protozoan, trembling beneath the lens, revealed openings to other worlds and to what I've come to call the habitat of the heart. The storytellers were often surprised by the meaning they discovered in their own tales. But that act of telling was part of the process of knowing, one that our ancestors would recognize.

There are at least two good reasons for further exploration of our personal relationships with other animals. One is human health and well-being. Since 2005, the number of studies indicating the psychological, physical, and cognitive benefits of nature experience has grown from a relative handful to nearly a thousand. Most of these studies have focused on the general impact of green nature in our lives—for example, how the proximity of trees can help reduce the symptoms of attention-deficit disorder in children. Today, researchers—including those within the traditional disciplines of biology and ecology and also those working in the relatively new and exciting fields of anthrozoology, ecopsychology, and animal-assisted therapy—are exploring the evolving relationship between humans and other animals. These studies reveal what Indigenous people have known all along. Though an encounter with any animal, wild or domestic, can sometimes be dangerous, our relationships with other-than-human beings can also have a profoundly positive impact on our health, our spirit, and our sense of inclusiveness in the world.

A second reason centers on the current condition of the natural world. In her Pulitzer Prize–winning book, *The Sixth Extinction*, science writer Elizabeth Kolbert describes the five mass extinctions during the past billion years and interviews the scientists monitoring the sixth extinction, which some predict will be the largest since the time of dinosaurs. Between 1970 and 2014, the global wildlife population shrank by 60 percent, according to the World Wildlife Fund.

To a species so familiar with the corrective features of Photoshop, the threat seems impersonal and unreal. In 2016, a year after Kolbert's book was published, the electronic gaming magazine *ZAM* reported that the "explorers" of a self-generated universe depicted in the online game *No Man's Sky* had discovered ten million virtual species in the first twenty-four hours after the game's release. Creating or discovering new species seems easy in the imaginative space of a video game. Taking action in the physical world will require a more demanding leap of imagination, a journey into the habitat of the heart. By that, I mean that reversing or slowing biodiversity collapse and climate change cannot be accomplished solely through science, technology, or politics. We have much of the information we need already. Success will require a far larger constituency than what exists today, one with greater emotional and spiritual connection to the family of animals, recognizing in all nature the "inescapable network of mutuality" that Martin Luther King Jr. called for among human beings.

I'd like to think that the fox knew what it was doing that day. Its gaze snapped me awake to what I was already dreaming. It suggested a path.

Or perhaps I was just in its way, and it was telling me to pay attention.

Oceanographer Paul Dayton telling his
grandchildren the octopus's story

PART ONE

Beautiful Acts

Life-Changing Encounters with Species Not Our Own

And only then, when I have learned enough,
I will go to watch the animals, and let
something of their composure slowly glide
into my limbs; will see my own existence
deep in their eyes....

—RAINER MARIA RILKE, "Requiem for a Friend"

ONE

In the Family of Animals

Right now, my wife, Kathy, and I are living temporarily in an old stone cottage in the Cuyamaca Mountains sixty miles east of San Diego. The house's twenty-nine-inch-thick walls were quarried from the site; at the end of the nineteenth century, the structure was an apple storage barn, and in the 1940s it was converted into a house.

The cottage once belonged to the late Scott O'Dell and his wife, Dorsa. O'Dell wrote *Island of the Blue Dolphins* here. Based on a real event, the novel tells the story of an Indigenous girl who lived for years stranded and alone with her dog on an island off the California coast. The book became one of the classics in young adult literature. After they divorced and Scott moved away, Dorsa continued to live in the cottage with her dogs. Up until her death at age ninety-six, she was known in nearby Julian, population fifteen hundred, for her feisty political views and her support for local artists, whose work and art, much of it devoted to the animal life in these mountains, decorates this book-filled home known as Stoneapple Farm. Kathy likens it to Snow White's cottage.

Now, in the early morning hours and toward dusk, a flock of wild turkeys pokes and scratches and moves like an extra shadow through the live oaks and pear trees. Four mule deer arrive. They dip their heads to grass that has survived a long drought. One of the deer, a doe, limps. Two red-tailed hawks circle. One of them is particularly vocal, repeating plaintive cries to its mother, who is training it. An acorn woodpecker with his bright red helmet knocks on the woody parts of the cottage. I answer the woodpecker's knock by pounding my fist on the inner wall. The woodpecker squawks what sounds like a four-letter word, then goes silent. When our sons visit, Jason, the older one, calls this a "neighborhood of animals."

I have bonded with the barn cat on the property, who each morning brings us exactly one gopher head and, placed carefully two inches from the head, the gopher's innards. Yesterday at dusk, I stepped in the latest gifted gut sack. In bare feet. This is not the kind of animal connection I currently have in mind.

At sunset, I walk alone a few miles along the narrow roads through the mountains and long stretches of brown grass. The fields and hills of oak darken. I watch the red strip over the distant Pacific fade. Bats flick through branches. On the darkening road, I meet a mother and her daughter dragging a deer's leg. It's a long story, the mother says.

Back at Stoneapple, I sit outside with the cat on my lap and stare up at the handwriting of the Milky Way. The cat looks up, too, then to the side and down. Later Kathy and I can hear thumping and skittering in the walls and attic. Squirrels, wood rats, mice, or raccoons from the neighborhood of animals.

In the morning, the property's handyman arrives to plug entry holes and set live traps. As he packs up his tools, he asks me what I am working on. I tell him about this book. The handyman pushes his ball cap back on his head and says, "Yeah, I sometimes kind of think about animals as omens. I was driving up Pine Hills Road and this golden eagle swoops down right in front of my car, and I think, 'Yup, that's an omen of good things to come.' Couple weeks later, I get the license to open my video store up there in Julian." The handyman's tale is an offhand remark. He didn't consider it particularly unusual, just something that happens in everyday life. No big deal. But still.

When some people talk about their spiritual relationships with animals, it can be mildly off-putting. What if a person has never had a spiritual experience in nature? Such a story can be "alienating because it might sound so far out, hippie and silly," says Mollie Matteson, a practical wildlife biologist. Or because it is told to cast an air of specialness on the storyteller. Or it suggests that an experience with another animal must be larger than life: a bird in a burning bush, an encounter with a four-legged deity on the road to Yellowstone. Matteson has a point. Then she too admitted to a profound experience of her own, with bats—actually, the bones of a bat. That story, which I share with you later, redirected her career and life.

This afternoon, I'm staring at the ground squirrels from the kitchen window. They dig their burrows under large slabs of granite that have been smoothed by wind and water and the feet of deer and long-ago Kumeyaay and present-day suburbanites from San Diego. Young or old, the squirrels scurry across the rocks, dip into holes, pop up from the leaves, do their work, talk their squirrel talk, and walk their squirrel walk, always vigilant. Their pups bounce, jump, and wrestle, filled with what seems like teasing humor. They remind me of my sons when they were small and how Jason and Matthew, now men, still grapple playfully in the first hours of a visit with their parents.

I realize in this moment that I have never really *seen* ground squirrels. I had looked but dismissed them as poor excuses for squirrelness. But here they became personal. I Googled them (of course) and learned that California ground squirrels lead a complex life. They try to protect themselves from their nemesis, the rattlesnake, not only with watchfulness and conversation but also by chewing shed snakeskins and licking the scent onto their fur. Then they lick the bodies of their pups, passing along the chemicals that may provide some protection. The wiry, common little ground squirrels enrich my day. I find them to be beautiful.

For years, Jan van Boeckel, a Dutch artist and naturalist, has argued that science and the environmental movement need art and heart, that without a commitment to beauty both are diminished—and so is morality. Recently he wrote to me about the work of Norwegian ecophilosopher Arne Naess. Following Immanuel Kant, Naess makes a distinction between a beautiful act and a moral act. When people fulfill a moral obligation, they often feel compelled to go against their own inclinations, against what they would normally want to do. "A beautiful act, in contrast, is an act where one acts *with* one's inclinations; one acts in a moral way because that is what one wants to do," wrote Van Boeckel. "We can learn to identify with other humans, with animals and plants and even ecosystems. This takes a process of spiritual and psychological maturation. By thus identifying with the earth, we want to protect it and by doing so we are actually not acting against our deepest inclinations." The desire to act beautifully—rather than merely morally—is something that can be nurtured at a very early age. It is, he continued, "a way to go forward for the environmental movement." And, setting politics aside, for all our relationships.

To fully protect anything, we must know it, love it, act in mindful reciprocity—giving back to animals as they give to us. Engaging with animals and then telling our stories of these encounters can be beautiful acts. Our future with other animals and each other, as individuals and within society, are in fact shaped by the stories we tell. They can offer redemption and hope if the heart is generous. In our everyday lives and in our organizational and civic policies, we can choose empathy over separation or superiority. We can take strange comfort in the knowledge that zebra finches experience REM sleep, that dolphins recognize themselves in mirrors, that our early ancestors may have been domesticated by wolves.

Through critical anthropomorphism, a process explored in more detail in chapter 5, we can *become* the bear from that wild world. We can be mindful of every experience with animals, even in the most densely populated cities, and by doing so begin to imagine a different future for the children of all species. We can learn from the wisdom of our pets and the languages of birds and be touched by the mystery of the wild animals that pass through our neighborhoods at twilight; we can choose to go forward to nature while combining new technologies, "biophilic design" (which incorporates natural elements into our built environment), and the rest of contemporary science with ways of knowing that are older than humankind. We can create places of healing for our own and other species. We can share all this with the young and with children who might otherwise never hear the profound near-silence of an owl's wings in flight.

Through these beautiful acts and the stories we tell, each of us can experience a deeper connection to our own lives and then give thanks. The poet Mary Oliver writes:

> Whoever you are, no matter how lonely,
> the world offers itself to your imagination,
> calls to you like the wild geese, harsh and exciting—
> over and over announcing your place
> in the family of things.

A few days ago, I heard from my friend Anne Pearse Hocker: "I have wanted to ask you for a while, why don't you and Kathy have pets?"

We did have pets for most of our lives, but two final trips to the vet, for Rex the wonderdog and Binkley the cat, were two too many. Then, when Kathy's mother was dying, that caregiving consumed her for a long while. Now, however, we're thinking about pets again—or companion animals, as some people prefer to call them. Anne wrote back encouragingly:

> Even with a travel schedule, a couple of rescue cats would fare just fine. They need "staff" more than constant interaction. I hope your cat or dog (or both) finds you. Adopting a rescue animal saves two souls, usually. I have rearranged my life to accommodate the critters who share it. But I'm kind of a nutcase for animals. They die young, in our terms. But their lives are still rich and meaningful if we let them have the chance.
>
> If you are going to be away a lot, I'd suggest you adopt two animals, so they have each other. I adopted two who had been given up when their owner went into a nursing home. The easiest adoption I've ever done was my thirteen-year-old black Lab rescue from Idaho, Old Bob. Nobody wanted a thirteen-year-old Lab. Bob fits in like he's been with me all his life, and for whatever time he has left, he is having fun, chasing balls and patrolling the perimeter. He was already trained, mellow, grateful, and sweet. His teeth are awful, but everything else seems to be working. He will not spend his final months or years in a shelter wondering what the hell happened.

In kind, loving, conflicted ways, people are reaching out to animals, our fellow travelers. Around the world, good-hearted people are becoming the New Noahs, creating new habitats for wild animals or operating rescue centers for abused dogs and birds with broken wings. As animals save us, we discover new ways to save animals. The Book Buddies program of the Animal Rescue League of Berks County, Pennsylvania, for example, invites children to visit the shelter and read to cats waiting for adoption. This helps the children practice reading and offers the cats affection while they wait. Simple. Effective. Literacy and empathy are surely related. As we include more of Earth's creatures in our lives, the definition of family grows richer. I'm thinking of two older women in our former neighborhood who have lost their spouses and are living alone. Each of them rescued a dog from the pound and cannot imagine life without them.

Consider again my friend Anne. She has lived a life of adventure and conflict and loss. She has experienced the world through innumerable prisms, often through the senses of other animals and people who touch her heart. In 1974, she talked her way into the American Indian Movement's church occupation at Wounded Knee in South Dakota (the site of the 1890 massacre of three hundred Lakota by the U.S. Cavalry) and brought her camera. Her photos of the occupation are now housed in the Smithsonian. She later became a news photographer for national TV networks, married a country doctor, moved to the mountains of Virginia, and became a wildlife rescuer. She remembered:

> I would be up all night bottle-feeding orphaned infant squirrels, doing my best to be a surrogate mom and worrying about them when they were old enough to release. Taking care of injured wildlife took me from a life of TV journalism, where I always had a bag packed and my passport current, to analyzing the protein composition of various wild mammals' milk and facing a constant chore list of cages to clean. I knew I had crossed the divide when CNN called me to be part of an all-woman crew for a trip, and I hesitated a second, looking at the four baby fox cubs someone had just brought me as the only licensed wildlife rehabilitator in the area, and I told the caller that I was booked and gave them the name of my fiercest competitor to call. Never heard from them again.

Anne continued to care for injured animals, including an old red-tailed hawk with deteriorating vision, possibly a released falconry bird. "Had I followed the regulations to the letter, I would have been forced to have her euthanized," she wrote. "I chose instead to let her live out her days in a covered flight pen in the woods next to the house, surrounded by the sounds of nature with which she was familiar. She learned to know my voice and touch and would eat unencumbered off my fist." From falconers in the area, Anne also learned about the ancient art of hunting with trained birds of prey. She tenderly cared for the old hawk until it died of old age, after which she went through the lengthy training and regulatory process to become a falconer.

She understands the moral objections many people have to hunting, but she does not agree with all of them, particularly when related to falconry. "Hunting with a raptor for its food took me from being an observer of the surrounding habitat to active participant in the daily life of animals," she said. She explored the woods in the surrounding region with a mission, taking mental inventory of who lived where. Finding fields where her hawk could hunt rabbits or squirrels became a consuming journey, and when some of those fields were bulldozed for a strip mall, the rabbit nests, fox dens, and old oaks with squirrel nests felt like a personal loss. "I had seen how hard these animals had worked to stay alive. And when the dozers and chain saws arrived, it was game over for them."

Not long afterward, widowed and in her sixties, Anne left Virginia and roamed the western states in an Airstream trailer with the companionship of two falcons, two old dogs, two rescue cats, and a very nervous pigeon named Pauline. They are her family now.

TWO

The Aching Heart

The cacophony and distraction of modern times make it difficult to experience life fully. Bleating car alarms, grinding leaf blowers, and the nearby freeway interrupt sleep, thinking, emotions, and conversations. Social media does have certain charms and in some cases brings us together. But for many people, electronic connection is metastasizing into electronic *overconnection*, overwhelming our capacity for patience, interrupting the focus required to build real-time relationships, and herding people into unforgiving political tribes.

This state of constant interruption began long before the internet or power tools were invented. In 1802, the English Romantic poet William Wordsworth composed a sonnet titled "The World Is Too Much with Us," in which he blames the Industrial Revolution for substituting our connections with nature with the dissipations of materialism:

> The world is too much with us; late and soon,
> Getting and spending, we lay waste our powers;
> Little we see in Nature that is ours;
> We have given our hearts away, a sordid boon!
> This Sea that bares her bosom to the moon,
> The winds that will be howling at all hours,
> And are up-gathered now like sleeping flowers,
> For this, for everything, we are out of tune;
> It moves us not. . . .

In the so-called information age,* humans are even more out of tune. As during the First Industrial Revolution, technology is a primary suspect, but not the only one. A thirteen-year-old girl told me once that she was tired of hearing people say that technology is ruining children, insisting instead, "*Children* are ruining technology." Only a teenager could say such a thing with such authority. But she had a point: digital tools do not kill souls; people do, with a little help from their gadgets.

Nonetheless, a perfect storm of digital distraction, fear of strangers, poor urban design, competitive overscheduling, and economic insecurity does tend to separate us from one another and the natural world. As a result, alarming new research suggests the growth of what some health officials call an epidemic of loneliness. Epidemic may be an exaggeration (and creativity often depends on solitude), but as former U.S. surgeon general Vivek H. Murthy writes, "We live in the most technologically connected age in the history of civilization, yet rates of loneliness have doubled since the 1980s."

A 2006 study by the University of Arizona and Duke University revealed that surveyed Americans had a third fewer close friends and confidants than they did two years earlier, and the number of people who had no friends more than doubled during that time. In a 2010 survey on loneliness, AARP estimated that 42.6 million American adults over age forty-five suffer from chronic loneliness. According to recent census data, more than a quarter of the U.S. population lives alone, over half are unmarried, and marriage rates and number of children per household have declined. Of course, solitude or singlehood does not automatically indicate social isolation, and many adults would argue that being single can be less isolating than living in a dysfunctional nuclear family. But the *Economist* reports that in Britain "half a million people regularly go up to a week without seeing anybody." In 2017, at the 125th annual convention of the American Psychological Association, Julianne Holt-Lunstad, professor of psychology at Brigham Young University, presented an analysis of 148 U.S. studies showing that greater social connection can reduce the chance of early death by 50 percent. A second review of 3.4 million people in North America, Europe, Asia,

---

* Or, rather, the disappearing information age, as all magnetic media degrade over time. Old-fashioned acid-free paper remains the trustworthy, long-term storage medium.

and Australia, found that isolation, loneliness, and living alone were equal to or exceeded other well-accepted risk factors such as obesity for early death.

The findings of other research are particularly disturbing. Psychologist Jean Twenge at San Diego State University found that people who spend more time in front of screens and less time in face-to-face social interactions are more vulnerable to depression and suicide. A 2018 generational study by Cigna, the global health insurance company, surveyed 20,000 U.S. adults and concluded that each generation, oldest to youngest—from the Greatest Generation to boomers to millennials to Generation Z—is more socially isolated, with the Greatest Gen the least lonely and Gen Z the loneliest. It's possible that older people are more likely to minimize their feelings and younger people are more likely to reveal them, but these findings challenge the traditional assumption that social isolation is experienced most acutely by the oldest generation. No generation should feel isolated. But what does it say about the direction of society when the younger adults are, the lonelier they may feel?

Species Loneliness

At the same moment that social interactions among people are becoming more digital and less personal, there is an isolation of another kind forming: *species* loneliness—the gnawing fear that we are alone in the universe with a desperate hunger for connection with other life. Believers in a personal God may feel they are not alone, and yet as we move away from nature, they too sense an absence. All of us are meant to live in a larger community, an extended family of other species.

The term *species loneliness* was introduced in a 1993 article in *Environmental Ethics* by Michael Vincent McGinnis, an author and editor of books about ecology and bioregionalism. Nearly two decades later, he writes, "Species loneliness in a wounded landscape moves us to want to restore our relationship with place and others, or to put it another way, modern humanity yearns to reestablish and restore an ecology of shared identity." An individual or family cut off from positive social contacts with other people is more vulnerable to alcoholism, depression, bullying, and abuse and is more easily controlled. Cult leaders understand this too well. Likewise, our species' vulnerability to all manner of pathologies grows with our distancing from other species. Without contact with other-than-human kith and kin, the family of humans loses comfort, companionship, and perhaps even the sense of a higher power, however one defines it.

This hypothesis is supported by over a decade of research showing the positive impacts of nature connection on individual human health and cognition, as well as the health of communities. This body of research is relatively new, and proponents of a new nature movement are taking it to heart. An increasing number of physicians—particularly pediatricians and psychologists—are no longer satisfied that pharmaceuticals and traditional counseling alone can reverse the social isolation, depression, and substance abuse experienced by so many people, especially young people. Some now write "nature prescriptions" to encourage families to spend more time outdoors, preferably in a natural setting. Parks with the most biodiversity have the greatest beneficial impact on human psychological health. While green spaces can bring joy and reduce our stress, a deep connection to other animals has a special power to deliver us from our isolation, both as individuals and as a species. To a degree, some people are self-medicating with animals. Consider the dramatic growth in much of the Western world in the number of pets and the industries that surround them. Over the past decade in the United States, the growth in pet ownership has outpaced total household growth. Younger generations lead the pack: eighteen- to thirty-four-year-olds are the most likely to own a pet—and of young adults who don't have a pet, a whopping 43 percent say they want one in the future.

One might ask: If our pet population is growing, why would someone need more contact with wild animals? Companion animals differ from us in ways that are easy to forget, and we tend to perceive them as part of our immediate family. To assume that pets and other domestic animals alone can fill the void of our species loneliness is like saying the only human social contacts we require are within our own nuclear family—that we don't need our extended family, friends, or neighbors. The truth is, we humans need all the other-than-human friends we can get.

Like wind in advance of a storm, the approaching choices offer danger and possibility.

Identifying the names of geologic periods can be tricky, but the most generally accepted version holds that the current epoch began at the end of the Paleolithic Ice Age, when Earth warmed and the world's human population began to expand rapidly, leading to ten thousand to twelve thousand years of human development, including the rise of civilizations. In 2000, atmospheric chemist Paul Crutzen, among others, focused public attention on human activities that had become so powerful a force that we now shape the very systems and conditions that regulate life on our planet. Scientists can point to empirical evidence: half the world's large rivers are dammed; 20 percent of our planetary landmass is used for agriculture; our plastics, and their derivatives, permeate nearly every living thing; our carbon pollution is largely responsible for the rapidity of climate change*; our habitat destruction contributes to biodiversity collapse and ongoing mass extinctions. Perhaps 95 percent of the land-based vertebrate biomass is made up of pets and livestock living in human-created monocultures.

American biologist and researcher Eugene Stoermer came up with the term "Anthropocene" to define an age of human domination, and Crutzen brought it to public attention, beginning with a conference in 2000. In 2015, a working group of the International Commission on Stratigraphy—the largest and oldest scientific body within the International Union of Geological Sciences—formally recommended that the commission declare the end of the Holocene epoch and the beginning of the Anthropocene epoch, and this was endorsed in 2016 by the Anthropocene Working Group of the International Union of Geological Sciences, but the official determination has, at this writing, not been made. Nonetheless, Crutzen and many other scientists believe the planet has already transitioned into the Anthropocene—with suggested starting points ranging from the beginning of the First Agricultural Revolution thousands of years ago to the first detonation of a nuclear weapon in 1945. Harvard professor E. O. Wilson imagines the logical conclusion of the Anthropocene as a planet on which only people, agriculture, and domesticated animals remain. "Will we stop the destruction for the sake of future generations," he asks, "or go on changing the planet to our immediate needs? If the latter, planet Earth will enter a

---

* Climate change terminology is fluid. In 2019, the *Guardian* newspaper replaced "climate change" with "climate emergency" and "global heating" in its stylebook. Other terms are also used, depending on context, including "climate breakdown" and "climate disruption." Currently "climate change" remains the most commonly used term.

new era of its history . . . time for and all about our one species alone." He refers to that interpretation of the Anthropocene as the age of loneliness.

But wait, isn't there a more aspirational way to think about the next epoch?

The late Thomas Berry, a Catholic priest whom in 1989 *Newsweek* called "the most provocative figure among the new breed of eco-theologians," often used the word *communion* to describe what he considered our connection with the divine in nature: "The universe is a communion of subjects, not a collection of objects." An object can be owned, abused, or thrown away; a subject, by his definition, is not inferior to other subjects and can have rights. In this spirit, he proposed an alternative age. Rather than an age when humans assume total control of nature, he offered the "Ecozoic era," a geologic era of mutualism in which humans use both technology and spirituality to live in harmony with nature.*

Similarly, the Australian ecophilosopher Glenn Albrecht argues for a new epoch that he says should be called the "Symbiocene" (from the Greek *symbiosis*, or "companionship"). He introduced this concept in 2011 "as an almost instinctive reaction against the very idea of the Anthropocene." The scientific interpretation of the word *symbiosis* "implies living together for mutual benefit. . . . As a core aspect of ecological and evolutionary thinking symbiosis, and its associated symbiogenesis, affirms the interconnectedness of life and all living things."

Though they use different terms, Berry and Albrecht point in the same direction: away from an age of loneliness and toward an age of connectedness.

An Altered View of Human Exceptionalism

To compress the almost incomprehensible enormity of life into easier-to-digest pieces, we tell ourselves stories. Nearly every society's origin myth—its primary story and the ongoing mythology that follows—features

---

* The concept of the Ecozoic era was developed by Brian Swimme and Thomas Berry in their coauthored *The Universe Story from the Primordial Flaring Forth to the Ecozoic Era: A Celebration of the Unfolding of the Cosmos* (San Francisco: HarperSanFrancisco, 1992) to describe a geologic era in which humans once again live in a mutually enhancing relationship with Earth and the Earth community but using new tools and a higher power to get there. "What Does Ecozoic Mean?," Ecozoic Times, ecozoictimes.com/what-is-the-ecozoic/what-does-ecozoic-mean/.

animals in starring roles, including talking animals. This is because they have something to say to us, or at least we think they do.

In distant ancestral time, writes John Berger, "animals constituted the first circle of what surrounded man.... Animals first entered the imagination as messengers and promises." They continue to live in our imagination, a territory easily forgotten or unacknowledged. In today's contrasting era of algorithms, life is tested, sorted, branded, and polled; experience is reduced to that which can be counted at the most basic level. The habitat of the wild heart defies numerical measurement and so goes undervalued—or demands a different system of value.

For centuries, at least within circles of industrial power, the dominant cultural and sometimes scientific frame for nature has been reductionist, mechanistic, and exploitative. However, today a new generation of researchers, therapists, and educators is challenging human exceptionalism. As toolmakers and communicators, we once thought of our species as sole proprietors of planet Earth. No longer. Humans are still generally considered fundamentally different from other animals—in that a wolf does what a wolf does while a human makes moral or intellectual choices of a different order. But even those distinctions are being questioned.

We humans are not the only story. Intelligent life populated Earth long before we came on the scene. Now we know that humans and whales share specialized neurons associated with higher cognitive functions, including self-awareness and compassion, and that these neurons may have developed in parallel. These neurons bloomed in whales thirty million years before our own. Long before Genghis Khan or René Descartes walked the earth, dolphins were conversing and communing.

Interest in the powerful and mysterious bond between humans and other animals is expanding. So is the research. A relatively new multidisciplinary subset of ethnobiology called human-animal interactions, or anthrozoology, also known as human–nonhuman animal studies (HAS), is cutting new trails at the forward edge of this frontier. HAS spans several disciplines, including social sciences such as social work, sociology, anthropology, psychology, and political science as well as veterinary medicine, zoology, and other natural sciences. It focuses on the development of an expanding consciousness of the beneficial and detrimental relationships between humans and other animals. As environmental philosopher David Abram puts it, some people are defying the dehumanizing aspects of modern time by "becoming animal," pursuing an integration with what he calls the "greater than human" world. Researchers are deepening our understanding of interspecies and extraspecies communication, and the coevolution of humans with other species. They also study animal intelligence, zoonotic diseases (passed between humans and other animals), and how human settlements can be integrated with other life.

It's true that some people still believe we are at war with the rest of nature. They point to the "invasion" of raccoons and deer and coyotes in our cities; or, from another side of the battlefield, factory farming or the destruction of biodiversity. And yet other people are becoming gentler with the animals around them.

In 2016, a research team led by Kelly A. George of Ohio State University updated groundbreaking research done nearly four decades earlier by ecologist Stephen Kellert. Kellert had examined American attitudes toward nature, and George's work revealed substantial and unexpected societal change since that 1978 survey. The work of George and his team detected what appeared to be growing public concern for the welfare of both wild and domestic animals. Why? Writer Brandon Keim offers a possible explanation of the study's findings in the journal *Conservation*, in an article with a surprising title: "America Is Becoming a Kinder, Gentler Place (toward Animals, Anyway)." Since Kellert's earlier survey, "the loss of biodiversity has accelerated," Keim notes, citing George's study. At the same time, he adds, "the science of animal cognition has produced overwhelming evidence for intelligence" within the animal world. Partially as a result, animal-welfare issues have moved into the culture's mainstream awareness, "people in the U.S. generally feel more kindly toward wild animals," and attitudes have improved most toward "historically stigmatized species" [, including] sharks, bats, vultures, wolves, and coyotes." He adds, "The only species whose reputations dropped substantively are raccoons and swans, though people still quite like them."

Perhaps the most powerful factor is human loneliness and, undergirding that, our species loneliness. People once lived closely with other animals, but over the centuries and particularly in the past half century, people withdrew from contact with wildlife and farm animals. As our lives become more technological and fearful, we adopt more pets and pull them closer. And yet we still feel drawn to the wild ones. Now something is turning. Chickens, ducks, and goats are returning to backyards. Our disconnection from other humans and other species fuels the growing use of animal-assisted therapy to help people with mental and physical disabilities. And as if called, wild animals are appearing in our suburbs and cities in unprecedented numbers. This new proximity is driven by development patterns and the rule-changing forces of climate disruption. New rules present dangers to both people and to other animals. They also offer new opportunities to rediscover our lost intimacy with the living world, including our fellow humans. In the darkness at the edge of town, or even next door, wild animals begin to change in fascinating ways. So do we.

THREE

The Mind-Altering Power of Deep Animal Connection

One morning Lisa Donahue walked into her dining room and saw her six-year-old son, Aidan, and their large retriever, Jack, stretched out together on the dining room carpet. Both were facing away from Donahue. The boy was stroking the dog's side. Then she heard her son say quietly, matter-of-factly, "Mommy, I don't have a heart anymore."

Startled, she asked her son what he meant.

"My heart is in Jack."

She watched them for a while, in the silence and peace.

This permeability of the heart (or soul or spirit or neurological connection) occurs naturally when we're very young. Some people continue to experience it throughout their life, though they may have no words to describe it. They experience it with their companion animals and, if receptive and given a chance, with wild animals, too.

Each animal we encounter has the potential to become part of us or part of who we could become. If we meet them halfway.

Indigenous traditions are fully accustomed to this approach to physical and spiritual existence. The American transcendentalists of the nineteenth century also saw the divine in nature. That movement's leader, Ralph Waldo Emerson, wrote of the "great nature in which we rest, as the earth lies in the soft arms of the atmosphere; that Unity, that Over-soul, within which every man's particular being is contained and made one with all other; that common heart."

More recently, nature essayist Barry Lopez, in "A Literature of Place," wrote, "If you're intimate with a place, a place with whose history you're familiar, and you establish an ethical conversation with it, the implication that follows is this: the place knows you're there. It feels you. You will not be forgotten, cut off, abandoned." Our attachment to the natural world is "a fundamental human defense against loneliness." Lopez was primarily describing the ways land shapes our inner landscape. Animals, wild and domestic, also do this.

Habitat of the Heart

We live in fragile worlds. Two are familiar. The first world is the outer habitat of land, air, water, and flesh, the one that supports biological needs of humans and other animals. The second world is our highly individualized and private inner life.

Then there is a mysterious third world, the shared habitat of the heart. This is the deep connection between a person and another animal. It is the permeability of empathy. It is the connection that extends from within us, across the mysterious *between*, and into the other being. If we're lucky, we feel something almost indescribable in return. We can learn to enter this habitat at will. This transportive leap can change our lives and the lives around us for the better.

These definitions are imprecise, not an exact map but more of a metaphorical guide to thinking about our relationship with the natural world. The naturalness of this border-defying communion, as Aidan experienced with his dog, tends to fade when childhood ends. A teenager, before the demands and realism of adulthood set in, may still yearn for such encounters, even subconsciously. What if more young people experienced such transcendent, mind-altering encounters with urban birds or suburban coyotes or a rescue dog? Might a so-called at-risk teenager—or any of us—experiencing such a rite of passage set out on a different path to the future?

A few years ago, I had coffee with my friend Scott Reed at a local bookstore. By profession, Scott builds relationships. He works as a community organizer, often through churches, in poor neighborhoods around the United States. Scott is fascinated by transformative encounters. Paraphrasing twentieth-century German Jewish religious philosopher Martin Buber, Scott said, "The soul is over there—not in heart or head. But over there." Buber's mysticism focuses on the encounter and dialogue between humans:

"When two people relate to each other authentically and humanly, God is the electricity that surges between them."

"This is what Buber called the sacredness of the 'I-Thou' relationship," Scott explained. "The divine is in you as well as me, and you discover it in relationship."

The I-Thou relationship is quite different from the more common "I-It" relationship, which is based on what one can get from another person. In his famous 1923 essay, "Ich und Du," Buber writes, "No purpose intervenes between I and You, no greed and no anticipation; and longing itself is changed as it plunges from the dream into appearance." Buber is primarily focused on the power of relationship between human beings and between humans and a Western definition of God. But his description of the I-Thou relationship might also be applied to the relationship between a human and a member of another species.

Recently diagnosed with aggressive stage 3 cancer, Scott continues to work and travel. He described how one evening when he'd returned from a long trip, even before his family could welcome him, his large dog leaped up and did what he had never done: pushed Scott back and held him, wouldn't let him go. "What *was* that?" he asked. He felt it was something older and larger than recognition or affection. "That relationship is in the web of life I sense when I'm in nature. My breathing is easier there, the oxygen is plentiful, the smell of the leaves, the breath of life—all of it is connected."

We finished our coffee and stood up to leave.

"How do you articulate such a mystery?" he pondered aloud. "The philosopher [Kurt] Gödel has written about the 'incompleteness theory,' that in any system there are truths that cannot be proven. That's what you're getting into when you try to name the essence of divine relationship. Trying to show something that all the evidence points to but still can't be proved. This is familiar to those of us who are convinced that there is a mystery beyond us."

This essential connection or communion with other creatures—this habitat of the heart—is fragile. It needs nourishment to survive, as do they and we.

The heart is a useful metaphor, and perhaps more. An emerging area of neurological inquiry suggests that the heart is a mindful muscle; it resides in a complex physiological part of our body where we feel emotions in ways not yet fully understood. Living more in the moment, as other animals likely do, we are more mindful—more *heartful*. The heart—in reality or as metaphor—does not exist in isolation. It exists in its own habitat, which contains it but extends beyond self-awareness to other hearts.

In other contexts, this space of connection goes by other names. In the arts, the word *lacuna* describes the seemingly empty but powerful space in a story; in music, it is the pause or passage in which no notes are played, allowing the listener to feel or project meaning.

Michelle Brenner, a pioneering conflict manager in Australia, prefers the word *liminality*, a concept developed in the early twentieth century to describe the threshold stage between a previous and a new way of perceiving one's identity—sometimes referring to the between stage in an initiation. "In some cultures," she writes, "the liminal space is seen as sacred, to be respected and is holy, something 'out of this world.' . . . In other cultures, it creates anxious uncertainty, fear and disapproval." This betweenness can be found everywhere in nature: between the seasons, at the river's edge, between bioregions, at the borders of things, between two living beings, and, in Brenner's words, in "the undecided moments when we are neither here nor there."

The liminal space is where relationship occurs, where it breaks and can be healed. When Brenner applies the concept to conflict resolution, she describes this space as not fixed. It can be created, it can morph, and it can be perceived as a safe place for curiosity and repair. "In fact," she argues, "it is this very state that is required for relationships to shift, raising questions such as are we still enemies, or are we now turning towards repairing and reconstructing trust?"

There are as many descriptions of the place of connection as there are cultures, including especially those of Indigenous peoples. It is at once strange and familiar.

In human relations, love alters reality. We go mad with love. *Limerence* is the word for that. The chemical reaction that accompanies human love is measurable but defies full explanation. So it is with our deepest bond with other animals.

A friend who spends most of her waking hours in New York City once told me about an encounter with a pigeon—"a *pigeon*!" she emphasized—that left her speechless. As she walked to work, she passed the bird on the sidewalk. They looked at each other, and she felt "transported." She used that word. *Transported.* My friend is not a person inclined to seek a shift in consciousness, but there she was on the sidewalk, with that pigeon. In that moment she felt inexplicably touched, elevated. She felt as if she had entered that bird's world, and it had entered hers.

"It's like an *altered state*. But without drugs," she said.

And unlike drugs, it's generally free of charge, and with no known negative side effects. Depending on the animal.

The Land of Giant Ants, an Unexpected Urchin, and a Moving Protozoan

In "Why Look at Animals?," John Berger observes that the animal scrutinizes the human, and the human sees the animal, even if the animal is domesticated, "across a similar, but not identical, abyss of non-comprehension," of ignorance and fear. "And so, when he is being seen by the animal, he is being seen as his surroundings are seen by him. His recognition of this is what makes the look of the animal familiar. And yet the animal is distinct, and can never be confused with man. Thus, a power is ascribed to the animal, comparable with human power but never coinciding with it."

Some have argued that the human gaze across that divide disrupts the world of the other animal, harms it. Surely, in many cases, that does occur. But here's another possibility: when two creatures, one of them human, meet each other halfway across the abyss, both enter a world of potential.

Writer Jay Griffiths studied English literature at Oxford University; spent years living in a shed on the outskirts of Epping Forest, a former royal forest on the border between northeast London and Essex; and, to research her book *Wild*, journeyed among the Inuit people, spent time with Amazonian shamans, and researched other Indigenous cultures. She is now based in Wales. When I asked her about her most illuminating experience with another animal, she spoke of ants:

I once spent hours watching ants in my garden. It all began with a fleck of apple which fell to the ground, and one ant approached. It tried to move it and couldn't. Then another arrived, and they pushed and dragged at the little crumb. The more I watched, the more the scale of the world altered, as the tiny piece of apple started to look larger and larger to me, as I felt the effort of the ants to move it. More ants arrived, one climbing on top of the tiny bit of apple, almost as if it was directing proceedings, or just curious. They did, together, begin to move it, and the episode became a strangely intense time, as I realized that in the nature of deep concentration, I had lost track of time, but also that I had, in the end, utterly lost track of scale. After some long time, I suddenly looked up, and my garden (a tiny little plot of land) looked like a massive and endless forest.

For those gifted hours, Griffiths was released from ego. How many of us remember, when we were three or four, losing ourselves among the ants?

This suspension of time and scale often occurs amid peak experiences with other animals. At the time Griffiths was thirty-eight, though she felt as if she were eight. For her, the encounter not only stopped time but reversed it as well.

For generations, Siddharth Iyengar's family lived in Bangalore, India. Growing up as an urban child, he considered insects "just things to be avoided! Kitchens were always in constant battle against ants and cockroaches. Mosquitoes were a constant irritation while sleeping," he recalled. Later, as a biology graduate student in St. Paul, Minnesota, he awakened to the lives of insects. "We discussed how cockroaches will most certainly outlive human beings on this planet, even if we have a nuclear war. That gave me new respect for them, and I began to watch them instead of immediately trying to crush them."

Returning to India, he was taught by a friend to move slowly outdoors, to shift his focus from the birds, and to pay attention to what was just ahead of his feet. "The two of us were always the last in any hiking group." While doing fieldwork in a tropical rainforest in northeastern India, he and his friend would sit down to rest. "A dazzling variety of butterflies would settle on our socks, shirts and hats, feasting on the salt left from our sweat. I learned then to be absolutely still at the end of a long field day, sit quietly and let the butterflies slowly get comfortable and settle on me." All of this happened in slow motion. Like Griffiths, he learned that scale is the cousin of time. "It still humbles me, when I think about what I appear to be, in the perception of an insect."

Adriana Gonzalez told me about a similarly affecting experience. Born and raised in Lima, Peru, where she studied marine biology, she went to work for a marine conservation organization in 2012. One morning at a beach at Los Frailes, an Ecuadorian marine national park, she put on her mask and fins and headed to the deep blue water, determined to spend an entire day under the sea. Beneath the waves, colorful fish surrounded her. The bubbles above were, as she put it, "the only sight of airy Earth." She surfaced and a monarch butterfly hovered in front of her. Turning, she saw the green riparian forest in the distance. She dived to the bottom, where something grabbed her attention.

I swam straight to it. It was round, purplish and rosy with hundreds of little inquisitive tube feet. I was enthralled; I held this strange creature on my hand. I noticed hundreds of small and blunt spines.... With her tube feet, she was knowing me by touching every part of my sensitive fingers. It felt so good. She was massaging me. I was so mesmerized by her presence that I forgot that I was not a mermaid. I had to go up for air. Sadly, I said good-bye. But she didn't let me go. Her hundreds of tube feet suck hard and stubbornly at my skin. Finally, I nestled her at a nice spot at the bottom and said, 'Farewell beautiful strange thing!'

Some weeks after that, my old marine biologist mentor told me that this sea urchin was a poisonous species. The one I encountered had a hidden, stinging spear. But that day I never felt threatened.

Or was she simply lucky that she didn't give it a squeeze? Had Gonzales known the danger, she probably would have—and should have—avoided touching the sea urchin. She had never been interested in urchins before that dive, had in fact found them repellent. But because of what she brought to the moment, she discovered the animal's beauty and more. She felt a kinship with it, which may have been her own projection, or something shared beyond reason, but that matters less than the fact that her unexpected urchin has never left her.

Through a lens brightly, Rick Kool experienced a similar moment of enlightenment with a most unlikely creature. Kool is an associate professor in the School of Environment and Sustainability at Royal Roads University in Victoria, British Columbia. He combines brilliance with fun and a streak of the contrarian. He grew up in Boston, with a love of all living things. "But in truth, my feelings have never been really strong for anything with a backbone: vertebrates are overrated, and I've known that since I was little," he said when I interviewed him in 2015. "It is the beasts without backbones that have always grabbed my attention, and some of my most powerful teachers have had neither hair, fur, feathers, nor scales."

He was the first member of his working-class family to finish high school or go to college. His dream as an eighteen-year-old was to become a marine biologist. To help support his studies and finances, he looked for a work-study job, hoping for something better than stacking trays in the school cafeteria. That search took him to the lab of Arthur Borror, a zoology professor at the University of New Hampshire, who offered him his dream job. Borror studied the ecology of single-celled marine animals, "critters," as Kool put it, that ranged in size from around one-tenth to three-quarters of a millimeter. From Borror, Kool learned the skills of a microscopist and field researcher.

He spent long, immersive days out in the salt marshes of coastal New Hampshire collecting samples and bringing them back to the lab for study. "I loved the hours I spent investigating these tiny creatures," he recalled. But he didn't really get the connection that Borror had made with the protozoans until he had spent a year working with him. One day Borror introduced Kool to Roman Vishniac, "a wonderful Russian microscopist" famous for, among other things, returning the water from the ponds he studied back to the ponds. "Concerned about the needless loss of life amongst those little tiny creatures, he returned them, after study, to their native habitat." To Kool, that underscored a reverence for life. And then a protozoan jolted Kool's view of the world and of himself.

I was nineteen or twenty years old, and I had been studying a tiny ciliated protozoan, one that, under the microscope, looked like a glittering star. This critter just twinkled away under my gaze and then seemingly instantaneously moved to another location and resumed its twinkling. It seemed to accelerate in an instant and then come to a dead stop. That was the moment I got it—this creature, this single free-living cell, had an *intent*. Somehow this creature decided that where it was, was not where it wanted to be: "I (can a single cell have a sense of 'I'?) want to be there . . . and there." My sense was that something was going on inside that cell, something that wasn't all that different in quality from what goes on in me. Both that little animal and I have intents and purposes, and we both can express them. And then all of those little things, many of whom I would stick onto slides, became very and *differently* alive to me. They were doing things that I might not understand, but I felt a consciousness, and an affiliation, with those tiny cells.

The motives of a protozoan are beyond our ken. None of us will ever be able to know what an ant, a sea urchin, or a protozoan knows, but we can try. This state of alterity, the encounter with the "other," bends the mind. In the hours Jay Griffiths spent watching the ants, she felt an altered sense of scale, like Gulliver in his quest. Siddharth Iyengar was humbled by butterflies. Adriana Gonzalez found herself in an alien underworld, where she felt unrealistically safe and overwhelmed by love. And Rick Kool was shocked by a universe that defied both time and space.

Crossing Over

True *connectedness* is not a simple thing to describe; it can be a charged encounter, a web of relationships among friends and family or with other life-forms, an ongoing love—or, for some, coming in contact with a universal power or presence. At any age, it's possible to step momentarily into the world of another creature and then return to everyday life, changed or restored.

John Peden, a down-to-earth and taciturn associate professor of recreation and tourism at Georgia Southern University, described to me the initiatory moment that brought him to a language beyond words—it was the first time he recognized sentience in another animal. He was twelve years old, hiking with his father to a lake in Yellowstone National Park. They passed a rockslide, and Peden lifted his camera to take a photo of a pika, a high-altitude mammal that looks like a cross between a rabbit and a guinea pig. As he clicked the shutter, he noticed movement from the corner of his eye. There, stepping into his field of vision, was a bull elk.

The elk stopped and looked at the boy. Then another elk, then a whole herd, stepped out of the forest and stood behind the bull. "That first bull elk seemed to be thinking about what he would do," Peden recalled. "After the elk watched us for a while, they began to relax. Either they thought as a group, or one of the elk sent an invisible signal." The elk moved forward and split into two groups. The females, with calves, went up the rim past Peden and his father, while three bulls, majestic and powerful, moved below. "I realized that these animals were thinking and making decisions in much the same way that people do," Peden said. "It was clear that the elk were intentionally moving in two streams around us, and on the other side of us. They came together and disappeared into the forest. The sun was going down, the sky was a vivid red-orange. My father and I were surrounded by this herd of elk, and then they passed."

For Peden, this was more than a learning moment, more than an intellectual acknowledgment of the intelligence of another creature. It was a doorway into another world.

FOUR

The Octopus Who Stopped Time

Paul Dayton sensed something large gliding above him and felt when it paused. He turned his head slightly and saw the end of a long tentacle reaching down, like a flag unfurling. Or an alien finger.

"This," he thought, "is not going to be a good thing."

One of the world's most respected oceanographers and marine ecologists, Dayton, who is based at the Scripps Institution of Oceanography, is renowned for his work on coastal Antarctic habitats and the marine ecosystems along the rocky shoreline of Washington State. Dayton has documented the environmental impacts of overfishing and is the only person to win both the prestigious George Mercer and W. S. Cooper Awards from the Ecological Society of America.

Passionate about his field yet self-effacing, Dayton often talks with dismay about the devolution of natural history at the university level: the diminishment of flesh-and-blood taxonomy and the demotion of traditional studies of biology, such as zoology, in favor of the molecular sciences and bioengineering, fields of study that can, with public dollars, produce products in the lab to be patented for profit by research universities and professors.

Dayton started diving in the 1950s, using a homemade air tank. By the 1960s, he had moved up to a single-hose commercial regulator, which was not always reliable. At the time, he and several other University of Washington students spent hours on the floor of the Pacific Ocean studying marine biology. Wearing primitive wetsuits, the students, often alone, would climb down the rocks, enter the water, and descend eighty or ninety feet to where light levels were low. The divers would slide along the ocean bottom, hunting for clams or crabs to eat, collecting biological samples, or watching starfish move like constellations across the ocean floor.

Dayton had made hundreds of dives off Eagle Point in the San Juan Islands and had never felt any particular danger. But this time, on his hands and knees while turning over a starfish and inspecting its quivering tube feet, he realized that his air tank was almost empty. It was time to quit. That was when he felt a presence and looked up. "It was one of those huge northwestern octopuses that get to be fourteen feet across," he recalled. "It must have thought I was a crab. All of a sudden I'm covered with octopus."

When he tells this story, which his grandchildren often ask him to repeat, his eyes and his smile widen, and he's *there*.

Dayton could feel the octopus's suckers moving on his skin, exploring his body. Octopus suckers are capable of taste and smell, and an octopus may also be able to "see" with its skin, which contains gene sequences associated with light-sensing retina.* Each octopus contains some five hundred million communication-processing neurons—nearly as many as dogs. Some of these neurons reside in an octopus's central brain, between its eyes, but two-thirds are found in its semiautonomous arms or tentacles. As one neurobiologist writes, the arm of an octopus "is a brain of its own." In a sense, Dayton was being embraced by the octopus's mind.

> It pushed my mask down and I'm hanging on to my regulator with my teeth and I'm starting to panic and trying to rip its arms off me. An octopus's arms look soft and squishy, but they're not; they're like steel when they grip you. I was going to lose the battle.
>
> For some reason, I relaxed completely. I let the octopus pull me down, and I could feel him—her, probably—relax a little bit, too.

---

* In an article titled "Deep Intellect," Sy Montgomery writes that "new evidence suggests a breathtaking possibility. Woods Hole Marine Biological Laboratory and University of Washington researchers found that the skin of the cuttlefish *Sepia officinalis*, a color-changing cousin of octopuses, contains gene sequences usually expressed only in the light-sensing retina of the eye. In other words, cephalopods—octopuses, cuttlefish, and squid—may be able to see with their skin." Sy Montgomery, "Deep Intellect," *Orion*, November–December 2012, orionmagazine.org/article/deep-intellect/.

My legs were bent and my feet touched bottom. Then I just pushed off hard. The octopus and I started going up. She was wrapped all around my head. I was aware of her very large three-jawed beak, attached to a large poison sack. The beak was right behind my bare neck. Every ten feet or so I would take another sip of air. Then I didn't have any more air.

The octopus's face moved around my head, and she looked at me. She slowly began to disentangle from me, and we held eye contact all the way up. And then we popped up at the surface of the ocean, the octopus and I, off Eagle Point.

I pulled off my mask, and as I got my bearings and put my mask back on, here is this octopus with its big eyes just sort of pulling back. She's looking at me and I'm looking at her, and, at least in my mind, we communicated *something*—interest or respect. She slowly moved away from me. Without breaking our eye contact, she started to make her arms into what looked like the wings of a space shuttle. She was one of the most beautiful things I have ever seen in the sea.

As her arms came out, her big body flattened. And she started gliding down.

Then Dayton did the inexplicable. He took a deep breath and dived after the octopus. He followed her down as far as he could, straining to see her in the darkness. "As she disappeared, she was still looking at me. I remember thinking, 'We have our nonaggression pact.'"

When he told me this story, I was astonished and asked, "Why, after barely making it to the surface, would you do such a thing?" He said he did not know why. "But I do remember how that moment felt. Otherworldly, even spiritual. The memory still makes me feel warmth."

Following the octopus into the dark, he felt part of something larger than himself or the octopus, and time disappeared.

Time Bending

Our perception of scale, space, and time depends on context. In an interview, the Westerns author Louis L'Amour once told me about a time-related device he uses in his writing. "When you're at a moment of great stress, you notice things with great clarity," he said. "A seedpod rattles. You're full of adrenaline. I've been in situations like that. I try to bring that back, like an actor remembering his past." He leaned back in his chair. "Some of us think; all of us feel."

An octopus's beak sharpens that point. But danger is not the only time bender. An encounter with an ant or a protozoan does not threaten our immediate safety. A sea urchin does not feel threatening if we do not know about its poison. In a sense, each of these animals, as well as Dayton's octopus, live in otherworldly time zones. Every day, our dogs remind us that our time on Earth is relative in length and in pace. The maxim that one dog year equals seven human years is at best an oversimplification. In their youth, dogs mature faster than humans, and in later years they age slower than we do. Life bends time for its own use.

Paradoxically, other-than-human animals can be at once familiar and utterly strange—and the contrast of these two polarities alters our view of reality. Dayton felt, for those moments, that he came to know the octopus, even as it remained an awe-inspiring mystery.

"Meeting an octopus is like meeting an intelligent alien," writes Peter Godfrey-Smith, a diver and professor of philosophy at the Graduate Center of the City University of New York. An apt description for a creature with eight brains, three hearts, and blue blood (not to be outdone, the overcompensating leech has thirty-two brain segments, two reproductive organs, and nine pairs of testes), an animal that can wield tools, strategize complicated escapes, and possibly even alter the information encoded in its own genes.

Even if we never personally encounter a particular animal, knowledge of its existence in the universe touches us, shifts us, humbles us. In 2017, widespread news coverage reported that scientists had discovered a Greenland shark that was 512 years old—which means that the shark would have been born in the year 1505. Later this story was countered by Mindy Weisberger, a senior writer for Live Science, who said, in effect, Hold your horses—the original research had claimed that the sharks could *potentially* live to be as old as 512. The oldest examined were a spry 335 and 392 years old. And anyway, Weisberger added, "as long-lived as they may be, Greenland sharks don't even come close to the longevity of hydra—freshwater polyps," modest invertebrates who regenerate their own cells and just may be able to live forever.[*]

Beyond the individual animal, the interconnectedness of all life—as long as it lives—imparts a sense of the everlasting, itself an altered state. In 2018, researchers discovered a sprawling complex of two hundred million conical termite mounds, some perhaps four thousand years old, covering an area approximately the size of Great Britain. The insects, over the millennia, have excavated an amount of soil equivalent to four thousand Great Pyramids of Giza—visible on Google Earth but hidden from horizontal view all that time by vegetation.

In her 1937 essay, "Undersea," Rachel Carson describes life in the deep waters of one hundred to fifteen hundred fathoms, the "calcareous oozes" that "cover nearly a third of the ocean floor." Here, she writes, we see "hungry swarms of planktonic animals growing and multiplying upon the abundant plants, and themselves falling prey to the shoals of fish; all, in the end, to be redissolved into their component substances when the inexorable laws of the sea demand it. Individual elements are lost to view, only to repair again and again in different incarnations in a kind of material immortality."

Through communion with individual animals and plants, we feel touched by this larger web of life, even when it seems grotesque. In *The Log from the Sea of Cortez*, John Steinbeck writes, "An ocean without its unnamed monsters would be like a completely dreamless sleep." Knowing an animal at a deeper level does not diminish its mystery but opens our hearts to the unknowable and, in a sense, the divine.

---

[*] In Ralf Schaible, Alexander Scheuerlein, Maciej J. Dańko, Jutta Gampe, et al., "Constant Mortality and Fertility over Age in *Hydra*," *Proceedings of the National Academy of Sciences* 112, no. 51 (2015): 15701–6, doi.org/10.1073/pnas.1521002112, the authors show hydra could live in ideal conditions without showing any increase in mortality or decline in fertility, "which was thought to be inevitable for all multicellular species," according to Pomona College's report on the work of biology professor Daniel Martinez. "I do believe that an individual hydra can live forever under the right circumstances," said Martinez. "The chances of that happening are low because hydra are exposed to the normal dangers of the wild—predation, contamination, diseases." Stacy Liberatore, "Does This Creature Hold the Secret to Immortality? Scientists Claim the Hydra May Be Able to Live Forever," DailyMail.com, updated December 23, 2015, www.dailymail.co.uk/sciencetech/article-3372200/Does-creature-hold-secret-immortality-Scientists-discover-Hydra-able-live-forever.html.

As of this writing, the study of awe's impact on humans through the natural world has focused mainly on weather, great storms, and towering trees rather than on our relationships with animals. But researchers do know that people can become immersed in this magical sense of connection just by seeing the tracks or other signs of a wild animal that has passed nearby, or when a dog they love meets them at the door, or when the sea bulges and life rises.

John Johns, a retired California publisher and businessman, took his family whale watching at a Baja lagoon, where migrating gray whales gather. A large whale calf, urged forward by its mother, surfaced first feet, then inches, from their small boat. "Its eye was huge," Johns told me, "and when my family and I looked into that eye, we all burst into tears." That was wonder, of course. Participatory, intentional awe, intimacy, and the unknowable juxtaposed. They had chosen to enter the whale's world, through the shared habitat of the heart.

Resetting Our Sense of Wonder

Few people have a whale or a handy octopus available. But every day we encounter some kind of other-than-human creature, alien or familiar. A life-changing perceptual shift can occur in a sudden encounter or longer relationship with an ant that becomes a giant, or a hydra as immortal as Dracula; a week-old puppy; or the tiniest turtle carried gently to the sea.

Their mysteries can be partially conveyed through an article, a book, a documentary, or clickbait. But physically and emotionally, only *direct* experience with another living thing can elicit the most startling and personal sense of wonder.* This is possible especially when we're very young, but it tends to fade as we move into our teen years and beyond. Rediscovered, a transcendent connection with another animal offers a kind of reset.

Our situation today requires the mother of all resets. So far, our intellect and even our instinct for self-preservation have proved insufficient motivation for the preservation of the wild. Something at once old and new is missing.

---

* I say this while acknowledging Indigenous belief systems that consider all matter to be animate as well as the Gaia theory, which posits that living organisms interact with their inorganic environments to regulate the planet's system. Most of us, however, find it difficult to look into the eyes of Earth alone.

Joanne Vining, professor emerita at the Human Nature Research Laboratory, University of Illinois at Urbana-Champaign, has given considerable thought to our role in the family of animals. In a 2003 article in *Human Ecology Review,* she describes attending a workshop for children with autism and developmental disabilities, which used dolphins,* a golden retriever, and a manta ray as therapy animals. "The organizers of this session went to great lengths to emphasize the fact that there was no 'magic' involved in these programs," she writes. The children's favorite activity, used by the therapists to encourage desirable behaviors, was to prepare food for the dolphins, which "gave them the opportunity to dig their hands in buckets of fish." Even though the therapists "didn't want parents to have false expectations, and even though they were trying to maintain a psychological rigor in the therapeutic process, at least some of the program's success could be attributed to the magic of the human-animal bond," she concludes. Similarly, Louise Chawla, a professor in the College of Architecture and Planning at the University of Colorado, describes the magic of the human-animal encounter as a sense of union between self and other, a "silent intuition of the world's power and our own power."

Vining is careful to note that "magic" is not meant to suggest the supernatural but "rather the sense of awe and wonder that often accompanies such peak experiences," joined by curiosity. Scientists have avoided the study of the magic in human-animal interactions. Why? Because "magic consciousness defies rational explanation," Vining writes. "Therefore, it also tends to be ignored or dismissed as 'irrational' by the rational world of research." Until the 1970s, scientists ignored the study of emotions in other animals for much the same reason. Yet today the study of emotion, "both quantitative and qualitative, is thriving," and Vining suggests similar research on the sources and impact of the magical experience.

Awe is a safer term than *magic.* Psychologist Abraham Maslow defines *awe* as those "moments of highest happiness and fulfillment." During a peak

---

* Though the use of captive dolphins and other captured wild animals for human therapy has drawn criticism, the tourist industry continues to encourage people to "swim with the dolphins" as a form of guided therapy or self-medication. Using captive wild animals, however, is not the same as living in proximity with animals in the wild. Science has only recently turned to the psychological and social benefits of the latter.

experience, he writes, a person feels "disorientation in space and time, ego transcendence, and self-forgetfulness: a perception that the world is good, beautiful, and desirable: feeling passive, receptive, and humble: a sense that polarities and dichotomies have been transcended or resolved: and feelings of being lucky, fortunate, or graced."

Since Maslow's time, the study of awe has come into fashion. In 2003, in an article in the journal *Cognition and Emotion*, psychologists Jonathan Haidt, then at the University of Virginia, and Dacher Keltner of the University of California–Berkeley, described awe as "a moral, spiritual, and aesthetic emotion" found at "the upper reaches of pleasure and the boundary of fear." Awe is what we feel during or after an encounter with something unexpected, which stimulates a sense of vastness and possibility, such as hearing thunder, listening to a moving piece of music, sensing the infinite during prayer or meditation, or, as Keltner writes, "when experiencing the sacred during meditation or prayer, when viewing the Grand Canyon, touching the hand of a rock star like Iggy Pop." (By happenstance, I once sat next to the shirtless Iggy Pop at an airport shoeshine stand. Retrospectively, I can say I detected no upsurge of personal awe.)

Haidt and Keltner confirm Maslow's characterization of awe as transcendence, as a motivator of generosity, kindness, and hope. An awe-inducing event, they posit, "may be one of the fastest and most powerful methods of personal change and growth."

When struck by awe in the presence of a wild animal, most people feel both outside their comfort zone and, at the same time, the exhilaration of wonder. And some of us feel a paradoxical and profound sense of *comfort*.

Not long after I met the black fox in Alaska, I was alone on a lake in the mountains near San Diego. The morning air was just beginning to warm. I saw what appeared to be two turkey vultures on the shore picking at a dead carp. I turned the boat and used my quiet electric motor to move closer. The vultures were not vultures. They were large golden eagles.

For what seemed a long time, I moved back and forth, parallel to the shore, twenty feet from the eagles. I watched them watch me. I photographed them. One flew up and circled high overhead, then returned to its meal. The eagles ate while they watched. Again and again, their heads lowered to the carp, then rose, pausing to look directly at me. I felt something then that

I had first experienced when I was a boy, and many times since, but never so intensely. I cannot speak for the eagles, but I choose to believe that the encounter held a mysterious but essential truth.

Back home, I said to my younger son, "Whoever I say I am, I'm not. Who I was in those moments is who I really am—and I have no words to explain it." Except that during such moments, it is impossible to feel alone.

PART TWO

What the Wild Heart Still Knows

The Art and Science of Communicating with Other Animals

DR. DOLITTLE: 'ow come I can hear you talking?

LUCKY: I dunno. Maybe you're just weird or something.

DR. DOLITTLE: Shut up. You're a dog. DOGS CANNOT TALK.

LUCKY: What the hell do you think barking is,
an involuntary spasm?

—DR. DOLITTLE (1998 Film Version)

An animal's eyes have the power to speak a great language.

—MARTIN BUBER, *I and Thou*

FIVE

Becoming the Grasshopper

Robin Moore, one of the world's most prominent designers of natural play spaces, uses PowerPoint to convey intricate patterns of where and how children explore them. One series of photographs shows a little boy, still in diapers, moving through green growth and wildflowers. The child, pale and vulnerable in the sun, comes upon a large grasshopper (technically a locust) on a branch. The boy bends over, peers at the grasshopper for a long moment. Then the boy flings his arms outward and upward and locks them into place high behind his back. The arms are straight, rigid, like wings. The little boy seems to freeze in that position, still looking, absorbed.

"The boy becomes the grasshopper," explains Moore.

He employs this slide and story to illustrate what he and his colleagues consider a popular misconception about infants and early toddlers, that while they can be sensitive to the feelings of others, they are not yet capable of empathy. What the child did in that moment may rather have been a rudimentary form of mimicry. Still, this boy *became* the grasshopper; he imagined what it would be like to physically be one.

Sitting in the audience, we became the boy becoming the grasshopper.

Such identification is not the same as anthropomorphizing or romanticizing an animal, but it's related. Anthropomorphism attributes feelings or characteristics of a human being to an animal, a god, or an object.* In

---

* Closely related, theriomorphism ascribes animal characteristics to gods or humans.

many cases, doing so can reduce our appreciation for the true qualities of that animal and can be an act of disrespect, as noted by one participant on *Merriam-Webster's* online forum: "On Facebook someone posted a picture of a poodle wearing a bustier and tights, and a lady said anthropomorphism made her want to vomit." Clearly, one doesn't want to be caught being an anthropomorphist in public.

Anthropomorphism can also interrupt learning about the natural world. University of Toronto psychologist Patricia Ganea observed how three- to five-year-olds perceive nature when taught in a purely factual way compared to an anthropomorphized way. The children who were educated through the use of fantasy animals were more likely to attribute human traits to other animals and less likely to retain the facts. Her conclusion: anthropomorphism can lead to "inaccurate understanding of biological processes in the natural world." On the other hand, some scientists, like oceanographer Paul Dayton, contend that the rejection of anything resembling anthropomorphism may have gone too far. Had he shared his octopus story at a scientific conference in the not-too-distant past, he would have been reprimanded by colleagues (or at least some of them) for romanticizing nature, even though, beyond the conference hall, "marine biologists tell stories like this all the time and always have." But concerns about such criticism no longer bother him. "I've been around too long to worry too much what other people think."

Antipathy toward anthropomorphism is, in fact, relatively new. To early peoples, animals served as symbols, offered truth and understanding, not because of their biological limitations but because of the animals' relationship with humans.* Aristotle, in *The History of Animals*, attributes to "a number of animals" traits that, at least in the recent past, were reserved for human beings, such as "gentleness or fierceness, mildness or cross temper, courage, or timidity, fear or confidence, high spirit or low cunning, and with regard to intelligence, something equivalent to sagacity." This view, what some would now consider anthropomorphism, remained accepted wisdom

---

* John Berger argues that the spiritual spell of animals precedes domestication, noting that ancient people named eight of the twelve signs of the zodiac after animals and that for the Nuer people of the southern Sudan, as he quotes social anthropologist Roy Willis, "all creatures, including man, originally lived together in fellowship in one camp." John Berger, "Why Look at Animals?," *About Looking* (New York: Pantheon, 1992), 3–18.

until the nineteenth century, when French philosopher René Descartes's notion of *bête machine* (from the French, literally "animal machine") took the stage. In describing the difference between humans and animals, Descartes posits that animals are basically stupid machines. In the century that followed, this designation gave cover for industrial animal abuse—to mine operators, for example, who lowered caged and blindfolded mules into the tunnels, stabled them underground, and worked them there, often for the rest of their lives. Dayton rejects Descartes's dismissal of animals as machines.

As for anthropomorphism fouling the waters of education, Dayton says many of the students who came through Scripps Institution in past years lacked even the most basic knowledge of natural history. Even students majoring in marine science knew little about the animals along the coast. Today increasing awareness of the complexity and intelligence of many animals may be changing that trend. Dayton makes the case that knowing about animals begins not with specific factual knowledge but with personal, empathic contact—identifying with animals, understanding them, *feeling* as best as we can the traits that are shared between a human and another animal. The key is not to reject early anthropomorphism but to help students go beyond it, to transition from projecting human characteristics onto animals to applying the kind of identification needed to distinguish between what we have in common with other animals and what we do not, what the animal *may* be feeling or thinking and what we will never know.

Like Dayton, Carl Safina, author of *Beyond Words*, contends that extreme derision of anthropomorphism has held back science, preventing researchers from even speculating about the inner life of animals or their ability to communicate. "Not just held it back—it's ruined the field," according to Safina. "It prevented people from even asking those questions for about 40 years." In his book and in numerous interviews, he rejects the notion that other-than-human animals lack thoughts and emotions, "just like it's wrong to say they are completely the same as us." As for the public, lack of recognition of nuanced emotions and thoughts in other animals contributes to the very absence of empathy that leads humans to destroy other species at an unprecedented rate. None of this suggests any of us should see or treat another animal as a mini-me, which, taken to an extreme, is just as reductionist as Descartes's view of animals as machines.

Frans de Waal suggests a different approach. An Emory University professor of psychology, de Waal is an authority on primates and pro-social behavior, which is what occurs when, say, one animal *identifies* with another animal. De Waal breaks anthropomorphism into three categories:

- Anthropocentrism, an assumption that you, as a human being, are at the center of the universe, and all other creatures are there for your use or entertainment
- Anthropodenial, a blindness to the humanlike characteristics of other animals ("Are you in anthro-denial?" he asks)
- Animal centrism, an effort to understand and feel what life must be like for a member of another species

Patricia McConnell appreciates de Waal's approach. "Next time someone accuses you of being 'anthropomorphic,'" she advises, "ask yourself which category your behavior was in, and don't hesitate to stand up for yourself if you were being 'animal-centric.'" Seen this way, the boy who became the grasshopper was animal-centric.

Wearing the Shoes of the Snake (Critical Anthropomorphism)

In the 1980s, biopsychologist Gordon Burghardt introduced the concept and process of "critical anthropomorphism." Today, as Alumni Distinguished Service Professor at the University of Tennessee–Knoxville, his work centers primarily on reptile behavior and animal play. The idea of critical anthropomorphism is built on the classical German concepts of *Umwelt* and *Innenwelt*—German for an animal's perceptual environment. As Burghardt and his herpetologist colleague Jesus Rivas explain, they came to consider the animal to be studied "as an active participant, with the researcher trying to put himself or herself in the animal's situation." The scientist brings existing scientific knowledge about the animal, enters into the animal's environment, then attempts through the available information and imagination to sense what it might be like to be that animal. A prerequisite for studying a snake is "wearing the snake's shoes," as Rivas and Burghardt put it playfully. Doing so helps the scientist ask the right questions about the snake.

Proponents of critical anthropomorphism argue that its use helps scientists avoid poorly conceived animal studies based on the wrongheaded assumption that human beings and other animals always live in different universes. "Too often ethologists [those who study animal behavior usually in more natural conditions] and herpetologists regard snakes and other reptiles as robot-like machines or as animals so alien from us that attempting to put ourselves into their world, even heuristically, is both useless and a scientifically dangerous conceit," write Burghardt and Rivas; on the contrary, considering the perceptual world of the animal "may generate testable hypotheses that were previously unconsidered."

When I called Burghardt, I wondered how his thinking might apply to the lives of nonscientists, perhaps as a way to more deeply understand the world around us. If you were to sit down with a twelve-year-old or someone older and suggest ways to apply critical anthropomorphism, what would you say?

Burghardt began his answer with a caution: "It's impossible to know exactly what another animal, or even person, experiences." But, he said, by using scientific knowledge and a good imagination, the twelve-year-old might ask a series of general questions about the animal: How does it sense and perceive what is important to it? How does it solve problems and learn? Does it experience fear, anger, joy, or love? "We are animals ourselves and have brains organized similarly to most other vertebrates, so asking general questions is a good way to start. But we can't stop there."

Go deeper, Burghardt suggests, by asking what stimuli the other animal detects, beginning with the ones we can't detect. Not a small task for a layperson, but it just might motivate that twelve-year-old (and maybe the forty-year-old) to learn more.

"Bats, dogs, and mice can hear sounds we cannot," Burghardt said. "Dogs and snakes rely on chemical cues such as odors that we cannot perceive. Many mammals do not see colors; their world is black and white. Knowing this, we would not attribute color as important to them." Birds, on the other hand, can see colors well. "And honeybees perceive white flowers as full of patterns. They see wavelengths we cannot. Social animals will respond to and experience other members of their species in multiple ways." To understand the mind of another animal, "we need to learn as much as possible about their abilities and sensory worlds; we need to know what brain structures underlie their emotions, ones that are similar or different to ours." If, when they are hungry, thirsty, or scared, changes occur in their body and brain that are similar to the changes that happen in ours, "then it is a good bet that they experience similar—though certainly not exactly the same—feelings that we have."

In a way, to use critical anthropomorphism is, borrowing the word that science fiction writer Robert Heinlein coined in his 1961 *Stranger in a Strange Land*, to "grok," which is to "understand profoundly and intuitively." But Burghardt stresses that critical anthropomorphism is more than grokking. It is steeped first in scientific knowledge, then in imaginative identification, and it leads to better scientific inquiry.

To gain more insight into critical anthropomorphism, I spoke with Harry Greene, an affable and popular professor of ecology and evolutionary biology at Cornell University and one of the world's leading experts on snakes. A prolific author, Greene writes about snakes in a way that can make even the snake-phobic person understand a snake's beauty and its *Innenwelt*—as well as one's own. In our phone conversation, he revealed unexpectedly that he "had an uncharacteristic early encounter with violence." As a college student, he lived over a funeral home, worked as a mortician's assistant, and drove an ambulance full-time. He once delivered a baby for an eighteen-year-old woman and gave CPR to a dying girl. Later he was an army medic. As soon as he got out of the army, the woman he loved was killed. "Natural history has been a counter to all that," he said. "Feeling like a small part of a universe . . . all coming to terms." For him, the world of snakes is a place of healing and empathy.

As he spoke of his love of reptiles, I thought about the turtle pit that my father had constructed at the far end of our yard under the shade of a hedge. I would gather box turtles (similar to tortoises but actually members of the American pond turtle family) on wet roads in the spring, collect worms and berries for them, and spend hours watching them eat. I often thought that someone very interesting must be at home in those shells. They had individual personalities, and I gave each turtle a name. And every fall I let them go. I mentioned to Greene that some folks might say those turtles were simple minded and that by naming them I was robbing them of their turtleness.

"Bullshit!" he said. "Some people think doing something like that is pointless. I'm not one of them." He observed that many people are driven to study animals because they wonder what it's like to be an eastern box turtle or a black-tailed rattlesnake. To Greene, critical anthropomorphism "is in that middle ground; it's definitely not cutesy and definitely not 'Oh, if you're a good scientist, you won't name or identify with your animals.'"

He speaks of the character of snakes with poetic sensibility. In his field-work, he came to deeply admire one black-tailed rattlesnake that he had observed for twelve years. "She was a hunter, and the best mother, and she stayed out of trouble," he said. "She was the smartest and most caring of all fifty of those snakes that I watched for those years. Her number was 21, but to me she was Super Female 21. The favorite snake of my whole life."

Greene used critical anthropomorphism to sense the world as the rattle-snake might.

"First, I *shucked off the blinders*," he said. "Everyone else 'knew' that pit vipers don't have the capability for that kind of parenting, so I didn't at first see it. Yet it was right in front of me." Next came the opening of his own senses, which he also tells about in his classic book, *Snakes*. To imagine what it would be like to live in the "chemosensory world" of a snake, he assembled shards of his own memories, of moments in his life when his sense of smell had been the most dominant, as it is in snakes. He remembered driving down I-5 in the Central Valley of California, daydreaming about his mom's tomato soup when he was a kid. And then a few miles later, he caught up to an open load of tomatoes. "I think I was in the odor plume, unknowingly," he said. One difference here: a snake smells primarily with its tongue, which flicks out to capture smelly molecules and then delivers them to two small openings in the roof of its mouth for analysis. So Greene imagined what that would be like. What he described was quite a process, not unlike method acting, in which the actor pulls up personal memories in order to transport himself or herself into a character. He also imagined being "one of dozens of species of snakes in a tropical forest, all knowing each other as well as their prey and non-prey by odors" by thinking of himself blindfolded in an Andean market smelling "roasting corn, urine in the gutters [, and] encoun-tering a friend and recognizing her without sight."

Sometimes he imagines the snake in front of him as a human wearing a snake suit. "It's not a human being in there, but I have reason to perceive that similarly complicated things are going on inside that skin," he said. He once watched a different rattlesnake, number 41, stake out a mouse trail. The snake held perfectly still for hours waiting for food to move into its strike zone. So did Greene. After a long while, the snake lifted its head and neck in a position usually reserved for fighting another male snake, then pushed its head forward and used its chin to tamp down a dried fern. For the herpetologist, this was a moment of delight and respect. To his knowledge, this was the first scientific record of a snake clearing a sight line—or appearing to do so. Later he would write, "Will future studies confirm the tantalizing possibility that male 41 knew a dead plant might thwart his strike, hours or even days later, then he acted accordingly? Did that animal really exhibit what psychologists call inferential reasoning, whereby a novel problem is solved by generalizing from some previous experience, in this case perhaps the toppling of a rival male?"

The great reset in the relations between humans and other animals, and with each other, will require a new appreciation for observational empathy. Perhaps someday critical anthropomorphism will be taught to enthusiastic sixth graders, graduate students in biology, or to students of psychology, health care, parenting, education, or politics.

Like Gordon Burghardt and Paul Dayton, Greene believes that the human ability to sense the world of other animals will one day be considered essential to the protection of the life around us, that developing this capacity will be especially crucial for the protection of the not-so-charismatic animals, especially the critters that have the capability to kill us. "Empathy," Greene writes, "is understandably a stretch when it comes to animals without fur or feathers, the more so when they lack limbs and moveable eyelids. Nevertheless, if people can begin to appreciate rattlesnakes, then turkey vultures and badgers should be easy." Greene is guardedly optimistic about changing attitudes. If Robin Moore's photos of the mesmerized little boy in diapers are any indication, even grasshoppers might stand a chance.

SIX

Intimacy Is All around Us

Most people first cross the threshold into deep relationship with other animals during childhood, and then a kind of amnesia sets in. Some, however, never lose that passage. Others rediscover it. Through it, they enter other worlds.

When Alan Rabinowitz was growing up in Brooklyn, he stuttered so badly that he couldn't communicate with other people. Sometimes when he tried to talk, his body would convulse in painful spasms. At that time, in the 1950s, the condition was known as frozen mouth. As a boy he would "come home from school every day and yearn for the darkness and safety of his closet," he recalled in a 2014 interview with Diane Rehm.

But when he was four or five years old, something remarkable happened that would guide the course of his life. He realized he could speak to animals. At first, he spoke to his pets: "hamsters, gerbils, New York style pets." Then one morning his father took him to the Bronx Zoo, and he witnessed a transformation in his son. Alan felt comfortable there; his stress melted away. The zoo visits became a ritual.

"While all the other cats were charging the bars and roaring and screaming, the jaguar always stayed quiet." It would stand or lie near the back of the cage. "It stayed away from people coming up to the bars. And that's where I would go, and I would stay at those bars until the jaguar came up close to me." And then he would begin to whisper to it.

He spent many hours talking to the jaguar, and listening. During this time, he was treated by a hypnotist and other therapists. He was given drug therapy and even shock treatment, a remedy later discredited for stutterers.

Nothing worked. Adult expectations only made him nervous, worsening his stutter, and for a while he gave up trying to talk to people. "But the jaguar, the animals, had no expectations of me. They accepted me as I was. Words would come out. Sentences would come out.... I realized I could talk to animals and they had feelings and they couldn't express those feelings either. These animals were just like me."

As his stuttering improved, he made a remarkable vow: "I promised them if I ever found my voice I would be the voice for animals, and I never forgot that promise."

Rabinowitz fulfilled his vow, eventually becoming a zoologist and then working as the director of Panthera, a worldwide nonprofit organization that helps protect thirty-seven wild cat species around the world, including jaguars. He told his story to those who would listen, and there were many who were inspired. Rabinowitz (whom *Time* magazine called the "Indiana Jones of wildlife science") related to me a story of a personal encounter he had in the Central American country of Belize.

Tracks had been seen not far from his camp. "You shouldn't go in the jungle by yourself for all kinds of reasons. I figured I'd walk about an hour and follow the tracks and hope against hope to see the jaguar," he said. Sometimes the tracks would veer into the forest, then come back on the trail. He followed those tracks longer than he had planned. "Dusk was coming and I knew I couldn't be alone in the jungle after dark, and the tracks had disappeared into the forest again. So I decided to go back to the camp. I turned around and there was the jaguar."

Later Rabinowitz realized the cat had disappeared into the forest and circled back; it had been walking on Rabinowitz's tracks for twenty minutes. "I'm not going to say it was an exhilarating moment because that would be a lie. A jaguar will kill you without a second thought. It was terrifying. And the jaguar was blocking my way back to camp, and I was blocking its way back into the jungle."

In a large-cat encounter, normal protocol is this: Don't run away (that triggers the animal's chase instinct). Instead, back away slowly and become bigger than you are—raise your arms, wave them, shout. If all that fails, protect the back of your neck and head. That protocol is what Rabinowitz should have followed. He did not.

"I did what you do with primates," he said. "I made myself small. I sat down." And then something remarkable occurred: the jaguar sat down, too. "I was amazed. I can't tell you why I sat down. Inexplicable. As soon as I squatted down, both of us were looking into each other's eyes. I knew right then that it wasn't going to attack me. That moment reminded me so poignantly of all the days I went to the Bronx Zoo. The eyes of a wild jaguar are so different from those of a zoo jaguar.... I saw the *power* in those eyes."

One interpretation of the encounter is simple, an animal scanning for signals of intent: *Is that a predator who wants to eat me? Or is that potential food?*

Along with the light, Rabinowitz's fear faded. But unlike the light, his fear returned. He needed to make a proactive move. He stood up. "The jaguar was about twenty or twenty-five feet from me. I started walking backward and fell on my back, like a turtle. I thought, 'This is it.' The jaguar let off a growl, a guttural low growl, and got up, and then it just walked off sideways toward the forest. At the edge, it turned and looked at me."

In the years that followed, Rabinowitz thought often about his highly charged moment with the jaguar and believed that, at least for him, it was worth the risk. Similar to what Dayton experienced with the octopus, Rabinowitz's communication with the jaguar was not heard so much as felt—like the bass notes too low for human ears to detect. Truth often remains hidden or below the surface. He thinks of this as a place, the place of knowing.

Beyond the Threshold

Later in life, Rabinowitz coined the word "jaguarness" to describe a way of knowing the world beyond his human capabilities. At this point in our conversation, his voice sharpened. "People can accuse me of anthropomorphism, but I'm a hard-core trained scientist." Further, "nothing is going to save the species until we break through and realize that our emotional health, physical health, is based on that bond—one that can also occur between humans."[*]

---

[*] Sadly, on August 5, 2018, Alan Rabinowitz died of the cancer he had battled during the years he fought for the survival of the world's large cats.

Does jaguarness characterize some kind of interspecies telepathy? Some people promote that idea. Whatever one thinks about the claim, telepathy isn't really the point. *Recognition of the other* is the aim, and meaning can be a consequence. While our interpretations of those moments may have no relation to what an animal is thinking or feeling or sensing, the found truth is *ours*. It can help us read our own mind.

Author and scientist Aldo Leopold was one of the primary shapers of the modern environmental movement. In *A Sandhill County Almanac*, his masterpiece published shortly after his death at sixty-two in 1949, he describes his awakening to natural intimacy. In one of the most affecting passages, Leopold tells a story about how he and a friend, young and trigger happy, shot at a pack of wolves, because in those days few hunters or ranchers would pass up the chance to kill a wolf, either to protect cattle or the deer the ranchers hunted for meat and sport. Aiming downhill, they shot with "more excitement than accuracy," and by the time their rifles were empty, an "old wolf was down, and a pup was dragging a leg into impassable slide-rocks." What came next changed Leopold's life.

> We reached the old wolf in time to watch a fierce green fire dying in her eyes. I realized then, and have known ever since, that there was something new to me in those eyes—something known only to her and to the mountain. . . . Since then I have lived to see state after state extirpate its wolves. I have watched the face of many a newly wolfless mountain and seen the south-facing slopes wrinkle with a maze of new deer trails. I have seen every edible bush and seedling browsed, first to anemic desuetude, and then to death. . . . The cowman who cleans his range of wolves does not realize that he is taking over the wolf's job of trimming the herd to fit the change. He has not learned to think like a mountain.

Such an experience is similar to the insight that an artist, musician, dancer, or writer feels when visual pattern, sound, texture, movement, and memory come into focus.

At Scripps Institution of Oceanography, Paul Dayton teaches students about the "X-ray" tradition of Australian Aboriginal art, which exhibits an elaborate understanding of the bone and organ systems of animals, "even showing the split lengths of snake lungs." He marvels at their mythology of animals, plants, and even rocks, and their concept of Dreamtime, where all lives and stories exist forever. "These people were and are spectacularly accomplished naturalists. When you look at those images, if you let yourself fantasize, what do you think these animals dream about?" He challenges his students to go beyond the lab, to have the courage to dream the lives of other animals, an ability they were perhaps born with but atrophies in a society and education system disconnected from nature.

Robert Bateman, a Canadian icon famous worldwide for his paintings of wildlife, is deeply concerned about that disconnection. Now in his eighties, Bateman began his artistic career as a boy painting birds viewed from his bedroom window. He saw the world as a bird would and for the rest of his life experienced the world from that viewpoint, of how a bird might sense the world combined with his own insights. Such sensitivity is felt both from outside one's own body and from deep within it. At the opening of the Bateman Center in Victoria, British Columbia, I realized for the first time how his paintings were truly meant to be seen—as portals. Some of them are wall sized. On the walls, yes, but also coming out of the walls, which seem to bulge: a bear turning toward the visitor; a bison exhaling clouds; wolves; eagles—all of them *alive*. I was stunned. Later I asked Bateman how he accomplished that feat. He said, "Think about the Ice Age artists of Europe twenty-five thousand to thirty-five thousand years ago."

Look carefully at those ancient stalking lions, he added, those hulking cave bears, those magnificent horses flying through the millennia with their heads together, legs straining, manes flowing in the wind, mouths open and breathing, their eyes looking straight ahead. Describing these animals, Bateman's voice grew distant. "I can practically smell them, they are so real." Then he answered my question directly: "I become the bear."

Intimacy is often defined as a person's relationship with one other person, a soul mate, a lifelong partner, a close friend or family member. For the purpose of research, some scientists have narrowed the definition of intimacy to physical closeness or sexual relations.* Thomas Patrick Malone and Patrick Thomas

---

* Even this form of intimacy may be threatened. In 2018, the *Atlantic* magazine published a cover story titled "The Sex Recession," reporting that millennials are having less sexual intimacy than prior generations—attributing that change, in part, to the easy availability of online substitutions for personal intimacy.

Malone, father-and-son psychiatrists, take a broader view in their book *The Art of Intimacy*, defining intimacy as "the experience of connectivity."

One example of this expansive idea of intimacy is described in *The Art of Happiness* in which coauthor and psychiatrist Howard C. Cutler asks the Dalai Lama if he is ever lonely, especially considering the role he must play, one that places him seemingly at a distance from other people. To Cutler's surprise, the Dalai Lama answers, "No." The reason he is never lonely, the Dalai Lama goes on to explain, is that his model of intimacy is based on a willingness to open oneself to family, friends, and even strangers, to form genuine and deep bonds based on common humanity. Though people may spend their lives waiting for that one true other, Cutler writes, there "is incredible diversity among human lives, infinite variations among people with respect to how they can experience a sense of closeness. This realization alone offers us a great opportunity. It means that *at this very moment* we have vast resources of intimacy available to us. Intimacy is all around us." Not only with people but also, in an expanding circle of relations, with all those cats and sparrows and bees and box turtles who are available to us even when people are not.

Have You Ever Seen a Box Turtle Drink?

Like us, animals can send mixed signals. They can feel or think something one moment and something else entirely the next. They're capable of nuance. They can show empathy and compassion and selfishness and aggression. We have a lot to discuss with them.

Today we see a surge of scientific interest in how animals communicate with members of their own species and even with members of other species, including humans. Researchers exploring animal intelligence and emotions of animals have found that the brains of several species share information-processing neurons similar to the ones associated with empathy in humans. For example, elephants sacrifice their own well-being for the good of other elephants in their group and grieve for their dead, and young elephants show signs of posttraumatic stress disorder after losing their parents to poachers.[*]

---

[*] In addition, a classic 1964 study revealed a kind of moral code among monkeys. The monkeys refused to pull a chain that would produce food if doing so would hurt another monkey; one macaque avoided pulling the chain for two weeks and nearly starved. Jules H. Masserman, Stanley Wechkin, and William Terris, "'Altruistic' Behavior in Rhesus Monkeys," *American Journal of Psychiatry* 121, no. 6, 584–85.

Ravens may have what is called a theory of mind, the ability to understand their own state of mind and emotions and even the motives of another animal. Scrub jays hide their food and are so skilled at second-guessing competing birds that their abilities are likened to espionage and counterespionage. As for the domestic animal world, researchers at Emory University's Dog Project, using a brain scanner, have identified regions in the brains of dogs that give them the ability to understand complex combinations of facial expressions in other dogs and in humans.

Dogs get the lion's share of attention for facial communication. A team at the University of Sussex hypothesized that because a horse's elongated face is so radically different from humans that their facial communication would also be radically different, but they discovered otherwise. Using a program called Facial Action Coding Systems, they fully mapped an equine head and its communicative expressions. To their astonishment, they found that a horse's expressions are surprisingly similar to the facial signals that humans send. Sometimes in micromovements difficult for the "nonwhisperer" to detect, horses smile, pout, raise their inner eyebrows (as humans do when they're surprised, scared, or sad), and widen their eyes in fear. They also do what humans can't: use their ears to broadcast signals. Horses, researchers discovered, have seventeen separate facial expressions, second only to humans, who have twenty-seven. Chimpanzees have thirteen expressions, and dogs have sixteen. When it comes to rubber faces, a horse is the Jim Carrey of the other-than-human world, though its humor is more subtle.

These and other studies verify what many of us already know, at least subconsciously, and raise this question: What would human life be like if the ability to communicate with animals were brought consciously to the surface of our days—to the position it once held in older cultures? The horse whisperer today is revered as a kind of telepathic shaman. But *most* of us could become whisperers. This lost language still exists.

When we enter the habitat of the heart, we tap a primal chord first sounded long before humans appeared on Earth, the patterns of bleeps and signals and images that predate, and may yet outlast, the narrower verbal languages of *Homo sapiens*. The sheer variety and overlapping patterns, complications, and future possibilities of animal communication can seem overwhelming. Unless you're six.

Patty Born Selly is an extraordinary professor at Hamline University, in St. Paul, and author of nature-related books for children, parents, and teachers, including *Connecting Animals and Children in Early Childhood*. She has served as the executive director of the National Center for STEM Elementary Education. Selly sometimes brings injured reptiles and birds to her classes, where students help care for them before they are released back to the wild. She told me a story about a classroom experience she once had with young students.

"Have you ever seen a box turtle drink?" she asked.

She was referring to a specific eastern box turtle missing her back legs. Because of that injury, the turtle could not be released back into the wild. Selly had taken care of this turtle for two decades and sometimes brought her to elementary classrooms.

"It's always striking to me how children seem to read an animal's cues," she said. "They seem to intuitively know how to respond to a turtle. They speak in quiet tones, and they remind each other to move slowly. They don't want to startle or scare it."

To drink water, a box turtle may submerge its head and keep it there, taking in water through its nostrils, Selly explained. "Small bubbles float up to the surface."

While this was happening, a girl in the third grade said, 'I think that turtle is experiencing joy right now!"

Selly asked her why she thought that.

"I can just feel it coming from that turtle, like those little bubbles floating off."

Next, the girl invited over several other children to see the turtle drinking, so they could, as she said, "see what a turtle looks like when it experiences joy." The children agreed that the turtle did look joyful.

"This turtle is not fearful in the classroom," said Selly. "She often scoots around with her head out, looking around and taking it all in. Over the years, I've heard a number of children remark that she is 'curious' or 'wants to know what is happening' or 'checking things out.'"

Selly has noted that the comments from adults "seem to reflect an assumption that the turtle's actions are all about people—themselves, usually." This reaction fascinates her. "Adults seem to assume that whatever an animal is doing it is in some way shape or form a response to humans. Children do not demonstrate this tendency—unless their responses are influenced by adults." Selly's students just accept the fact that a turtle can feel joy, not for their sake but for its own.

She asked me to ask myself a question: If I see a raccoon trotting down the street, do I see it as a threat or as something whose habitat I helped destroy?

"Either answer suggests that *you're* the central character in the experience," she pointed out. Both ways offer valid perspectives on the existence of that raccoon, but the binary approach is narrow and insufficient. With kids, it's different: "One of the wonderful things about children is that they do typically see themselves as the central character of an experience, but *not* when it comes to animals. Children can see that animals are important just because they're animals."

Selly then said something that I have thought about ever since: "At the end of your life, your understanding of life will depend on how many lenses you've seen the world through."

Awash in secondary experience, surrounded by avatars, we hunger for authenticity—to wake up every morning and see the world through new eyes, hear it through new ears, understand it through a rediscovered language, use senses forgotten or never known, and, then as life progresses, to become a larger vessel for others. Such a pursuit can become a way of life. Animals help us through the passage.

SEVEN

Earth's Oldest Language

Decades after he was surrounded by the herd of elk, John Peden, now a professor, was hiking with a companion on a similar windblown ridge of rock outcrops and bunchgrass. This time, he was walking over the Sable Mountain pass in Alaska's Denali wilderness. It was early spring, in grizzly country, so they were on high alert. After completing the hike, they made their way to a road to wait for the bus that was scheduled to pick them up. The bus, stuck in the snow on a pass, was late. Peden and his hiking partner sat down next to the road and waited.

Suddenly his companion pointed down the road, and the man's mouth opened and closed. No words emerged. A large male wolf was not more than twenty feet away, staring at them.

After a few long moments, the wolf turned and began walking slowly away from the road. He kept looking back over its shoulder at the men. "It was as if the wolf was saying, 'Come with me.'" So they did. As they followed, the wolf periodically stopped and looked back at them. "Every five minutes or so. If we stopped, the wolf knew. Then it would turn and look at us again." After a while, the wolf disappeared into the willows. The men headed back to the park road.

And there it was again, standing at the edge of the road. It stared at them, then turned, looked back. Forgetting about the bus, Peden and his friend once again followed the wolf.

"We heard another wolf howl. It was up on a ridge, and we could see it, a female with two cubs," Peden said. Two more adult wolves appeared.

Repeatedly, the first male would walk a few feet back and stare at them, apparently "to get their attention, to get them to continue following it, and they did."

Three hours later, the men returned to the road. Now five wolves, including the big male, gathered in a circle around them, watching. When a park ranger happened to pull up in his truck, the wolves became agitated but did not leave. Observing the wolves' behavior, the ranger called a state biologist, who advised the ranger and the other men to look for a kill in the immediate area. "We did. There it was, a dead moose. We believed the wolf was trying to lead us away from the kill."

The ranger closed the area to hikers and didn't reopen it until the wolves had completely eaten the moose. I asked Peden what he made of this experience, which had lasted four hours.

"I'm certain that they were leading us away from the food site," he said. "I felt no fear. And the wolf didn't either, as far as I could tell." What did he see in the wolf's eyes? "I saw determination. Maybe a better word is 'intent'? It knew exactly what it was doing."

To Peden, this encounter felt like a conversation.

He regularly takes his students on adventure-learning treks through the Great Smoky Mountains, the Outer Banks, the Everglades, and the Gulf Islands National Seashore, where they experience their own animal encounters and tell stories of them later. What does he tell his students about the meaning of his wolf story?

"I leave that up to them."

Call and Response

The exchange between Peden and the wolf may not have been a verbal conversation, but it *was* communication or at least manipulation. When the wolf pointed with its head and body, Peden followed it. If, however, Peden had pointed with his own head and body, the wolf would have been indifferent. A dog can understand what we mean when we point; a wolf cannot. That ability coevolved in the human-canine relationship. Still, the normally taciturn Peden understood the reticent wolf's intention, and the wolf understood the same in Peden.

"We make the assumption that other animals can't have language. So we don't look for it," according to Con Slobodchikoff, professor emeritus at Northern Arizona University. An animal behaviorist, he is an expert in prairie dog communication, which he calls language.

By any definition—communication, manipulation, language—the whisper surrounds us, even when we're not listening. Maybe especially then. Wolves howl to contact and reconnect with pack mates over long distances. Bees broadcast using a different kind of signal, odor plumes. Lizards also employ chemical signals for choosing mates and communicating with other lizards in the lounge. (*Lounge* is, in fact, the collective noun for a group of lizards.)

Researchers at Tel Aviv University applied a modified algorithm designed for human voice recording to analyze the calls of fifteen thousand Egyptian fruit bats, sometimes called flying foxes, matching their vocalizations to bat videos to detect what behavior the calls were associated with. A fruit bat's tongue is so long that when the bat isn't feeding, it remains coiled inside the bat's rib cage. Even so, they're never tongue tied. Living in colonies of more than one thousand members, fruit bats hang around upside down in their caves, arguing. The contentiousness comes in four varieties, each with its own sounds. The bats argue about food, about their sleeping quarters, and about sitting too close together, and the males use one call to protest unwanted sexual advances. Bats blurt slightly modified call versions to the individuals with whom they are communicating.

Animals detect and study each other and us in humbling ways. Ants send complex messages with the release of ten to twenty pheromones. "It's almost like sentences being formed," according to E. O. Wilson. Using underwater microphones, Russian scientists report that dolphins create "words" by changing the volume and frequency of pulsed clicks and that one dolphin will listen to an entire "sentence" without interrupting and then respond with its own string of words. The sentences include up to five words, though scientists still don't know what the words mean.

If we could increase the audio intensity of this vast, whispering "outernet," infinitely more powerful than the human-created internet, it would turn to a roar, overpowering all our senses, including some we don't know we have.

Elephants generate seismic activity with their feet and trunks to communicate with one another. The tiny coqui frog can produce a sound nearly as loud as a pneumatic drill. Male alligators try to attract females by emitting low-frequency sounds that, as the BBC puts it, "cause the droplets on their backs to 'dance' at the surface." Try that on your next date. Then there's this:

Newsweek reports that scientists have recorded the "thunderous sound of 1.5 million fish mating in Mexico.... [T]he Gulf corvinas' machine-gun mating call can deafen dolphins and sea lions.... When they sing in chorus, the sound is loud enough to hear from fishing boats"—sometimes loud enough to awaken fishermen from deep sleep, transporting them from one dream into another.

Most animals communicate only with members of their own species. Others, like John Peden's wolf, prefer to talk to members of their own kind but will, if necessary or even out of curiosity, make themselves understood across the barrier separating them from another species. *H. sapiens* is that kind of animal. Or can be.

Because of our close coevolution, humans and dogs are remarkably communicative. In one experiment, John Pilley, a retired Wofford College psychology professor, taught Chaser, a border collie, to understand more than one thousand words, many of which the dog was able to associate with particular objects (specifically, eight hundred toy animals, 116 balls, and twenty-six Frisbees), and even some rudimentary grammar.* However, the neural mechanisms necessary for dogs to analyze and integrate the expression and intonation of human words has evolved even in the absence of a shared spoken language. Cats probably have a larger vocabulary than dogs. Purring turns out to be more complex than most of us assume. For example, cats purr not only when they're content but also when they're hurting. A purr can be a way for a cat to say "Stick around. I need you." By feeding various sounds back to us, cats train us to know what they're saying. They may, in fact, develop "a secret code of meows," as John Bradshaw, a University of Bristol anthrozoologist, writes, a code "between each cat and its owner, unique to that cat alone and meaning little to outsiders." In coming years, phonetics experts at Sweden's Lund University hope to further decode feline language. One question they'll ask: Do cats prefer humans to use pet-directed speech or to speak to them as people do to human adults? The researchers are also studying feline use of melody for communication.

Other domesticated or semidomestic animals communicate across species, too. Goats can apparently distinguish the broadcasts of our facial expressions—and exhibit a preference for smiling human faces. And wild

---

* His website, Dognition. was created for people who want to test their dog's intelligence, www.dognition.com/chaser-dog.

animals also communicate beyond the borders of their own species. In 2017, Russian scientists reported that a beluga whale, while living in captivity with a pod of bottlenose dolphins, learned their vocalizations of whistles and clicks and ceased using some of its own vocalizations. Over time, the dolphins' fear of the whale was no longer expressed, and the beluga began to swim alongside a dolphin calf. The researchers did not claim that the beluga learned dolphin language, but it did put the dolphin sounds to good use.

Since the 1960s, marine mammal veterinarian Sam Ridgeway, cofounder of the U.S. Navy Marine Mammal Program in San Diego, has trained marine mammals to locate and retrieve sunken torpedoes in the Arctic. In a 2012 article in *Current Biology*, Ridgeway reports progress in studying the vocalizations of beluga whales, often called the "canaries of the sea." At the Vancouver Aquarium, a fifteen-year-old beluga was capable of speaking his own name, Lagosi. "Other utterances," Ridgeway writes, "were not perceptible, being described as 'garbled human voice, or Russian, or similar to Chinese," but he further notes that one whale's "sound recordings and analysis . . . demonstrate[d] spontaneous mimicry of the human voice, presumably a result of vocal learning, by a white whale." The whale's name was NOC. According to Smithsonian.com, within days "NOC's voice was burbling from computers around the globe." Heard today, the sound is disconcerting, oddly moving, like a small child who has not mastered language but has something she is desperately trying to say. Whether NOC is doing mere mimicry or actually saying something is not known. But oceanographer Paul Dayton is convinced from his own experiences that marine mammals are communicating with us in ways we do not yet understand.

Con Slobodchikoff hopes to tap into the language of prairie dogs and make it accessible to humans through the use of digital technology. Prairie dog communication, he related in a 2013 interview in the *Atlantic*, is "the most sophisticated animal language that has been decoded." Studying prairie dog colonies over time, using sound-frequency analysis, he found that the animals call to one another by stringing together clusters of sounds into something like sentences. They put this ability to good use. For example, they can warn one another about predators—with observed details, including kind, color, and size. They can tell other prairie dogs whether they're seeing a dog or coyote, distinguishing between the two. "I personally think that whales and dolphins and monkeys are going to be shown to have very sophisticated languages," he said. "I think that we're just plumbing the very surface of things, and we'll find that their language is far more sophisticated than even we know right now, today."

Slobodchikoff is working with a computer scientist to use artificial intelligence (AI) to build a record of each prairie dog call, analyze it, and then translate it audibly, potentially in English. "So the prairie dogs could say something like 'thin brown coyote approaching quickly.' And then we could tell the computer something that we wanted to convey to the prairie dogs," transforming the human comments into prairie dog talk and playing it back to the prairie dogs. "We have the technology now to be able to develop devices that are the size of a cellphone and that would allow us to talk to our dogs and cats," he continued. "But I think we can get to the point where we can actually communicate back and forth in basic animal languages to dogs, cats, maybe farm animals— and, who knows, maybe lions and tigers." He imagines a computer-augmented future in which humans and other animals renegotiate their relationships.

> What I'm hoping, actually, is that down the road, we will be forming partnerships with animals, rather than exploiting animals. A lot of people either exploit animals, or they're afraid of animals, or they have nothing to do with animals because they don't think that animals have anything to contribute to their lives. And once people get to the point where they can start talking to animals, I think they'll realize that animals are living, breathing, thinking beings, and that they have a lot to contribute to people's lives.

Interspecies and even extraspecies communication is not limited to animals. One-celled bacteria can "talk," using "quorum sensing," the passage of signaling molecules from individual cell to individual cell; this is similar to how our brains use electrical signaling to communicate with other parts of the brain and the body.

In the 1999 edition of *The Whole Earth Catalog*, Paul Stamets, a much-honored mycologist based in Washington State, proclaimed mycelia fungi "Earth's natural Internet." One mycelium colony in Oregon was twenty-four hundred acres in size before logging roads cut through it, Stamets reports. It is estimated to be twenty-two hundred years old. In symbiosis with trees and plants, mycorrhizal fungi provide mineral nutrients in exchange for carbon. Researchers in the United Kingdom describe how mycorrhizal mycelia can serve "as a conduit for signaling between plants, acting as an early warning system for herbivore attack." And pines do whisper. Suzanne Simard, a professor of forest ecology at the University of British Columbia, has studied Canadian forests for three decades and has concluded that Douglas fir trees "recognize their kin." So-called mother trees send excess carbon through the living internet of fungi to their seedlings and reduce their own root systems to make more room for them, says Simard. She considers these symbiotic trees and seedlings to be "families."

To complete the loop, plants and trees, and possibly bacteria, communicate with animals. Plants may be rooted in one spot, but periodically they need mobility to spread their seed and for pollination, so they use animals as mobile units to do just that. Some plants release chemical cocktails into the air that send signals out to specific, cooperative animal species. The plants call, and the animals respond.

Hanging Out in the Tatooine Cantina

Remember the *Star Wars* bar scene on the planet Tatooine? Motley characters from different galaxies gather to argue and make mayhem. In the cantina, different languages and ways of communicating dissolve into interspecies inebriation. The result isn't pretty. Nor is it boring. Think of it as interspecies communication at an interstellar crossroads. The drinkers don't require translators. Between and across species, they seem to communicate in a preexisting superlanguage of visual, auditory, and other patterns of behaviors, mostly beyond words. Something like that seems to be what's happening for us, too, back home on the Blue Planet.

I use the word *superlanguage* to describe a nonverbal way of communicating that allows different species, including humans, to understand one another in a basic way. The word is usually applied to a spoken language shared by Ice Age Europeans fifteen thousand years ago, one that allowed groups to communicate across cultural and linguistic chasms.[*] Some words of that language are still used today. Among them: *you*, *we*, and *man*.

---

[*] Another superlanguage, Esperanto, was created in the nineteenth century and promoted by the League of Nations and, for a time, the United Nations. It was designed to be a common language of the human species, easy to learn and speak. Gone were all those pesky irregular verbs, complex conjugations, and redundant words. Esperanto never quite caught on.

Here is a speculation: Humans and other animals have modes, gestures, sounds, bleeps, and blurts—identifiable patterns—that predate just about every species that exists today. We and our fellow creatures use it all the time, without any particular awareness. Some use it more than others. Perhaps if we were more aware, we could parse its modulations, run it through computers for translation, and even teach it.

Patricia H. Hasbach, an ecopsychologist in private practice and a faculty member in the Graduate School of Counseling and Education at Lewis and Clark College, has been working for several years on a catalog of these patterns, which she calls "nature language." At a 2017 conference on connecting children to nature, she described her concept as a work in progress. Coauthor of two books on ecopsychology, she is a pioneer in the practice of ecotherapy—a method of treatment that recognizes the healing benefits of interactions with nature.

A few years ago, Hasbach and her coauthor, Peter H. Kahn Jr., were inspired by the concept of "pattern language," a term coined by architect Christopher Alexander to describe a design approach for buildings and cities. His work taps into the inherent wisdom of interconnected, repeating patterns found in nature. Alexander says these patterns express an aliveness that he refers to as "the quality that has no name," which produces a sense of wholeness and spirit. Applying pattern-language architecture, Alexander uses words from linguistics to describe the basic elements, including "syntax" (place) and "grammar" (patterns already successful in nature). To him, nature is language. Hasbach picks up on the linguistic roots of Alexander's pattern language, suggesting the existence of recognizable interaction patterns that occur in nature again and again. Currently, Hasbach is identifying many of these shared interactions along a "continuum of wildness" and applying them to her therapeutic work.

Here is a partial and rudimentary list of communication and engagement patterns shared by humans and many other animals. The list is based in part on the work of Hasbach but also includes patterns detected by others, and in some of the stories of animal encounters and relationships collected in this book:

- "Recognizing and being recognized" (Hasbach's phrase for taking time to engage or observe, see and be seen)

• Displaying mutual curiosity, including demonstrations of tolerance or indifference
• Engaging in playful interactions with another animal or animals
• Exhibiting empathy
• "Crossing the threshold" (Hasbach's expression for entering the psychological or spiritual space that exists between two animals)
• Becoming the animal (e.g., for humans, the practice of critical anthropomorphism)
• Using intonement—singing tones or monotones

The Song of the Wild

Not all scholars consider animal song to be music or analogous to it. However, the interpretation of animal sounds as music—long rooted in Indigenous thinking and ancient myths—has led to a new interdisciplinary field called zoomusicology. The journal *Current Biology* describes this field as a study of "the music-like aspects of sound communication among non-human animals." For example, researchers have found that elephants may be as musically inclined as people; when neuroscientists studied music played by the Thai Elephant Orchestra (assembled by a conservationist), they found that pachyderms keep better time on drums than humans do.

Long before videos of dogs singing became ubiquitous on the internet, the rare New Guinea singing dog was yodeling in the wild. In a family group, one dog begins, then is joined by others, each at a different sound pitch, in a synchronized chorus. Sonograms reveal an eerie similarity to the song of the humpback whale.

Recent research also suggests the following: The brains of birds and humans show some similarities when listening to music, fish react differently to different human composers, and cows produce more milk and dogs are less stressed when listening to soothing classical music.

Cats, on the other hand, don't like or care about our tunes. Middle-aged cats are the most indifferent—they say *meh* to music—though I've recently learned about a psychologist and composer team who have created music that some cats *do* like, using frequencies and tempos similar to the ones that cats use when they communicate with each other or with us. (But cats, of course, are contrarians.) Once, I found an abandoned and sick kitten huddled in a sandstorm. She was tucked behind a board outside a cafe in the Navajo Nation town of Chinle, Arizona. I took her home, named her Chinle, and raised her. She had no sense of balance and would fall from every available window ledge. In her middle years, she didn't mind when I sang to her. In fact, every time I sang Don McLean's song "Starry, Starry Night" about Vincent van Gogh, and only that song, she would sit on my lap and sing along. More or less in tune. Halfway through the song she would begin to caterwaul, ending with what sounded pretty much like an orgasm. She was exceptional.

Bernie Krause, a bioacoustician, is one of the leaders of another new field, "soundscape ecology." Krause records all the animal and plant sounds in the environments they inhabit, listens for patterns, and analyzes the communication of animals and plants. When he speaks at schools, Krause reminds students that in the places where they ride their bikes, there might once have been the sounds of bison, deer, elk, moose, foxes, wolves, bobcats, mountain lions, dozens of kinds of birds, and thousands of insects, all singing together in a kind of collective chorus he calls a "biophony." He believes that localized biophonies seeded and shaped the development of human music, from the songs of Indigenous peoples to Mozart to Madonna to Drake, and influenced the creation and evolution of our instruments, from a fifty-three-thousand-year-old hominid flute made of bear bone, to a four-thousand-year-old French vulture bone flute, to George Harrison's crimson Les Paul guitar. Krause also tells students how people who live in the wilder places of the globe make their instruments from the natural resources available—flutes from bamboo or drums from animal hide—and that the rhythms, melodies, and harmonies these instruments make are based on the sounds of the nature around them. Some Indigenous people, when playing their music, use the forest "as a kind of back-up band," he told me. On the Indonesian island of Borneo, "the gibbons sing beautiful duets that echo through the rainforest at dawn. You can hear the singing of these tree-dwelling apes for miles. When you listen to the music created by the people of the Borneo rainforest, you can hear the influence of these duets." He continued:

> The music of people living in South American rainforests has no
> doubt been influenced by a bird like the musician wren. This bird

whistles a repeated melodic tune that is really quite striking and surprisingly beautiful . . . a tune that sounds like a flute playing the blues. Over time, the musician wren learned to sing these notes in a way that said many things to the other creatures living nearby. He was telling other male wrens that the tree he was singing in was *his* tree and no one else's. But this same song, if it was pretty enough, might attract a female to become his mate. He was telling other birds that this was *his* vocal territory and that others needed to find other ways to sing and stay out of his way. He's also saying, "But if you're a female musician wren, you can cross the line and we'll check things out." At the same time, the musician wren's voice becomes part of the creature chorus where his song blends with all the others— but to do this in a way that no one else's sound blocks his own from being heard.

Humans and other animals share a variety of vocal expressions, but one animal's Bach can be another animal's rock. When birders in the field fire up their birdsong apps, the calls can disrupt the communication of birds nearby and stress the target species. Songbirds have had to adapt their songs to their rackety new neighbors—us. Some birds, including American robins, sparrows, and wrens, are able to change their voices so that they can be heard in spite of human-made noise. Krause teaches young people to listen for those adjustments. "Learning about the natural world without the soundscape is a bit like trying to watch *Star Wars* without the soundtrack," he said.

The oldest language—all those patterns and signals we share with other animals—continues. When we answer the call of a coyote or owl with our own, we sing the oldest song. Most of the time, it remains hidden from us, between the words, behind the notes, in the air surrounding the gesture.

In 2018, the Royal Society, an independent scientific academy of the United Kingdom, published the results of a study from the University of Neuchâtel, which offered evidence of what may be a kind of linguistic common ground between species. In a Royal Society interview, Raphaela Heeson, the lead author of the study, explained that "human languages are characterized by common statistical patterns, known as linguistic laws." One of those is the law of abbreviation, whereby the most commonly used words tend to be shorter, and for words with more syllables, those syllables tend be shorter. "Work on animal vocal communication has indicated that humans are not the only species whose communicative system is under-pinned by these laws," she said. "In our paper, we show for the first time that these laws also hold in animal gestural communication." The research-ers identified fifty-eight different types of gestures used by chimpanzees in social play. When they analyzed videos of the gestures, they found that the law of abbreviation applied to the chimpanzee gestures. According to Heeson, the study revealed that chimpanzee language, based primarily on gestures, and human language, dependent mainly on vocalization, share "some fundamental mathematical properties and that linguistic laws may apply beyond the vocal modality of communication."

Conservation, engineering, medicine, art, and our personal lives might be enriched through a deeper understanding of the oldest language. Gaining that understanding will be easier said (or gestured) than done. As A. A. Milne, best known for his Winnie-the-Pooh books, once observed, "Some people talk to animals. Not many listen though. That's the problem."

EIGHT

How to Talk with Birds

On a warm summer afternoon in Atascadero, California, Kathleen Lockyer and her seven-year-old daughter were in their backyard at the edge of the Salinas River. Her daughter was pounding a stone against an acorn when she suddenly looked up.

"Mama! What's he saying?" she said.

Lockyer's stomach fluttered. Was someone hiding in the backyard or watching them? Was her daughter hearing imaginary voices?

"Who?" asked Lockyer.

"Him, that guy," her daughter said without looking up.

The uneasiness in Lockyer's stomach turned into a small knot. She stood, then walked to one side of the house and peered down the driveway. Still no one. She walked to the other side of the house and peered between the fence and the house. No one.

"Who are you hearing?"

Her daughter went back to pounding the acorn, Lockyer recalled, "and as condescendingly as a seven-year-old can," she looked up at her mother and said, "That guy! *Liisssten!* Don't you hear that guy?" The little girl stood up and pointed with the stone in the direction of the front yard. "That *bird*!"

The knot in Lockyer's stomach unraveled. "Oh yeah, now I hear him," she answered, exhaling.

"So what's he *saying*?" the girl asked with a demanding tone. She watched her mother with catlike attention. Lockyer closed her eyes and turned her head in the direction her daughter was pointing.

She heard road noise, a distant leaf blower, an airplane, the river, and other random noises before tuning into the *cheep cheep cheep*. Once she heard the sharp metronome-like chime, she wondered, "How had I not heard it before? Why is *she* so tuned in?"

What was it about the sound that had clued her daughter into the call, to hear it and to be alarmed by it? And what did it *mean* to her daughter?

It was an alarm call.

Lockyer knew what a bird's alarm call sounded like. But her daughter, still at an age most sensitive to nature's signals, had heard it first.

What the Animals Say

For more than two decades, Lockyer has worked as an occupational therapist, helping children and teens with sensory processing disorders. She believes that bird language is the tangible representation of just how complicated and layered the human auditory processing system is. "It may have been the first auditory language that our ancestors tuned into," she says. "Bird language was part of what probably developed the auditory processing capabilities, which we needed for survival."

Those moments in the backyard underscored what she already knew, that nature connection could be a powerful therapeutic tool. In 2004, as a way to incorporate bird language into her work, Lockyer began to attend field courses offered by 8 Shields, a nature connection and mentoring program founded by Jon Young and headquartered in Santa Cruz, California. There she had learned about baseline birdcalls and the calls that birds make when the baseline is disturbed, especially when a predator is nearby. And, of course, she discovered more than that.

Science knows more about bird language than about the communication methods of reticent sharks or voluble dolphins, in part because birds are easier to study and are available nearly everywhere. But research on bird communication offers new surprises every year. For example, in 2016 researchers at Australia's Deakin University discovered that native zebra finches sing to their eggs during hot weather, and because of these fast, high-pitched "incubation calls," as the scientists call them, the embryos are somehow protected from the heat and grow more slowly in their eggs than they otherwise would, and when the chicks emerge from their long awakening, they are healthier because of the songs they have heard or absorbed in some way we do not understand.

I first met Young in 2013 at a conference on connecting children with nature. Though he often speaks in a Santa Cruz dialect, he has always seemed to me to be more of an enthusiastic, down-to-earth middle-school teacher than a New Age guru. His self-deprecating grin is infectious. We began a conversation then that has continued ever since.

Young grew up in Monmouth County, New Jersey. Starting at the age of ten, he learned wildlife tracking from an exceptionally talented tracker and mentor. At Rutgers University, he majored in natural history, with an anthropology emphasis that explored how Native cultures help their children understand and connect with the natural world. Over the years, he founded several nature connection programs, including 8 Shields and the Wilderness Awareness School in Duvall, Washington. To help people understand bird language, he teaches them specific patterns of sound and behavior, which he calls "shapes of alarm." He then asks them to sit quietly in order to journal and map the "shapes" and, finally, to share their observations with one another. This process reveals the larger patterns of the birds' alarms and behaviors as related to the movement of hawks, cats, people, and other disturbances. In this way, he says, birds are participating meaningfully and predictably in something resembling a conversation. "Deep bird language," as he defines it, refers to the specifics of bird life but is also about a different frame of mind and awareness, a practical combination of observation and feeling.

One basic step is to recognize alarm calls. Robert D. Magrath, an ornithologist and behavioral ecologist at the Australian National University, studies bird communication patterns. Almost every bird species that his team has studied responds not only to alarm calls from members of their own species but also to those of other bird species in the same locality. Magrath suspects that birds' eavesdropping on other species' calls is common—not surprising, as he points out, "given that almost all species are vulnerable to predators and so should use any available cues that predators are around." His research has revealed that red-breasted nuthatches understand chickadee warnings and can precisely decode the level of danger in those calls.

When a raptor approaches overhead, the tufted titmouse, a songbird, sends out an alarm that is understood by squirrels and chipmunks, who not only flee but who are also capable of imitating the titmouse warning to let still other animals know about the pending threat. Magrath contends that these calls are learned rather than innate. Either way, birds and small mammals have been living and dying and coevolving with one another long enough that they share communication patterns.*

Young explained to me how he has his students enter the birds' world by sitting quietly rather than "plowing through." He advises them to choose a "sit spot" in, say, a forest or backyard. "As a kid, I had the same sit spot from early summer 1971 to the fall of 1978, rarely missing a day," he said. Others have outdone him. Max Allen, a naturalist, tracker, and nature photographer, racked up more than 2,555 consecutive days in ad hoc sit spots he would visit everywhere he traveled. "As Allen told me," continued Young, "it's difficult to put into words the life lessons and wisdom we learn from this kind of practice, and it's best *felt* rather than *thought* in the head. So it's not essential that you make it to your sit spot every single day, but it is important to go there as regularly as possible."

In your sit spot, if you're quiet, many of the birds and other wildlife that hid or disappeared when you arrived will return when they realize you're not a threat. Unseen birds become visible; some will search for food close to your feet. "Do this often enough," said Young, "and over time the birds will come to know you as an individual: *Here comes Kathleen again, a little late.*" A single bird may, in a sense, adopt you. Your connection to that bird will draw others to you, and your knowledge of their patterns and personality can be applied to other birds of that species and then to animals of other species.

The 8 Shields bird-language immersion program teaches the "routine of invisibility": Imagine two spheres, one representing your *awareness* of the natural world and the other representing the *disturbance* you cause. Slowly expand the sphere of awareness and shrink the sphere of disturbance. As the beneficial sphere becomes larger than the detrimental one, you'll start seeing and hearing more birds; you'll become more invisible, more welcome in the animals' home.

Similar methods are taught by several nature connection and tracking programs around the country. In 2016, Kathleen Lockyer founded her own

---

* As I write this, I hear a high-pitched repetitive call outside the stone cottage where I am staying. It sounds like a bird, but not quite. I go to the door to look for the bird and see a ground squirrel with its babies gathered around it; the squirrel is making what surely sounds like a bird alarm. Its tail twitches with each tweet. From the grass beyond, I hear the chittering reply, presumably from other squirrels. I'll spend the next few minutes scanning the trees for a hawk.

nature therapy program, Rx Outside. All these programs practice their own approaches, but there is overlap. Young's includes these features:

- Wandering. Practice timeless, unstructured exploration with, in Young's words, "nothing to accomplish, nowhere to go."
- Questioning. Here journalism basics come in handy. Ask who? what? where? why? how?
- Tracking. Develop powers of pattern recognition not only by learning to identify animal tracks but also by getting down on all fours and following them.
- Mapping. Learn basic orienting skills, perceive the landscape from a bird's-eye view, and draw maps not simply to establish landmarks but also "to reveal gaps in what we notice," according to Young.
- Journaling. Keep seasonal records; create personal field guides that incorporate writing, drawing, and even sound recording to retain what is noticed and learned.
- Listing. Keep a list of observed animal patterns—how they walk, run, fly, eat, dance, mate.
- Mind's-eye imagining. Develop the ability, *with eyes closed*, to reexperience events gathered from all senses.
- Allowing for complications and moral friction. These are part of every relationship.
- Recognizing, in advance and afterward, patterns of contentment or distress. This is what Young calls "making ripples" in the environment of another animal.

These interaction patterns are practiced by many animals, including humans. The list could go on, but the last item is particularly relevant to conservation and environmentalism. To be successful, those who love nature must first become aware of the animal pattern changes our presence makes—whether through the intrusion of a bulldozer or a single footstep or the climate crisis—and then determine what we can do to avoid or reduce that distress and thereby reduce our own. To this we should add the humbling act of encountering animals higher than us on the food chain (ones that can have the last word, so to speak), practicing reciprocity by giving care and protection to animals partly in return for the gifts they give us, and sharing our experiences with other people through the oldest social networks—in-person storytelling, art, and music—and through Instagram, too.

Young recommends that individuals and families make storytelling a dinner table ritual, emulating the campfire gatherings of our ancestors and current camp counselors. Through that ritual we reflect on outdoor experiences, which is easier to do when the experience is relived and told to another. A person may hear a bird but not listen, and when asked later if birds were heard, the answer will be no.

Young travels often to Africa, to the Kalahari Desert in Botswana, where he learns about an older, deeper connection to nature from a people who have no collective name for themselves. They're usually called Sān, at least by outsiders. From them, he has learned about the practice of "storycatching." By practicing storycatching, a person learns to pay close attention to every detail observed, heard, or sensed in any way; perhaps then to ask the bird a question; and, afterward, to bring the experience back to the campfire or dinner table. In telling the story, they not only use words but act the story out physically—including the bird's actions. By catching and telling stories, people become progressively more sensitive to all that happens around them, and in them, in nature. This is only one of the exercises that Young teaches at his gatherings.

In an informal email survey, I asked recent 8 Shields participants to describe what they had learned during their weeklong session in the forest around River's Bend Retreat Center in northern California and how the experience had changed them. The group of 120 students consisted mostly of adults but also some teenagers and a few children. Some camped in the woods, and others slept at a nearby motel.

One woman responded: "When I'm doing a bird sit, I have a feeling in my body that has no intellectual connection to what's going on around me. I'm not just an observer. I'm actually a participant in the landscape." She now interacts with animals in a different way. "Yesterday I saw a robin. I was careful and conscious that I wasn't disturbing it as I passed. It was looking at me, and I was looking at it off and on in glances." By not staring too long, she was trying to protect its sense of safety. "In that way, we were communicating, although all the robin was saying was, 'What are you going to do next?'" Opening herself to the language of birds has reinforced her awareness that she creates "a ripple everywhere I go." Another participant, a musician, described his experience this way: "One of the takeaways from bird language is the capacity to see events as patterns instead of random, for example, being able to watch the room when someone tense enters, see the ripple of that go through the room, and watch as that ripple hits people and changes the quality and movement of the conversation."

Learning bird language, and about one's own ripple, builds capacity for understanding and compassion. "My energy may cause a bird to flee. That fleeing bird may be picked off by a predator hunting in the wake of my disturbance," said a yoga instructor. "So we say, 'Some days you feed the songbird, some days you feed the hawk.' When I hear a series of bird alarms or see a bird fleeing for its life, it grabs me right in the heart. I feel empathy for the prey and for the hunter, who also needs to eat to feed its young." Back at home, in their yards or other open areas, the participants create "threads of connection to the songbirds in [their] yard, and over time these threads become ropes," as one bird language student put it, echoing one of Young's key lessons. And one participant, a choreographer, summed up the experience this way: "At first you can't hear the tiniest bird in the bush next to you. Through sitting and listening, expanding your awareness, little by little, you hear a song, softly at first, but soon it's a chorus and your heart is part of the song."

When the students describe the relationships and ripples that come with bird language, they conjure the image of a fluid map. In fact, for hunting and gathering cultures, bird language provides a mental chart of types of birds seen or heard, their numbers, specific vocalizations, and other details that may reveal running water or still water, fish, insect hatches, dead trees, fruit, carcasses, predators, and more.

For some people in Young's class, the process translates into caring more about other human beings, including themselves. A seventeen-year-old boy wrote to me that the week he spent learning bird language helped him connect with peers, a struggle for him in the past. He can still "get lost looking for connection" with people yet "can always rely on going to [his] sit spot, to listen to the birds and let them be a mirror to look inside [himself] for connection and love."

Awakening the Seventh Sense

Some aspects of interspecies communication resemble the sixth sense, usually defined as intuitive perception. Without discounting the extrasensory aspect of that definition, deep communication with animals is more likely a collection of practical knowledge, empathy, and intuition, and the use of senses we have forgotten we have or could better develop. We might call that collection of talents, emotions, and knowledge the seventh sense.

It's true when it comes to the senses that humans are generally outclassed. Elephants can hear thunderstorms from 310 miles away. Grizzlies can smell *you* from 18 miles away. Bloodhounds can even smell across time: they're able to create a detailed history from layers of scent in one spot. In addition to seeing the same spectrum of light we detect, mantis shrimp can see in ultraviolet, infrared, and polarized light. Jumping spiders have tetrachromatic vision, which means that they see four primary colors (we see only three). No wonder they jump.

Still, we're no slouches in the senses department. In my research for a previous book, I found that scientists who study human perception no longer assume we have only five senses: taste, touch, smell, sight, and hearing. They conclude, conservatively, that humans have (but do not necessarily use) nine or ten senses and perhaps as many as thirty or more, including, among others, proprioception (awareness of our body's position in space) and echolocation (use of reflected sound to locate objects). In one study, human subjects, just like bats and dolphins, proved capable of locating objects through the echoes of their own tongue clicks. The echoes were perceived through vibrations in ears, tongue, and bones. Our familiar senses can be far more acute than most of us have assumed. There's a reason we have two nostrils. We smell in stereo, side to side. A study at the University of California–Berkeley required a group of undergraduates (the study's subjects) to wear taped-over goggles, earmuffs, and work gloves to block as many senses as possible. These students were able to follow, accurately through every twist and turn, a thirty-foot-long trail of chocolate scent. And they zigzagged, a technique employed by nearly every animal, domestic and wild, that makes its living with its nose.

South African Anna Breytenbach travels the world as a professional interspecies communicator. She reports brief mental pictures that come to her when she touches an animal's track in the field, which she calls "sudden knowings." Most scientists would be leery of giving credit to animal telepathy, but Breytenbach might be onto something.

Migrating birds and fish use Earth's magnetic fields to navigate; now some researchers theorize that humans have the same ability, called magnetoreception, in which our brains hold "grid cells" that keep track of where we are. Another possibility is suggested by Ron Rensink, an associate professor in psychology and computer science and director of the Visual Cognition Lab at the University of British Columbia–Vancouver. He calls it "visual sensing without seeing," or an added visual system that some people subconsciously use along with their everyday visual ability. They sense something occurring in the split second before the brain can make sense of the incoming light and turn it into an image. While respecting his data, some scientists remain skeptical. However, scientists do acknowledge synesthesia, a phenomenon that occurs when the use of one sensory or cognitive ability, such as hearing, forces the activation of another sense, say, vision. We think we're seeing what we're actually hearing. In addition, scientists know that all animals produce small levels of bioluminescence (created when electrons lose energy, which emits light photons); in 2009, Japanese scientists using a special camera discovered that our bodies emit light. This human bioluminescence is a thousand times lower than what the human eye can detect, but it is there nonetheless. The researchers reported that "the human body literally glimmers." If these theories are correct, there's more than one way to see a cat. And presumably for the cat to see us.

Others have taken this controversial idea further. Daniel Goleman, author of *Emotional Intelligence*, suggests the existence of "a kind of neural wi-fi." Our brains continually react to people around us through our mirror neurons, a system that tracks our emotions and movements and "activates, in our brains, precisely the same brain areas as are active in the other person. This puts us on the same wavelength and it does it automatically, instantaneously and unconsciously." Digby Tantum, a clinical professor of psychotherapy in the United Kingdom's University of Sheffield, believes spoken language plays only a small—or at most partial—role in human communication and that the human "interbrain," as he describes it, is continually picking up microsignals from other brains and transmitting them. Echoing Goleman, he likens these signals to a Wi-Fi connection, a human wireless fidelity always working in the background of consciousness. Through it, we pick up "tells" from other people—not just a tick of the eyelid but also an actual signal that, he suggests, might explain why we have accurate hunches about other people, why laughter is contagious, and why we're attracted to large sporting events and religious settings where, he claims, we achieve an interbrain-induced sense of transcendence. He also claims that a grow-ing scarcity of face-to-face communication, due in part to the internet, is damaging our ability to use the interbrain.

Theories of neural Wi-Fi and other mysterious animal frequencies are fun to consider, but they still fall short of convincing scientific proof.

Meanwhile, science accepts the existence of interspecies communica-tion. Border collies and ranchers could not do their work together without collaboration and signals and "tells" too subtle for others to see. In Laguna, Brazil, one school of wild dolphins works with a group of fishermen by signal-ing with head or tail slaps where and when the fishermen should throw nets. The dolphins chase schools of mullet into the nets and share the catch. This is a way of life for these fishermen and their two hundred families, as well as for the dolphins—and it depends on intergenerational education by both species. The older generation of fishermen passes along their dolphin-fishing knowledge to the next, and so do mother dolphins, through social learning.

In 2016, a study published in *Science* reported "reciprocal signaling" between humans and birds who hunt together. *Science News* called this "the first solid evidence of two-way, collaborative communication between humans and a nonhuman animal in the wild." The evidence may not have been the first (see the dolphins example above). But it did describe a rare form of mutualism, according to Claire Spottiswoode of the University of Cambridge and the University of Cape Town, who studied how Mozambican human honey hunters call out a specialized vocal sound—a long trill and a sharp grunting "Brrr-hm!" A small bird, the greater honeyguide, answers with a chattering sound of its own. The birds flit from tree to tree, leading the hunters to bees' nests, where the hunters break up the hives, harvest honey, and leave chunks of beeswax for the birds. Spottiswoode and her team found that the people who use that sound end up being helped by a honeyguide and find hives up to 54 percent more often than when they mimic other wild sounds. The researchers' conclusion: "These results provide experimental evidence that a wild animal in a natural setting responds adaptively to a human signal of cooperation."

The history of dogs and humans illustrates how coevolution can produce a profound understanding between or among species, a deep and produc-tive identification with others, through a collection of senses and abilities we already own.

All this raises an intriguing possibility: future development and practice of enhanced forms of collaborative communication between humans and many other species. People might someday be trained how to use their collective seventh sense and to practice critical anthropomorphism, incorporating current human-animal communications programs—such as those already developed for military use, along with field courses in animal communication. Another ingredient could be technological augmentation. The oldest language would then become the newest language, marketable by universities as an essential tool for yet-to-be-imagined careers.

The journey from here to there will not be easy. In addition to the human disconnect from the natural world, cultural bias perception will present major barriers. Somehow, today, it's fine for Indigenous people or scientists to speak of interspecies communication, but for most of the rest of society, such talk can come off as New Age speak and therefore easy to dismiss.

Then there's the equity problem. Nature connection programs tend to attract the already converted and also those who can afford to take a week to learn in a course or at a camp. As a result, these efforts reach relatively few people, according to Ricardo Sierra, who has been running wilderness summer camps for three decades. Today he is executive director at Hawk Circle Wilderness Education, located in Cherry Valley, New York. He conducts after-school nature programs for elementary- and middle-school students. Another concern: over the past five years, he has witnessed a dramatic change in student attitudes and behaviors. "At least 30 percent of the students I see are too anxious to sit in a sit spot more than a few minutes," he told me. "They can't wait to get back to their cell phones for their next dopamine fix." Sierra believes that addiction to digital tools is a form of self-medication for deeper anxiety. He has added meditation, yoga, self-care, and service learning to his courses. In this way, he hopes, nature connection will reach new audiences and meet them—especially young people—where they are instead of where he wishes they were.

He also believes that the effectiveness of nature connection programs is undercut by low pay and underwhelming staff sizes, leading to a high burnout rate among people who work in them. "With ninety-four million children under the age of eighteen in this country, and only a small percentage of those kids getting outside in a meaningful way, how do we scale this work up?" he asks. "We need real funding and resources. I haven't seen that happening yet."

Sierra offers no easy solution. But, like Young, he continues to believe in the life-changing potential of communicating and connecting with wild animals—not only as a novel way to understand the world but also as therapy and as a long-term pathway to a new frontier of collaboration among species.

Kathleen Lockyer also envisions that future, born of simple wonder.

Back to the Garden

Later that day in their garden, Lockyer and her daughter discovered that the "he" who was sounding an alarm was actually two birds: a pair of California towhees upset and agitated as a gray squirrel crept closer to a nest with babies. Although Lockyer's daughter did not identify it directly as an alarm call, by asking what "that guy" was saying, she was acknowledging a disturbance to her own system, possibly a nearby threat. She couldn't ignore it.

In the not so distant past, such information would have been critical to physical survival. In the present, this form of alertness can help enable development and organization of our neurological foundations—and enhance our sense of being fully alive by making us more aware of our surroundings. "If a sound is not attached to sight or smell or given meaning," Lockyer reasons, "it never makes neurological sense and gets tossed away. We are designed to make sense of our world. Developmentally, the best response to a child who hears the alarm of a bird and asks, 'What's he saying?' is 'I don't know, let's go find out!'"

NINE

Playing Well with the Others

While technological visionaries devote their careers to developing higher forms of machine-augmented human intelligence, the biological whisper—the conversation occurring all around us, even when we do not listen—already augments our intelligence. Sometimes through play.

As a frequent diver, oceanographer Paul Dayton developed a special fondness for harbor seals. To him, they seemed smarter than dogs. And they liked to have their bellies rubbed. Sometimes he played with them, and with sea lions, too. Once, while diving offshore in Baja's Sea of Cortez, he was laying out a transect line, a rope with a lead weight on the end used to mark his progress and guide his return. He picked up a sponge from the seafloor and looked at it. Suddenly another sponge dropped from somewhere above and hit the sand directly in front of him—followed by a diving sea lion, turning its head to look at him, as if to say, "Want a sponge? Here's one." As Dayton continued to work, three more sponges dropped in front him. Then came the lead weight, followed directly by the entire transect line. Dayton is convinced that the sea lion was playing a joke on him. Messing with him.

Animals teach us with their language and their stories, and we teach ourselves in the retelling. *H Is for Hawk* author Helen Macdonald, in her essay "What Animals Taught Me about Being Human," writes, "The purpose of animals in medieval bestiaries [collections of real or imaginary animals with symbolic significance] was to give us lessons in how to live." And our minds, she contends, still work like bestiaries. "We thrill at the notion that we could be as wild as a hawk or a weasel, possessing the inner ferocity to go after the things we want; we laugh at animal videos that make us yearn to experience life as joyfully as a bounding lamb." But she offers a word of caution: "None of us see animals clearly. They're too full of the stories we've given them." Still, "the imagining? The attempt? That is a good and important thing."

Dayton agrees with McDonald's caution about overinterpreting animal behavior through the prism of our own stories. He told me he once knew a technician at Scripps Institution of Oceanography with a pet octopus who hated the office cat. The cat slept in a sun spot near the aquarium, and every day the technician would find a streak of salt from the tank to the sleeping spot. "The octopus hosed down the sleeping cat," the technician surmised. "There might have even been a sense of humor there, but I suspect the act was more about being defensive than playful." The cat had probably tried to pull the octopus out of the aquarium, and the octopus was launching preventive strikes—a serious business. So is football.

Dayton chooses to believe that in some node of its multiple brains, that octopus took pleasure from its sneak attack against the cat. But then, Dayton is a playful man.

The Labrador Retriever of Primates

Curious about the role of play in the bond between humans and other animals, I called Stuart Brown. A psychiatrist, clinical researcher, and founder of the National Institute for Play, Brown has spent years observing animals at play. For a time, he also worked closely with the National Geographic Society and primatologist Jane Goodall. "For two years I chased animals all over the world," he said. His pursuit of animals playing had more to do with humans than with animals. As we spoke, he was sitting in his office. "My tree house is above my head right now. It has a double bed in it, skylights, a stained-glass window. It's noisy up there, because every time there's a little bit of wind it squeaks." Fittingly, Brown spent more time in the tree house when his grandkids were young. "We'd go storytelling up there." He practices the play he preaches.

By nature, humans are "the Labrador retriever of primates," he said. He meant that in a good way. In an increasingly stressful society, many of us need to be reminded to play more and we need to relearn how. Which may be one reason that so many people now share their homes, yards, streets, and parks with Labrador retrievers.

In his book *Play*, Brown describes play as "preconscious and preverbal—it arises out of ancient biological structures that existed before our consciousness or our ability to speak." Defining play has always seemed to Brown "like explaining a joke—analyzing it takes the joy out of it." Still, partly to soothe "the restive natives of Techland" who show up at his presentations, he put together a chart that describes play as "apparently purposeless (done for its own sake)" and voluntary. Play also has an inherent attraction in that it offers freedom from time and diminished consciousness of self, has improvisational potential, and promotes a "continuation of desire," a fancy (or succinct) way of saying we want to keep doing it, and when it's over, we want to do it again.

Looking at Brown's chart, it occurred to me that every quality noted could be applied to most of our encounters or relationships with other animals—though, of course, some of those encounters are not voluntary or desirable. From an evolutionary point of view, he argues, research suggests that play is a biological necessity for health and that "the forces that initiate play lie in the ancient survival centers of the brain—the brain stem—where other anciently preserved survival capacities also reside." Brown cautions that all such definitions and charts fall short of capturing the *feeling* of play. Leave the emotion out of the science, he argues, and "it's like throwing a dinner party and serving pictures of food."

As a medical researcher, Brown's professional frame of reference is evolutionary heritage. "Our union with our animal cousins, our union with nature, our DNA as it goes all the way back to plant life—we're interconnected." And that interconnection, "especially when you add imagination to it," continues to shape us, not only in the far future but right now as well. "Again, whether it's a projection or something physical or spiritual that occurs between you and the animal, I don't know. It doesn't matter that I don't know. There is a phenomenon that seems to be good." Primal play can activate that moment.

Play is a form of enchantment, bringing us out of ourselves and offering a deeper understanding of another creature, an expanded experience, and, when we reenter ourselves, maybe even greater wisdom. Critical anthropomorphism—"wearing snake's shoes," as biologists Jesus Rivas and Gordon Burghardt put it—is a form of playacting and storytelling.

At this point in the conversation, Brown asked about the stories I had been collecting from other people about their encounters with other animals. I shared a few, including my own encounter with the golden eagles on the shore of the lake. And I explained the themes that seemed to run through so many of the stories, including the habitat of the heart.

"This touches things that are very deep in my soul," he said. "A number of similar stories have been sent to me. And I've had personal experiences that are not too different from what you described with the eagles. There are some moments in my life where an animal, and its proclivity to whatever emotion and circumstance was happening to me at the time, put me into a different state." This state is similar to what he calls the "play state," which is "a separate kind of existence that is as specific as dreaming. It is a whole altered space that we haven't fully defined. The 'habitat of the heart' sounds like something we all long for and don't often experience. What you described is preverbal knowledge. There is a wisdom about those moments that can't be described well in words."

Nevertheless, I asked him to elaborate.

"Say you're at a conflicted point in your life—a problem with your career or your mate or your family, emotional vulnerability—and that happens in the presence of an animal," he said, noting that he feels close to the ravens and crows outside his office under the tree house. Their behavior around him, he's observed, seems to change when he is experiencing one of those emotionally charged moments. While he can't offer "a linear conceptual paragraph" to explain the change in atmosphere between him and the animals, he acknowledges that human imagination can affect the circuitry of the cortex in the brain. "Whether what I'm feeling with the raven is a projection, the *process* will make new connections that are adaptive, and those adaptations may push cultural or personal evolution along."

Brown has come to believe that play is one of the most powerful forces in nature: "In the end, it is largely responsible for our existence as sentient, intelligent creatures."

Which brings us back to the Labrador of primates.

People and dogs are members of naturally playful species—juvenile, in a good way, in Brown's opinion. We meet on the same playing field. But the first time Brown came face-to-face with a wolf, he had "the shocking realization that this was not a dog." He was working at the time with a researcher in New Mexico whose doctorate in animal behavior he had helped supervise. "In contrast to the complex 'singing' in wolves, dogs sound off in response

to territorial invitations or frustration and as an attention-getting or emotional expression. Their play and their aggression are easily communicated
to us," Brown said. "Wolves do not need us for their own survival, so their
regard for humans seems blank by comparison, neither friendly nor angry.
Their social structure is complicated and hierarchical. . . . Yet as pups, wolves
and dogs are like rambunctious cousins. For a brief period of development,
wolf pups are compulsive retrievers."

In fact, during the pup stage, the muzzle and ears of a wolf cub are similar
to those of an adult Labrador retriever. As they age, their muzzles lengthen
and their ears become pointed. Some dog breeds, like German shepherds,
resemble wolves, but Labs and golden retrievers "die of old age primarily
still players and retrievers," said Brown. While wolves become bound by
clear rules of hierarchy, essentially serious animals, compulsive and narrow,
dogs generally retain the goofball side of their nature.

Similarly, chimpanzees more closely resemble us when they're infants,
but as they age, their faces lose some of their roundness, their foreheads
slope, their brow ridges grow heavy, their jaw juts forward, and they become
more inflexible and purpose driven in their behavior. Their mental development reaches a plateau and then tends to slow or stop. But because the
human organism insists on staying forever young through play, learning, and
peak experiences, the human brain appears to create new neuron growth
throughout life, especially during windows of neurological opportunity—
growth spurts of awareness that may occur until the end of life. Humans can
even bounce back from strokes through this ability to produce new neurons
used as shortcuts around damaged neural pathways. Chimps, no such luck.

Most, not all, animals grow up. Our inner child (as some people used to
say) does not go gently into assisted care. No matter how old we are or how
sour life may taste, we still need someone to play with. And we need to play
well with the others.

How Elephants Taught Sven Everything He Needed to Know about Business

In his classic book, *The Genesis of Animal Play*, biopsychologist Gordon
Burghardt writes, "Even eminent scholars have thrown up their hands and
considered play more a mystery than a specifiable phenomenon that can be

understood through scientific analysis." Still others claim that play doesn't really exist. As Burghardt sees it, "Play is a reality we have not effectively confronted in science or society. Yet it may lie at the core of who we are and how we came to be." It's also at the core of Burghardt's critical anthropomorphism, which depends not only on science but on imagination, too. "Committed herpetologists are only happy, in my experience, when they have the opportunity, or excuse, to get back to the field and personally collect at least some of their specimens," he writes. "The dirt, water, sand, heat, muck, cold, thirst, ticks, leeches, wasps, bites, scratches, and foul-smelling feces all are part of the treasured experience.... I trust that any field biologist will understand what I mean."

It's safe to say that play is a form of learning and that learning can be a playful adventure. Why else would people watch birds or cruise the Galápagos Islands?

Sven Lindblad is a most practical man, down to earth (or sea). As the founder of Lindblad Expeditions, he operates, with National Geographic, a fleet of ships that offer trips to the Galápagos, Antarctica, and other exotic places. His father is credited with inventing ecotourism, and Sven is one of the world's leaders in the business. He is committed to conservation, and I know him to be a kind and playful man. A few years ago, he invited a group focused on connecting people to nature on a Galápagos expedition. We became acquainted as the ship weaved between islands. One day, our group walked the paths ashore, careful not to step on the toes of blue-footed boobies and iguanas and lava lizards going about their business. Not having been threatened by our species, they barely noticed us.

As Sven was talking about Darwin's discoveries on these isolated islands, a lava lizard ran up the side of a large pointed rock. At the apex, the lizard froze and stared at us. Lava lizards, named for the rocks on which they often perch, look like miniature iguanas. This one had a bright red head and throat. It seemed friendly enough. I told a naturalist who was walking with us that the lava lizard was my favorite animal in the Galápagos, because of its seeming playfulness.

"You know," he said, "lava lizards are cannibals."

Surprised, I asked what possible evolutionary advantage there could be in eating a relative.

"Well, it's not as if they do it all the time. Sometimes they just say, 'Why not?'"*

As we moved along the path among the animals, Sven told me about his boyhood and young adulthood in Africa and the animals there who schooled him. "Elephants taught me everything I needed to know about business," he said. "They gave me my real education and were the best mentors I could possibly have had." As a young man in the 1970s, he spent a year and a half in East Africa studying elephants. Today he says that he aspires to be like an elephant. Sometimes he says to himself, "Think like an elephant."

Elephants play long into adulthood, as do humans. Males play with sticks, stones, and bones and invite one another to play. For them, play is a way to test the trustworthiness of potential friends. Female elephants use play as a strategy to maintain their leadership roles within their families and to survive. Sven noticed that older elephants were better at recognizing impending natural disasters and coming drought. Elephant herds with older matriarchs tended to last longer. This is probably because matriarch elephants, in particular, store massive amounts of social knowledge. They remember an elephant they met decades earlier, as well as paths to water discovered in prior droughts.

"Elephant governance is quite rational," Sven said. "I have never seen an elephant be mean to another elephant. I have seen them battle but not with lethal intent. I have seen a mother elephant kick her teenager out of the family because she knew she had to, and I have seen the reaction of the other young elephants to that—and to when she lets her son back in for a visit. There is a whole list of lessons I learned that I try to emulate. I always fall short, but that experience shaped my life, my attitude toward dealing with other people." And, he added, to running a business. "I only wish I could have developed the ability to, on all fronts, be as wise, compassionate, and strategic as they are."

He then told me a story about an encounter with another animal in Africa, one that saved his life. He was sitting on a rock and felt something

---

* Actually, there are a few advantages to cannibalism. One of them, over the long haul, may be genetic resistance to some diseases. The animal who has been invited to dinner, however, experiences only side effects.

on his bare foot. It was a green mamba, one of the most venomous snakes in the world. "One wrong move and I would have been dead. But then I heard a Third Voice, and I did what the Third Voice said to do."

Be calm and present. Be the rock he thinks he's lying on.

For a while, Sven and the Voice "had a discussion," as he put it, and they waited for the precise moment when a flick of his foot would send the snake flying. Had he heard the voice of a watchful elephant? Was it an auditory hallucination? Or the sound of common sense?

He didn't pretend to know the answer. "But ever since, whenever I'm in danger or under great stress, I go to that moment with the snake, and I hear the Third Voice."

Has he heard it recently?

He laughed. "Oh yes."

The whisper is all around us, the constant song of life communicating with itself. It exists in our mitochondria, in our inner ears and inner self.

Perhaps you first sensed the whisper as a small child, when you buried your face in the fur of a dog's neck; or, when you were twelve, encountering a bull elk on a high ridge; or maybe in midlife, as you sat on a park bench and watched a scrub jay watch you; or, in your final days, startled by the shadow of an owl you already knew was coming. You can learn to whisper, to turn up the volume, to sing within the family of animals.

Banner with friend in 1957, Raytown, Missouri

PART THREE

How We Co-Become

Wonderdogs and Werecats,
Therapy Lizards and Robot Pets

If we imagined that the between-space is just as charged with
possibility as outer space, we might be inclined to turn our attention to
the fecund depths of our co-becoming with earthbound critters.
What could turning our attention look like?

—BAYO AKOMOLAFE, *These Wilds Beyond Our Fences*

No animal should ever jump up on the dining room furniture unless
absolutely certain that he can hold his own in the conversation.

—FRAN LEBOWITZ, *Pointers for Pets*

TEN

More Than Human

For millennia, human beings lived with their livestock. In England, before there was an England, or on the African continent, in our thatch-roofed houses we lined our floors with straw; we slept with our beasts—and their fleas and flies—as if our lives depended on them, because they did, and we protected those beasts from the lions or bears that roamed the dark beyond the fields.

David Western is senior conservationist with the Wildlife Conservation Society in Uganda and founder and chair of the African Conservation Centre in Kenya. He was also among the first conservationists to insist that preservation efforts must include Indigenous peoples, in this case the Maasai of Amboseli National Park in southern Kenya, where Western conducted field research. The Maasai do not have a word for nature. Like the people of many traditional societies, they view humans as essentially inseparable from other animals. Because survival is so dependent on them, and so evident every day, reverence (or respect) and utilitarianism are also inseparable.

"Maasai love their cows," Western tells me. "They tattoo them, sing songs about them." They hold their cattle in such high regard that they believe that other animals came from cattle. Even so, the Maasai still eat their livestock.

This view of animals isn't limited to traditional societies, of course. Tania Moloney grew up on a dairy farm in Boorcan, a crossroads two and a half hours southwest of Melbourne. Pranksters would sometimes change the village's sign to "Beercan." Her family also had a utilitarian and sometimes affectionate relationship with their domestic animals, and the wild ones, too. "Everything had a purpose and a job to do," she told me a few years after we met in Australia. Tania was already one of the leaders in the Australian movement to connect families to nature. The family's dogs were loved, but they were working dogs. They mostly weren't allowed in the house as they were inclined to spend their days eating dead things "or rolling in cow poo." The cats' job was to catch mice and rats. "That's it. I never really felt a deep connection with our cats." Despite that, she loves animals, though her description of her childhood on the farm allows for more contradictions than you might hear from an urban animal lover:

> The girl calves grew up to become milkers; the boy calves went off in the calf buyers' truck with "the man." That was life. And death, I suppose.
>
> When a cow died, Dad always called Jacka the knacker to come and take it away in an already heavily laden truck of bloated dead cows.
>
> I remember one day trying to explain to a friend how we artificially inseminated the cows. She was mortified. We kids used to giggle our heads off when the cows had what we called piggybacks on each other. Then we got to see the miracle of the baby calves being born and sometimes giving them a helping hand. Afterwards we used to put on our rubber boots and go slipping and sliding in the afterbirth singing "Surfin' USA." It was funny until you fell over and landed in it.
>
> When we had pigs, they were for eating, eventually. Sheep, too. However, we always enjoyed feeding and playing with the lambs, feeding them from old glass Coke bottles with a teat attached and giggling at their madly wiggling tails. Until, that was, the inevitable time came for poor Lamby Lamb Chops to become one.
>
> We had ducks once or twice, and when they laid eggs, I remember one day Mum got the temperature slightly (very) wrong in her homemade incubator and they became "duckling à la cooked." She was guilt ridden for years. I did have two fish, but Mum mistakenly poured clear liquid into their tank, which she thought was water. But sadly it wasn't water, and Maverick and Goose (that was my Tom Cruise *Top Gun* crush phase) ended up getting the big flush. Last but not least, there were our many "pet" bunnies. Usually orphaned and unlikely to live for more than a few days at best. But we loved them while they lasted.

The Wild, the Domestic, and the Distorted

Making one's way through the moral maze of our complicated attraction to other animals and our overlapping lives is no easy thing. To eat or not to eat meat, to breed or buy designer pets, to feed wild animals, to catch and release a fish, to love a robot dog, to chase a snake—the maze goes on, passageways change, parts become overgrown and then cleared again. Though the path is as certain as day to some people, most of us feel our way in the twilight. "This question is the unconquered peak: What does it really mean to be part of nature in the twenty-first century?" asks herpetologist Harry Greene. "Will we be spectators, disruptors, or participants?"

In 2012, ecopsychologist Patricia Hasbach began to catalog human interactions with nature on a "spectrum of wildness," which she and colleagues described as a continuum of wild, domestic, and perverse. Today Hasbach admits that "perverse" may have been a poor choice of words. If you label someone's actions as perverse, well, that's a real conversation stopper. Or an argument starter. So, as an alternative, she suggests using the label "distorted" to describe the line we cross "when we move from what we think of as natural and into the purely technological, or when our part of the interaction needlessly harms the other life-form." What about when we eat other life? Her answer: "The question ought to be '*How* do we acquire the food we eat?' All animals must eat to survive. In this example, hunting would be a wild manifestation of this interaction pattern. Raising a farm animal for food would be a domestic example; and killing an animal raised in a factory farm slaughter house would be a distorted manifestation."

To further illustrate this spectrum, she points to the interaction pattern of "recognizing and being recognized," mentioned in chapter 7. A "wild" manifestation of this pattern might be an encounter with a bear or a lion in the wild, inducing feelings of awe or primal fear and a sense of profound humility. The "domestic" manifestation of the pattern could be an interaction with our family pet, such as when we come home at the end of the day and are greeted by a dog who clearly recognizes us as we recognize it, thereby producing a sense of joy. "A 'distorted' manifestation is one we've all witnessed at the local zoo. A person might be seen throwing a piece of food or a pebble at a caged animal or banging on the glass enclosure despite signage telling people not to do so. Most likely, the person engaged in this behavior is trying to get the attention of the animal in the enclosure—to see and be seen."

Regarding this spectrum, let me suggest an additional or standalone category: co-becoming. By this, I mean respecting the necessity of wildness while recognizing the blurred lines that have always existed between wild and domestic, human and other than human. We change other forms of life, and they change us. Nature is messy, nothing genetic is set in stone (except in the fossil archive), and the distinction among wild, domestic, and distorted wavers. Co-becoming is what we see happening all around us right now. It can occur within the span of a lifetime or this week. For example, when we take good care of a dog, it takes good care of us: it protects us, and our interactions with it lower our blood pressure and improve our mental health. We become each other in that sense. As we attempt to outwit the raccoon, it learns to outwit us. At least one of those two species is made smarter by that process.*

Others have used the term *co-becoming*, too, and one of the most interesting applications is found in the collaborative work of Indigenous people in Australia's Northeast Arnhem Land and a research team from Macquarie University and the University of Newcastle. Together, they challenge the "western, dualistic understandings of nature and culture that do not allow for other ways of conceptualizing the world or for the agency of nonhumans." In contrast, they refer to co-becoming as a way to move toward a more-than-human familial relationship with the world, in which divisions between humans and other animals, and even plants and rocks, time and space, dissolve. Clearly, this isn't the standard approach to conservation or biology, but it may well become widely accepted in the future not just as an idea but also as a way of life.

---

* Talk about communication and co-becoming! Recent research has shown that through a process called "crosstalk" plants emit tiny molecules (micro RNAs, or miRNAs) that pass through the gastrointestinal tract of an animal that eats them, make a hard turn right into the blood stream, accumulate in the animal's tissues, and begin to regulate the animal's gene expression, thereby changing the essence of the animal that ate them and its offspring. In the case investigated by this research, the process determined if a bee became a worker or a queen. Kegan Zhu, Minghui Liu, Zheng Fu, Zhen Zhou, et al., "Plant Micro RNAs in Larval Food Regulate Honeybee Caste Development," *PLOS Genetics* 13, no. 8 (2017), doi.org/10.1371/journal.pgen.1006946. "Transfer of miRNAs from one species to another may be a conventional mechanism to facilitate cross-talk and interspecies communication," according to the researchers at Nanjing University. *Cross-talk* is a term for how one molecule can change another one. Just why plants would want to do this to the animals that eat them—possibly including humans—has yet to be fully explored. Nanjing University School of Life Sciences, "Cross-Kingdom Regulation of Honeybee Caste Development by Dietary Plant MiRNAs, ScienceDaily, August 31, 2017, www.sciencedaily.com/releases/2017/08/170831140545.htm.

Every day, we co-become with the animals in or around our homes, creating a wider family. Like any complicated family, this one has arguments, splits, sacred cows, odd ducks, black sheep, and love.

It takes a while to become a good being. Sara St. Antoine is editor of the book series Stories from Where We Live, about bioregional flora and fauna, and author of *Three Bird Summer,* a novel for young people about the connection between twelve-year-olds and the natural world. When I asked her if she or her children had had any life-changing experiences with other animals, she was stumped at first. After considering the question for a few days, she proposed that for many of us one moment may not be life changing, but the *accumulation* of these small but intimate encounters over a longer period of time *can* be transforming. A single encounter with a wild animal can redirect the trajectory of a life, but in a long-term relationship the animal sticks with us on the journey, at least for a while.

This is a lesson Tania Moloney strives to pass on to the next generation. After living in Melbourne for twenty years, she returned to a farm near Noorat, population 162, with her partner, Michael, and their blended family of five kids. Noorat is only a seven-minute drive from the ancestral Boorcan farm. She started an organization called Nurture in Nature, which works throughout Australia to connect children to nature.

Moloney teaches her own children to "develop the same knowing" that she learned on her childhood farm, one that does not disguise or ignore the disturbances, the contradictions, and the moral friction of relationships with animals—or with other people.

The kids are starting to understand the circle of life and death and everything in between, just like I did growing up on a farm. We were out some time ago in the paddock picking up a dead calf. Taylor, then three, asked if it was asleep. I explained, "No, sorry, honey, it's dead. It's gone to heaven." Nash, then four, reassured his little sister by adding, "That's okay, maybe Grandpa can look after it in heaven." Oh, now we have a pet rabbit (a domestic one, not a wild one), and the kids' education will be taken to a whole new level when we get our girl rabbit, Bun Bun, a boyfriend.

The rabbit we had before Bun Bun sadly went to the afterlife thanks to the dogs next door; and a wild baby bunny that Taylor found recently, which lived about forty-three minutes and died in the palm of my hand, was given a beautiful funeral and decorated by Taylor in colorful loom bands. I asked her at the ceremony if she wanted to say anything about the bunny. Her reply: "He's dead."

Like I said before, life and death and everything in between.

ELEVEN

The Animal Lover

My mother called herself an animal lover. By profession an artist, she loved all animals—or most of them. Her eight-year-old son was studying to become a herpetologist, and she had a serious snake phobia.

One afternoon, the mailman delivered a box—about the size of a shoebox—postmarked Silver Springs, Florida. Something moved within it. I peeled back a corner. Curled up inside was large purplish-black indigo snake, a species now endangered. Just having that wild snake today, let alone selling it through the mail, would be a crime, and rightly so. But times were different. In those days, *Boys' Life* magazine hosted advertisements in its back pages for all manner of wild animals that you could purchase by mail order.

I had been set on a raccoon. My parents suggested a compromise. Perhaps they knew that a raccoon's personality usually turns from cute to aggressive after its first year. Despite my mother's snake phobia, they went with my second choice.

The snake was about five feet long, and I loved it. It made the perfect accessory—worn like a cowboy bandanna or a noose around my neck—as I walked past the bridge club ladies in the living room. It seemed to fancy me, too. But there was a problem. Inside the mail-order box, the snake had rubbed its nose raw on the chicken-wire lining, resulting in a bad fungal growth. Temporarily brushing aside her phobia, my mother came to the snake's and my rescue. It was an act of heroism.

Every afternoon for several weeks, I would take the snake out of its terrarium, sit on the edge of my bed with the snake in my lap, and pry its mouth open with my fingers. It never bit me. Approaching carefully, keeping her body farther away than anatomically possible, my mother would stretch her hand toward the snake and use tweezers to remove pieces of the fungus from its mouth. Then she would sprinkle the contents of a penicillin capsule along its teeth. I remember my father helping, too, but my mother was the one on the front line.

Given that this was a fungal, not bacterial, disease, the penicillin did not work, and the snake didn't make it. I was heartbroken.

I perked up when a neighbor gave me a baby pigeon to raise. I kept Petey (of course!) outdoors in an open birdhouse that my father built. When I rode my bike down the street, I would sometimes hear a whooshing sound, and Petey would land on my shoulder and lean into the wind. Petey also liked to fly *in* the house, gliding through the living room, hanging a right turn at the dining room, hurtling into the kitchen, and dive-bombing into the sink as my mother washed the dishes. My mother always thought that was hysterical. "Petey's into the suds," she'd say. She did not have a pigeon phobia.

We don't hear the label "animal lover" much anymore. Or at least that's my impression. In a cynical age, some people may find it vaguely embarrassing. But not all, not yet. The uncle with ten cats, the woman carrying the bejeweled teacup dog in a bejeweled bag, the pipefitter with the python, the farm girl who knows too soon that life will end for the prize-winning calf she loves, the fly-fisher who casts a fly just to watch the trout rise, the child who tells her hamster a fearful secret—all these are animal lovers. As was my mother.

Who's Raising Whom?

Keeping animals as pets or companions is not universal. Some Indigenous cultures in New Guinea do not keep pets. Nor do the Letuama of the Colombian Amazon. But other Indigenous peoples of North and South America kept a variety of animals as pets long before European settlers arrived. In some cases, keeping animals close by has more to do with survival than with sentiment. Even today, some people keep dogs primarily for security; others raise them for food. In 2017, the Humane Society International transferred more than two hundred dogs from an overseas dog meat farm, placing them for adoption through local shelters in the United

States. In the States and around the world, domestic animals are sometimes neglected, abused, and used for sport fighting. And yet these creatures
remain our friends. Sometimes our only friends.

A 2017–18 survey by the American Pet Products Manufacturers
Association showed that 59 percent of dog owners in the United States
consider their dog to be like a child or family member and that more than
half of cat owners feel the same way. Seven out of ten dog owners and 87
percent of cat owners buy gifts for their pets. Eleven percent host birthday
parties for their dogs (up from 7 percent in 2014). Going dancing? Take a
terrier. "Canine freestyle," where dogs and human companions dance in
competition, is a growing sport in the United States, Canada, and Great
Britain. Cannabis (specifically CBD oil) is now a mainstream medication for
dogs and cats. Pet diets can mirror the intake of upscale health-conscious
humans—Paleo and raw diets, for example. In 2017, pet industry experts
predicted that the biggest pet food trend would be natural foods, clean
labeling, and hypoallergenic and limited-ingredient diet products. That
same year, the online magazine *Petfood Industry* reported that consumers
want pet food to be "ever closer to the foods they put on their own dinner plates." These trends are all part of the "humanization" of companion animals, according to the pet food company that packages Jimbo's
Hypoallergenic Lamb.

Not long ago, I was missing our now-grown sons. Thinking about them, I
began to remember details about the pets we had when the boys were young.
This stoked my yearning to welcome a dog into our house once again. Or
maybe a cat. I mentioned this to my wife. Hoping to close the deal, I told
her about the ScoopFree ultra self-cleaning litter box I had seen online.
Using an electronic rake, it "self-cleans for weeks with no scooping, clean-
ing, or refilling" and comes complete with a "health counter" that "tracks
how many times your cat uses the box" and, to avoid freaking out the cat,
"safety sensors" that "automatically reset the rake timer if the cat re-enters
the box." Kathy raised an eyebrow. So I offered a second, more "natural"
option, also found online: a litter box disguised as a potted plant.

Aside from convenience, what explains the rise in the number of pets
and their humanization? One reason, at least for millennials, is that young
people are waiting longer to have children. A dog or cat will suffice for now.

As boomers enter into their seventies with fewer grandchildren than past generations had, they're increasingly likely to have pets.

Some of our companion animals are more than stand-ins for children yet to be born. Some serve as auxiliary parents. Gina Griffith described herself to me as a "retired full-time mom." She grew up in West Virginia with a border collie named Laddie.

People would ask me, "Is that your dog?" I always answered yes, of course. But I felt I was lying. A more accurate response would have been "I'm his child." Laddie "knew" I had no present father, and so, improbable as it seemed, Laddie assumed that role.

Once, the popular kids in our town actually invited me—me! the bookish geek!—to join them behind the dentist's office to smoke cigarettes. Hooray! I had finally arrived! I hadn't. Laddie did not approve. When I turned from the sidewalk to cross the street to the dentist's office and that sneaky, against-the-mountainside rear smoking spot, Laddie stood in my way. I walked around him. He stood in my way again. Repeat. Except this time he lowered his head and gave me that border collie stare. This went on for a while, but bit by bit, foot by foot, I was nearing the street.

That's when Laddie actually picked up my hand in his mouth, pushed his teeth down just to that initial pressure point, all the while giving me that stare. It was clear to me he decided it was better that he bite into my skin than let me go behind the dentist's office. Here the popular kids began to laugh at me for having a dog that saw himself as my master. So what could I do? I turned and went home, muttering and cursing at Laddie the whole while. Laddie just trotted along in front of me with his "I'm so happy" gait. When we got home, Laddie insisted on actually coming into the house (which he rarely did). My mom was on the phone. Laddie, who was always perfectly behaved when he was in the house, jumped onto the coffee table so he was at eye level with my mom, who was seated on the couch and talking on the phone. Laddie stared into my Mom's eyes. "I'll call you back," my mom said. "I need to see to something." She hung the phone up and said, "Thank you Laddie, I'll take care of it."

Then Mom let him outside, turned to me, folded her arms, and said, "Laddie tells me that you need to tell me what you were getting into."

Now, of course, I agree with Laddie's choice. And I marvel at how he knew that I should not go back there. So I know my story is not scientific and is just a random story, which may well be, as you point out, embellished with time. But, no, Laddie was not "my" dog. I was a border collie's "child." And he raised me right.

For a lonely or isolated child, especially, companion animals are good listeners and confidants. They keep secrets safe. For some, dogs can offer the unconditional love that might be in short supply in their lives. Pets help them build trust and can serve as a buffer against loneliness and stress. In 2014, Tufts University research found that parents with a deep bond to a pet reported better coping strategies in dealing with stress. Children who were more attached to pets were also more likely to seek social supports, invest in close friendships, and exhibit self-reliance. This was especially true for youth with a parent deployed in the military. "It isn't enough to be around animals—children need to be engaged in that relationship," writes the study's lead author, Megan Kiely Mueller, a developmental psychologist and assistant professor at Cummings School of Veterinary Medicine at Tufts University. "Strong attachments to pets may foster a more proactive attitude about handling stressful problems and could serve as a bridge to developing and maintaining peer relationships during stressful circumstances."

In addition to nurturing us, pets help us learn to nurture. As Gail F. Melson, professor emerita of developmental studies at Purdue University and the author of *Why the Wild Things Are*, writes, "People need a way to practice being caregivers when they're young. In many other countries, siblings look after one another, but in the U.S. that's not culturally acceptable. It's actually illegal in many states to leave kids in the care of anyone who is under 16 years of age." Melson conducted a time study of children over age three. During a twenty-four-hour period, the youngsters invested 10.3 minutes providing care giving to siblings. For children whose siblings were significantly younger, nurturing time dropped to only 2.4 minutes.

While she gathered no corresponding figures for time spent nurturing pets, she argues that kids need all the nurturing time they can get, and pets fit the bill: "Nurturing animals is especially important for boys because taking care of an animal isn't seen as a 'girl' thing like babysitting, playing house, or playing with dolls. By age 8, girls are more likely to be involved than boys in baby care both inside and outside their homes, but when it comes to pet care, both genders remain equally involved." So pets do (indirectly) teach some of us how to care for others, both by example and by providing opportunities to practice nurturing.

Jeff and Sarah Milligan-Toffler live in Minneapolis. Their son Jacob was a latchkey kid. When Jacob turned ten, they bought a Goldendoodle, Honey, so that someone would be there to welcome him when he got home from school. Honey ate money. She was a difficult dog, with multiple anxieties and hoarding behavior, which, according to Sarah, "meant that she would bite you if you tried to take something away, even poop." Nonetheless, Honey held up her end of the family bargain and continues to do so. "We all love her so much," she said, "that we've adapted our behavior to make it so that she can live with us." Which, among other adaptations, means forever hiding spare cash. Sarah has kept a running list of the items Honey has eaten. Among them:

Too many socks to count
Underwear
Gloves (including a pair of leather gloves)
Wooden game pieces
Playing cards
Trash of all kinds
Napkins
Whole flourless chocolate cake (potentially quite dangerous for dogs)
Jacob's homework (not kidding)
A bagel (which she retrieved from a two-foot-high snow bank)
Plastic bags
A relative's yarmulke

And, yes, money. Sarah recalls the time when Jeff was sick—running a fever—but had a gig with his band that he didn't want to back out of. He came home with sixty dollars in tips that he set on his dresser. The next thing he knew Honey was "surfing his dresser and had the wad of cash in her mouth."

Jeff grabbed a twenty-dollar bill, but Honey quickly polished off the rest. "This prompted the question, how much money do you have to lose to go through poop to find it?" Honey kept the change.

Sarah believes that the dog helped Jacob—and her and Jeff, too—develop keener attentiveness to the anxieties, fears, and imperfections of another being. And to have patience.

The Dog Who Taught Ethics

Thinking about co-becoming, an obvious question comes to mind: Do humans and their dogs really look alike, and if so, why? Sadahiko Nakajima, a psychologist and researcher at Japan's Kwansei Gakuin University, asked five hundred people to match photographs of dogs and their owners. His findings: yes, dogs and their owners resembled each other—not because of such physical characteristics as size, length of fur/hair, or jowls but because of some essence of personality or spirit in their eyes.

Dogs see us the way we want to be seen. Literally. When human beings encounter another person, we have a "gaze bias" in which our left visual field is dominant and directs our eyes toward the left side (from the gazer's perspective) of the other person's face. We inspect that eye first and longer. We do this reflexively, instantaneously, and then we look at the other side. Of all other animals, only rhesus monkeys do that both with one another and with us. But domestic dogs do that *only* with us. Perhaps, through shared experiences and emotional bonding over time, humans and other animals, domestic and wild, come to see the world in similar ways. We change each other over time, and not only in cosmetic ways.

The dog I grew up with was a moral teacher in our family. He saw me as I wanted to be seen, and he expected me to live up to what he saw. Perhaps you have a dog like that in your past, or now.

Many years ago, I asked animal behaviorist and trainer Dennis Fetco if other animals—dogs (appropriately named *Canis familiaris*), in particular—can be moral teachers to children. In addition to his work with animals, he had earned a doctorate in the psychology of human behavior and also had expertise on pet therapy for children. Pets, he said, are often moral teachers, "though that is not their intent." For example, pets teach children about death. The emotional price of losing a pet is, in most cases, not as great as the trauma felt when a parent dies. Children, he said, "can afford this price more than they can the loss of a parent." A dog can teach a child about unqualified love as well. Dogs may be the only source of unqualified, unearned affection that some children ever have. Dogs also teach about the difference between essence and behavior, about human forgiveness. A child may have trouble reading the intent of even a loving parent, but a dog is always straightforward. "Dogs do not deceive well. They don't lie. The most they do is misunderstand," Fetco said. "When my kid does something wrong and I explode, it's hard for him to realize I love him. But when my child sees me punishing the dog and then twenty minutes later giving it treats, loving it, paying its vet bill, my child realizes that the dog's behavior is bad, but the dog is still good." On the other hand, when parents use corporal punishment on a dog, "it teaches a child that swatting a butt is a good idea." That is a lesson more children could do without.

I pointed out that his examples had focused more on parental behavior than pet behavior. I wanted to return to my original question. "Let me ask you about Banner," I said. Banner was two when he arrived and eleven when he died, and in between he was my best friend and, I believe, my teacher. Is there any difference, in this regard, between how we perceive our friends and families and how we perceive other animals? To every parent or dog companion, extraordinary is in the eye of the beholder. And most are extraordinary.

To this day, I can remember Banner in fine detail. I remember him with *all* my senses or at least all the senses I'm aware that I have. I can remember the look in his eyes when, in the backseat of the car, I would come to the last bites of an ice cream cone, pause, and then hold out to him the last half-inch of the sugar cone, still with ice cream in it, and he would take it carefully in his mouth. Every ice cream cone ended with this ritual. I remember the scar on his nose from a dog fight and how it felt as I rubbed my fingers over the fur around it. I remember the rough lion collar of long fur around his head, my hands deep in it. I remember lying half-asleep and drifting into a dream, my head on his breathing side nestled in the blanket of his fur, curling my fingers in the thickness of it, listening to him breathe, and gently falling asleep to the rise and fall of him.

I also remember Banner as peacemaker, leaping up and down between my mother and me, or my brother and one of our parents, when my brother or I were being physically punished (although never cruelly). I recall his urgent barking and his odd, ambivalent grin when he intervened—so insistent that my mother often stopped in midswat and gave up, laughing in spite of herself. Where does that behavior come from? What evolutionary service does it provide? A research psychologist at the National Institute of Mental Health reports that some pets may worry as much as children do when the adults around them are distressed.

In retrospect, other Banner behaviors seemed deliberative, somehow less instinctive. Banner would never fight a small dog; sometimes he would protect the diminutive dogs of the neighborhood. Grumbling the whole time, he would walk out the basement door each morning with the cat between his legs. In a dog-infested neighborhood, perhaps our cat was using our dog for protection. Banner went along with it. Once, I watched him shoot up the street and catch the neighborhood's meanest dog in midair as it attacked a neighbor, who was holding her small dog in her arms. Banner would pull my brother by the diapers from the street. He would sit on us when we threw rocks. Sometimes, when we were away from the house and up to no good he would go home, but he would always come back.

I spent much of my boyhood in the Missouri woods with Banner. My parents didn't always know where I was, but Banner did. When I was eight, I fell through the ice of a creek deep in the woods. In water up to my waist, I tried to climb the steep and snowy bank but kept slipping back. Banner left.

But then he came back. The memory is vivid: Banner at one end of a fallen branch, tugging, as I pulled myself up the branch until I reached the top. I tell you this with some embarrassment, knowing the tricks of memory, realizing that neuroscientists contend that the brain tries to embellish memories until they become the story we want to be told. I don't know if any of this happened exactly the way I remember.

Children inflate the abilities of their pets, project all kinds of behavior onto them, Dennis Fetco said. And further, he explained, dogs often tend to fight the largest dog available. They are doing what dogs do; they do not think about championing the oppressed. The branch was probably there all along, and Banner was likely only trying to engage in a game of tug-of-war. "Your interpretation was the lesson," he added. "Perhaps you unconsciously aggrandized yourself by seeing his behavior as heroic. But who taught him to tug on the stick—an act that may have unintentionally saved your life? Probably you taught him that."

When I wrote about Banner in my newspaper column, and in an earlier book, one reader, Paul Roberts, who described himself as a "lifelong naturalist," offered another possible explanation for Banner's tugging on that stick. "My dogs over the years have used this form of displacement often," Roberts wrote. "It was usually when they were frustrated (like when I'd climbed a tree—and they couldn't come, too), or when they were excessively energetic and I wasn't moving, sitting for periods or playing something they couldn't participate in." At such times, his dogs would "displace or expel the frustrated energy by tug-of-warring on branches, pulling up and snapping sticks, or digging, often worrying stubborn rootlets found in the process."

Then he added something that I think gets to the root of my relationship with Banner. "Even when we are at our worst, the dog's lack of judgment from without is a mirror on ourselves, which begs for action from within," he said. "What we do with that is the measure of whether the animal has become a moral teacher or we have become a moral learner."

Such rationality is appealing, but so is the unknowable. Some Buddhists, I am told, believe that a teacher or priest who fails to live a good life can find himself demoted in the next life in the form of a dog, still with the urge to teach.

One dark morning, I awakened to the sound of my mother crying. I was sure that something had happened to my father. I ran down the stairs and out to the porch to find Banner, carried from the road by my father, lying cold and stiff on a bench. I cried, but the crying was fake—I was relieved that my father still lived. For a long time I felt guilty for that secret fakery. In that final lesson, Banner taught me about the confusion and untidiness of death, and more.

Homo homini lupus*

Did I inflate Banner? Romanticize him out of need or self-aggrandizement? A few years ago, I looked up the history and the characteristics of collies—specifically "rough" collies, like Banner. They were bred to be smart working dogs but also to be loyal and gentle with kids and fiercely protective of their human families—the hallmarks of a good person or parent, I thought

---

* *Homo homini lupus* is a Latin proverb meaning "A man is a wolf to another man." It suggests situations in which people behave like a wolf and usually assumes a negative outcome. But in the context of this chapter, it could also have positive connotations.

at the time. At first, I was pleased to learn that Banner and his ancestors had been bred for these traits, but then came the seed of doubt: If Banner had been bred for loyalty and to protect my brother and me, was he, in a sense, *programmed*—like, say, a robot—for those inclinations? Even now, I do not like that conception of my friend. But dog and cat breeding does pose certain questions about the relationship we have with the pets of our lives.

How, and even if, humans domesticated wolves into dogs remains in dispute. There are multiple theories about where and how dogs emerged. Some scientists make the argument that between ten thousand and thirty thousand years ago, wolves picked us. By this scenario, wolves scavenged the bones, scraps, and carcasses that human hunters left behind as they moved through forest and plains or threw beyond the firelight in their settlements. Gradually, some wolves and humans became partners, and certain traits of domestication, such as relative gentleness and direct eye contact, emerged. One intriguing theory has it that wolves, in fact, adapted us to their needs, that they domesticated *us* and, to an extent, even civilized us.

In 2003, Wolfgang M. Schleidt, retired director of the Konrad Lorenz Institute of Ethology in Vienna, and his coauthor, Michael D. Shalter, offered this alternative to the standard view of the domestication of wolves, "with emphasis on companionship rather than human superiority." According to them, "The closest approximation to human morality we can find in nature is that of the gray wolf, *Canis lupus*. This is especially odd in view of the bad reputation wolves have in our folklore." They cite wolves' ability to cooperate, noting their well-coordinated hunting drives—how they help one another carry items too heavy for any one individual, provision not only their own young but also other pack members, share babysitting, and more, which "is rivaled only by that of human societies." It is reasonable to assume, then, "that canid sociality and cooperativeness are old traits in terms of evolution, predating human sociality and cooperativeness by millions of years." This offers the authors a sharper interpretation of the Latin proverb *Homo homini lupus*: "Man to Man is—or at least should be—a kind of Wolfe." Instead of assuming domesticated animals are "intentional creations of human ingenuity," Schleidt and Shalter argue that early contacts between wolves and humans were mutual, leading to changes in both species that were part of a process of coevolution.

They also maintain that wolves were the first pastoralists, following Ice Age reindeer herds. As humans moved from Africa into Eurasia, they learned hunting and shepherding skills from wolves, along with the practice of cooperation and hierarchical ranking. Schleidt, in an earlier article, calls this the lupification "of human behavior, habits, and even ethics." He and Shalter contend that we value more than a dog's intelligence; we prize its warmth, playfulness, and loyalty—its ability to live in harmony within a pack, to work in a team "not only during the hunt, but in denning together and raising pups together." Members of the pack can accept strangers, but woe be to a stranger or even close kin who disrupts the harmony. Rather than adopting these traits from our own behavior, they came with the canine package. (What about our more direct forebears, apes? Primates, they argue, tend to be more selfish than wolves or dogs; their "Machiavellian reasoning gets in the way of [their] behaving communally.") They maintain that what we call humaneness "was invented millions of years ago by early canids," that the "impact of wolves' ethics on our own" may equal or even exceed the power that humans had on the slow transformation of wolves into dogs.

In the millennia that followed, humans also bred themselves for certain characteristics as they coevolved with the generations of wolves, wolf dogs, and dogs. So it's not outlandish to speculate that dogs—in my case, Banner—continue to influence our ethics, our ability to cooperate, our sense of order, and even our ability to love. I prefer to think Banner was special, that he was not designed only by breeders, and that this specialness came from deep within him, from tracks laid down long before the cosmetics and surface behavioral characteristics of modern breeding offered a final veneer (before it veered toward overbreeding, resulting in recurrent genetic maladies such as hip dysplasia). I want to believe that Banner's basic character was rooted more in his communal wildness, in the collected memory of gray wolves who loved and protected their own families, even as they edged toward the firelight of early people.

Until the genetics can be nailed down, the details of domestication or coevolution remain hypothetical. In the meantime, let's just assume that dogs and cats and, to a lesser extent, other pets and even wild animals have been coevolving with us for millennia. They are part of us. We are part of them. We made one another in each other's likeness and still do.

Andreas Weber has thought long and hard about the value of animals to children. Weber is a German scholar and writer with degrees in marine biology and cultural studies. He is respected around the world for his work in the fields of popular science and environmental sustainability. In *The Biology of Wonder*, he explores what he and others consider a new understanding, in science and the arts, of "biopoetics," or "life as meaning."

His focus extends the traditional study of biology to seeking personal and societal truths through biology. That search begins in our earliest moments of consciousness either through direct contact with nature or on an adult's lap watching pages turn. "Nearly every kid's first picture book is crowded with animals," Weber writes. "And this is a fact across all cultures.... Indeed, many 12-month-old toddlers would enthusiastically throw themselves from their buggy just to touch a passing dog.... Amidst our elaborate concepts of early childhood development lingers a gigantic blank spot. Its presence is a consequence of the merciless underestimation and misjudgment of everything that cannot speak with words."

Children's literature serves as evidence of the importance of animals in children's lives and development, though one study suggests the link may be fading. In 2011, the journal *Sociological Inquiry* published a study by researchers at several universities who reviewed 296 children's books, all Caldecott Medal winners and honorees, from 1938 to 2008. In the first of those decades, built environments made up only about a third of images. By the 2000s, images of natural environments had shrunk by almost half. Today natural environment and wild animals "have all but disappeared in these books," according to one of the study's authors. Granted, Caldecott Medal winners are a narrow representation of children's books, but the study raises this question: Do images of nature embedded in children's imaginations come from nature itself or from culture? E. O. Wilson's biophilia hypothesis—that we are genetically wired to be drawn to the rest of nature—suggests the former.

"Children . . . unconsciously know what they need to understand the world," writes Weber. "Every crawl under the dining table becomes an expedition. Every game played becomes the seed for a new experience. Therefore, children can meet their own future anywhere. If this is accurate, then their obsession with animals must have a meaning." Weber argues that we humans—first as children, then as adults—understand ourselves by borrowing the categories of thought "from an affiliation with the giant, and unfathomably entangled, web of other beings." Other animals "are like us, yet entirely different." Learning to relate to animals "means to become more deeply human, and is comparable to learning to walk." This process, he believes, "is the longing of a body that cannot behave any other way because its logic stems from the way it is made, which is mirrored by other beings made of flesh and blood."

The right animal can give a child a deeper capacity for wonder and empathy, as well as a set of symbols to help make sense of the world. We are more than walking genetic code; we are biological poems, and so are the creatures around us. We do not create the code or language, but we do make meaning out of it. We write the first lines of that poem as children. Our companion animals humanize *us*. They can offer unconditional love and show us how to give it. They give us the gift of shared imperfections, the seed of sympathy and humor. They join our pack. Or we join theirs. They and we co-become. We are not alone.

All these years later, Banner remains within me because of the care he gave us, the deeds he did, and what I imagined him to be. Whenever I think of Banner, I experience a sensory flood, just as I do when I think of my parents, now gone. He lives in me, his black-and-gold fur moving in waves of energy along his back and sides, shooting above the snow, cutting through the bitter wind, an arrow of joy.

TWELVE

Reptiles and Ambivalence

Rounding the end of an aisle, I stopped in my tracks. *An indigo snake!* There in a heated terrarium at eye level was the same kind of snake my snake-phobic mother once helped nurse: *Drymarchon corais*, also known as "forest ruler," with good reason. North America's longest nonvenomous snake, the indigo snake can grow up to nine feet long. Mostly immune to venom, it eats rattlesnakes for breakfast and invasive pythons for brunch, albeit after a long digestive break, but they seldom bite people. Today you can't capture or move a wild indigo snake across state lines without a permit. But here a glossy blue-black captive-born five-foot-long indigo was for sale for six hundred dollars.

San Diego's Reptile Super Show seems at once anachronistic and cutting edge. Collecting wild animals, even bred-from-the-wild critters, is frowned on by some animal lovers. And yet the civic center conference hall was packed.

Two boys with wide eyes and hair gelled like iguana combs raced past, hurtling down an aisle lined with plastic containers of blue-tongued skinks, $180 each; tiny vanilla black Mojave snakes (a ball python designer morph), $300; more lizard breeds than I had ever imagined existed; and scores of Styrofoam cups filled with mealworms and crickets. In that same aisle, under the watchful eye of a solid-built tattooed man, a five- or six-year-old girl wearing a polka-dot skirt and a single flower in her hair, embraced the neck of a python with a girth as large as her waist.

"Several thousand people here today," dealer Sean Evans told me. A tall, polite man, he was manning the booth for his Santa Barbara company,

Sensational Pets. "The show in Pomona, California, attracts fifteen thousand to almost twenty thousand attendees a weekend, twice a year." Reptile shows haven't caught up with bird show attendance, he added. "But we're getting there. People are busy. Reptiles are easier to maintain than other pets. They need less attention. They're quieter, not as messy. As long as you are staying with the smaller reptiles and not doing a seven-foot monitor lizard."

Right. Nothing captures the ambivalence—the attraction and repulsion and several stops in between—that we feel toward other animals (including people) quite like a reptile show.

The indigo snake's terrarium was bracketed by equipment for the reptile hobbyist: racks of UVB lighting, spot lamps, habitat heaters, ReptiSun lightbulbs, a ReptiBator digital egg incubator, and a Mini Mister —a spray bottle for moisturizing your exotic pet.

"Indigo World." That's what Evans called the fan base for indigo snakes. I asked him if there were other snakes with their own fan bases. "Oh yes. 'Python World,'" he said. "You have subgroups of enthusiasts for specific breeds, like carpet pythons [a South Pacific breed with varied skin patterns], just like you have with dogs." He turned to his coworker. "Riley, how many carpet python fests have there been?" Riley, a Sensational Pets employee, didn't know the exact number, but he did know about the carpet fan base. "Lineage is very important for the carpets, which get more beautiful as they get larger. So, as babies, you can't really tell what you've got unless you [know] where [they came] from."

Are different snake breeds marketed to different types of people?

"Yes, definitely. Like carpet pythons," said Evans. "They're a great snake but more for somebody who has a higher attention span than an eight-year-old. It's more sensitive. A hardier snake such as ball pythons or corn snakes would be a better match for most kids. Bearded dragons are also a great option. They grow super fast. They're hardy. You can take one out for six hours and walk it around. As long as it stays warm, it's great." In his booth, you could buy a Fluker's six-foot adjustable Repta-Leash for walking your lizard. Also for sale were "tall-tree systems" for boreal snakes and larger outside enclosures.

I mentioned the indigo snake I had as a kid and said I was surprised to see one here. "They're not very easy to breed. They're hard to come by," said Evans.

My last question: Do you see people getting truly emotionally attached to their reptiles? "Oh yes, definitely. And reptiles recognize people and associate differently with you. Not all reptiles do this, but, like, bearded dragons—100 percent. Same thing with some snakes. We used to have a fourteen-foot Burmese python. He would normally be fine with everybody touching him. Once he got fed up with all the touching, he would just bring his head—and I'd be sitting cross-legged on the ground—he'd bring his head into my lap, and then that meant, 'Oh, okay, I'm done.' I'd know it's about time to go."

One last nostalgic look at the indigo snake, and I moved along.

Wild Blood Transfusion

An aisle or two over, I visited the Kammerflage Kreations booth, a company "dedicated to supplying you with the most incredible 'living art' via our spectacular panther chameleons!" Alec O'Brien was wearing art on his arm: a Madagascar chameleon, the size of a kitten, with turquoise skin, yellow lips, a nubby beard-like structure under its chin, feet that gripped like human hands, revolving eyes, a sawtooth ridge down its back, and a little knob on its head. It looked like a character in the Beatles movie *Yellow Submarine*.

The indigo snake may rule the forest, but the chameleon is, according to the Greek origin of its name, the "earth lion." O'Brien, twenty-five, works part-time for a veterinarian who specializes in exotic pets and part-time at Kammerflage, a business owned by his girlfriend's family; he works in the breeding lab and at the shows. His hair is dark, short, hip, neatly combed. His ears are pierced with silver double studs, and his smile is pleasant and sincere. I was struck by his orchid-illustrated flowered shirt, buttoned at the top, mainly because its colorful print almost matched the complex yellow-and-red chromatophores and reflective guanophores of the art piece that now crawled down to his fingers, rotating its eyes.

O'Brien grew up in Richard Nixon's hometown of Whittier, California. He haunted the nearby hills, flipping boards over and looking for reptiles and amphibians underneath. As a child, he preferred them as an alternative to the norm, and he still does. "As far as dogs and cats, sure, a lot of people like them, but the reptile movement is gaining momentum. It's really a community. There are more and more kids coming to the shows. Facebook, Instagram—so many people connect through them. They trade animals, they sell animals, they breed, and they can post and update pictures, and everyone can follow along and get excited about it."

He still goes reptile hunting—"herping," as it's called by hard-core, well, herpers. He cruises desert highways at night with his high beams on, watching for snakes, toads, and geckos crossing the road. "I'll just look at them, take pictures of them, document them, and let them go. Some people will take them for breeding colonies, and if you have a California fishing license, you're legally able to collect certain reptiles. There are places where people go consistently. Some are "operations," he said, "laying board lines"—like fishing trotlines, only instead of a cord strung with multiple hooks between two trees, board lines are pieces of plywood distributed in reptile territory. Smaller reptiles often like to hide under boards.

I asked him where the animals at this show came from, and he said that the vast majority of reptiles sold as pets are bred and raised in captivity. "They're not wild blood," he said. "People correlate that term with wild-caught chameleons." And what's the opposite of wild blood? "Generationally captive-bred animals. We try to breed the healthiest, prettiest, most colorful individuals with each other."

About then I noticed the chameleon looking at me with one eye. The other eye was staring at the ceiling.

O'Brien emphasized that his company breeds responsibly and does not take from the wild. But some breeders believe that an occasional infusion of wild blood helps. Wild blood. A hint of danger. Unexpected behavior in a programmed world.

A few months earlier, I'd attended a cat show held at the nearby Del Mar Fairgrounds, where rows of booths displayed a dizzying variety of products, including Almost Invisible Cat Litter ("anti-icky-poo"), pet hair picker-uppers for house and garment care, and, for cats and their owners, water filtration systems. (The ScoopFree ultra self-cleaning litter box was nowhere in sight. Too bad. No demonstration. "But wait! There's more!")

Wild blood was there, too, including the Chausie, a mixture of nondomestic species of jungle cat; the Egyptian Mau cat, a naturally spotted breed that looks like a miniature cheetah; and the Pixie-bob, said to be bred from the natural offspring of bobcat hybrids. A pleasant young woman, wearing a knit cap with cat ears, showed me a photo on her smartphone of the recently popular breed, the werecat, also known as the Lykoi cat (*lykoi* being the

Greek word for "wolf"), which looks like a little wolf or, depending on the stage of the moon, a werewolf. This breed, which sells for as much as twenty-five hundred dollars each, is said to act like a canine.

Meanwhile, breeders are producing oversized cats as dog surrogates. (Who knew the need existed?) These long-legged creatures, called Savannah cats, are designed, as the website The Dodo reports, to "walk on a leash, play fetch and snuggle up to you at bedtime." They're "a cross between a regular domestic cat and the wilder (and larger) serval—which accounts for the animal's stupendous proportions." Savannahs are commonly "compared to dogs in their loyalty and they will follow their owners around the house like a canine," a breeder told the Dodo's reporter. "Some owners even shower with their Savannah cats." The problem is, they're still wildish. They tend toward sudden viciousness. Susan Bass of Big Cat Rescue in Florida told the reporter, "You have to go through at least five generations to get a cat that's even remotely docile enough to live in someone's family. They are notorious for howling at night. They bite. They can't be controlled. They are going to spray all over your house. They aren't safe to have 'round children or elderly people." In other words, a Frankenstein cat.

Planned or unplanned, an infusion of wild blood is occurring in every state in the union. Since the 1970s, the exotic pet trade has imported, legally or illegally, some two million constrictors, including boas, anacondas, and pythons. In 2015, the National Park Service estimated that as many as one hundred thousand nonnative constrictors were loose in the Everglades.

Some of these critters returned themselves to the wild by slithering down toilets, drain pipes, and heating ducts. Or the owners, realizing that reptiles aren't always as easy to keep as advertised, released them outside. The care and feeding of a Burmese python, which can, on rare occasions, grow to twenty feet and 250 pounds, can be, well, consuming. In Florida, feral pythons are a serious threat to indigenous species, cats and dogs, and small humans. In 2009, a two-year-old toddler in Florida was killed by an escaped Burmese python that belonged to her mother's boyfriend. This eight-foot-long snake, which was later found to have been severely malnourished, broke free, coiled itself around the girl, and squeezed her to death. The mother and boyfriend were convicted of manslaughter and sentenced to twelve years in prison. Public python hunts have been organized in Florida, and snake hunters from India have come to lend their expertise, but there has been no appreciable dent in the population. Meanwhile, the snakes are reducing the number of raccoons, possums, bobcats, and even deer. Issues with the exotic pet trade go far beyond snakes to include lions and other large predators. Even pets indigenous to the United States, or parts of it, can and have been problematic. Take those little dime-store turtles that so many baby boomers kept in bowls in their childhood bedrooms. They were eventually banned because they spread salmonella, and when let loose, they overpopulated local waterways. All manner of other exotic invaders, or importees, are threatening native wildlife in America. Among them: Asian carp threatening the Great Lakes, Argentine tegus (a large omnivorous lizard), venomous Asian lionfish, African monitor lizards, and Russian zebra mussels.

Naturalist Paul Roberts once shared with me his conflicted feelings about keeping reptiles or any wild animal in captivity. He did allow his son to catch and keep a lizard "because of the lessons" a lizard could provide, "most immediately those of habitat needs: moisture, nutrition, lighting type, intensity and periodicity, and fundamental ecosystem requirements, especially important with aquatic critters. They offer a tangible experience in responsibility, knowledge, mindfulness." Roberts recently buried the lizard, which died in captivity. He does feel regret. "Our love for animals, our biophilic relationships, can be a direct passage to the deeper meanings we all want for our children. But the world is bigger than our own selfish thoughts and desires. It requires more of us and offers more for us."

Where would a reptile show rank on ecopsychologist Patricia Hasbach's human-animal interaction spectrum? Distorted, I suspect. Still, she would like and admire many of the people here, and she would recognize the therapeutic value for the humans, though probably not for, say, the blue-tongued skinks, known affectionately to herpers as "blueys."

Herping, USA

The folks of Reptile World are understandably sensitive to how other people see them. Reptile people are far from cold blooded; they feel the bond to other life every bit as much as those who cross any of the more publicly approved bridges to the wild.

Many hope to revive a connection with the particular animals who showed them the way, in their earliest years, to the other-than-human world. A blogger on one reptile community website writes, "Why is it that people who don't like snakes feel like it's ok to say such mean things to us that do like snakes? I get it, not everybody loves snakes—but that doesn't mean they have to be rude. Just imagine walking up to some stranger and telling them, for no reason, that you think their dog is disgusting!"

At a booth in the last aisle of the Reptile Super Show, I met Jimmy Cruz, owner of Ball Life. He raises and sells ball pythons. He wore a black Ball Life T-shirt with his company's slogan in white gothic lettering: LET THE ADDICTION BEGIN. Cruz is from Fresno, California, where he grew up, as he told me, getting into a lot of trouble.

"Ten years ago," he said, "my son was like six years old, and he goes, 'It's Father's Day. I'm going to get you a snake, Dad.' And I'm like, 'Really? *All right.*' So I got my first ball python." He was hooked. Six years later, he was in the mood for a radical shift in his life. He went shopping for pythons. "We had a pet store in Fresno called Reptile Room." Cruz became the owner's new best friend. That first week he spent just over two thousand dollars on snakes, tanks, equipment, and food. Two weeks later, he owned over forty snakes. "Then I was up to two hundred snakes. In one room."

Now wait a minute, you were living in one room?

"No, I had a house," he clarified, "but one room was devoted to snakes. Then, after that, I started doing a rack system. I'm currently just over one hundred snakes, and I've got another eighty to one hundred on the way. I've got my incubator filled and more females dropping eggs."

He started his own company, in part to pay for his reptile habit. He also works for a company called Freedom Breeder in Turlock, California, which manufactures acrylic racks, trays, and tubs for snake and rodent breeding. As he explained, reptile love isn't cheap love.

"People jump into this hobby without thinking. If you have a couple of snakes, it's one thing, you know. But then some people start getting up there, fifteen or twenty snakes, and then the feeding starts being really expensive," he explained. Live or frozen rodents called feeders (frozen baby mice are called pinkies) can cost $1.50 to $2 each. "With the ball pythons, you have to start getting rats. And that starts costing anywhere from $3 to $6 per live rat." Some companies will "send the feeders with dry ice. You stick 'em in your freezer."

What's the personal connection to snakes? Where's the payoff? Partly bragging rights, he admitted. "I like looking a little bit different. Tattoos, all that. I like the attention. Driving around Fresno, my town, walking around with a big old snake on. I would see guys that were six foot something, and they'd run. I'm like, dude, you're like ten times bigger than the snake." Cruz's smile was warm and kind. He was not a large man. But the ink that covered most of his right arm below the elbow read DO NOT START WITH ME. YOU WILL NOT WIN. "I'm forty-one years old and I kind of grew up," he said. "I have three boys. My youngest is six, my middle is nine, and oldest is seventeen. So my seventeen-year-old and my six-year-old, they want to do this with me." Sometimes Cruz takes his boys herping on the land around Fresno. "My little one helps with the feeding. He's just as involved with this as I am."

I asked him to describe the essence of his relationship with animals, any animals.

"You just appreciate everything a lot more. Some people are afraid of spiders; some people are scared of bugs. And now, for me, it's like you want to preserve everything. You want to save it instead of trying to kill it, smash it, whatever. You are like, 'No, leave it alone, it's not bothering you.' . . . Even the rodents, you know, you're not trying to be mean. Scurry along, you know. It just changes the way your outlook is on a lot of things."

Including people?

"It actually does, you know what I mean?" he said. "In the reptile industry, it's just all walks of life. You have people who look like me, all tatted up. You have the people you would never imagine they would have reptiles. You get a little friendlier, I guess. You are not so judgmental anymore. People who don't have reptiles, they look at you like, 'Oh, you're just weird.' But ones who do have reptiles, and that's more and more of us, we're less judgmental. We don't look at you for your exterior. We're like, 'Oh, okay, how you doing?' "

Restricting pythons to a twelve-by-twenty-inch ReptiSun-heated terrarium may seem cruel, even with that cooling Mini Mister. Yes, the exotic pet industry has a dark side. But what I saw at the reptile show also reflected species loneliness, the hunger for a deeper connection—an injection of wild blood. As vampiric as that sounds, the thirst is real. For a connection to other species. For a larger family. For a kind of healing, as one sided as that may be.

Admittedly, I grew up conditioned to accept the show. More than once as I walked through the aisles, I saw my mother's trembling hand holding the penicillin capsule and my father standing next to her.

THIRTEEN

The Boy Who Said Horse

Several years ago, I watched a helmeted girl reach for a saddle horn as the horse she had mounted turned its head and looked with one eye— the largest eye of any land mammal—intently at the child, then turned back patiently, blinking slowly.

A volunteer led the horse by the reins around the corral. The girl on the horse sat stiffly at first. The horse was calm and steadfast. The girl relaxed. She began to smile. Other children joined her in a horse caravan. They leaned back slightly, some expressionless, others beaming, as the horses moved around a small circular track.

This scene, common around the country, took place at an equestrian therapy program at Anne Springs Close Greenway, a nature reserve in Fort Mill, South Carolina. The program serves children with a variety of physical and emotional disabilities.

That afternoon, one of the program's therapists told me a story. Among her favorite children, she said, was a ten-year-old boy on the most challenged end of the autism spectrum. She had worked with him every Friday for several weeks. On each visit, she would walk ahead and lead the horse around the corral and over a pasture. The silent boy would sway. The boy's mother told the therapist that on one Friday morning when she could not take her son to the scheduled session, he walked into his mother's room and said a single word: "Horse." It was the first word the boy had ever spoken to her. A horse had carried him into the world.

Animal-assisted therapy, formal or informal, is on the rise. "This is argu- ably one of the biggest health care strategies that people use informally every day," according to Philip Tedeschi, a clinical professor and executive director of the Institute for Human-Animal Connection at the University of Denver's Graduate School of Social Work. I met him in 2016 at the Animals on the Mind conference in Denver, sponsored by his institute. As a therapist, Tedeschi is particularly focused on interpersonal violence, including abuse of people and other animals. A former course director with Outward Bound, he believes in the therapeutic value of learning how to communicate with other animals, domestic or wild, on their terms. "In their relationships with us, other animals use almost every method except human vocal language to communicate with us or with other animals," he said. "Humans are, frankly, quite lazy communicators compared to many other animals." We can live with another human being who is having a horrible day or slipping into depression, and we may ignore most of the indicators "until they burst into tears or tell us they are having a hard time."

In this field, horses are veterans and therefore among the most studied therapy animals. Through equine-assisted psychotherapy (EAP), a patient grooms, feeds, walks, and plays equine games with the horse. EAP is conducted by both a licensed therapist and a horse professional.

For the psychotherapist, the horse's behavior works as a psychological barometer. Certainly, horses tend to calm anxious people. As herd and prey animals, they are extraordinarily sensitive to the animals around them. Horses can hear a human heartbeat up to four feet away, and research suggests that horses may synchronize their own heartbeat to a human's; to the specially trained eye, they can signal a change in the client before a therapist can usually detect it. By building a relationship with the horse, a person who is on the autism spectrum or suffering from addiction or posttraumatic stress—especially someone with limited verbal skills—can reestablish trust with another living being. And the relationship helps the therapist and the client model the work needed to improve relations with other people.

A year after I heard the story about the boy who said horse, I met Miyako Kinoshita, manager of farm education at Green Chimneys, an animal-assisted therapy institute with a campus in Carmel, New York, just north of New York City. She was also attending the Animals on the Mind conference in Denver. Kinoshita served five years as board president for the North American Riding for the Handicapped Association. "Our students live with the animals.

They're not just visiting and then going home. The animals are all part of their life. The kids are responsible for them, so they have a very deep connection," Kinoshita told me. Green Chimneys was originally a dairy farm. When the program began, it was a working farm; residents and students milked the cows and ate the pigs, "but as the program developed we began more therapeutic programs, and we stopped consuming animals and animal products." In addition to horses, Green Chimneys uses a full contingent of 120 farm animals—including goats, cows, sheep, chickens, and other domesticated fowl but also camels, llamas, rabbits, and guinea pigs; it also runs a dog shelter program and wildlife center populated with injured birds of prey and reptiles. Students and residents help train the dogs and rehabilitate the wounded wild animals.

Kinoshita's credential is in education, not therapy. Ninety percent of her work is animal-assisted education, though she has no doubt that her work is therapeutic. Through a residential center and a state-supported school, Green Chimneys serves about two hundred children with psychosocial disabilities who come from various economic backgrounds. Some are placed there by the state's schools when other educational environments have failed.

Though the animals collectively provide a healthy milieu, the key to the therapy is to make use of the special characteristics of each species, each individual. Kinoshita, an intense and deeply committed woman who once worked in a Cambodian refugee camp, elaborated. "You look for specific behaviors. Just about any horse or dog will behave similarly in certain situations. And working with that general behavior can be beneficial to a child—for example, learning how to halter a horse requires a certain skill set. You can't go in with too much energy. You have to slow yourself down, and you have to approach the horse in a certain way and then place the halter."

But beyond such general behavior and the lessons it imparts to the child, each animal and each child is an individual. Therapy is further customized based on the characteristics of the animal and the child. Some children will be more interested in the birds of prey; others show a preference for the dogs. Behaviorally, each species offers a different palette of interactions. Depending on the kind of interaction that the therapists feel is needed, they use animals with specific temperaments. "For example, if we want the child to experience one hundred percent success and to be happy at the end of the session, we will choose the oldest, kindest, gentlest sheep we have," said

Kinoshita. "If we believe it's best to frustrate the child a little bit, so the child can really stretch, we would want a slightly less satisfactory experience. In that case, we can choose one of the flightier sheep."

Such programs are gaining favor. A growing number of psychologists, psychotherapists, physicians, and occupational therapists view the presence of animals in the lives of people as helpful with both therapy and the prevention and detection of illnesses. For example, dogs have been trained to use their remarkable sense of smell to detect the onset of epileptic seizure and cardiac distress.

For many therapeutic applications, an animal's senses are essential, but relationship is the primary ingredient. A relationship with a domestic animal can also help smooth the edges of dementia, depression, and a host of other illnesses and challenges.

Naomi and Koba

Naomi, twenty-three, and her mother, Beth, visited me at a coffeehouse in Julian, California. Koba, a black standard poodle, accompanied them, wearing his orange service dog cape. Alert, focused, serious, he waited until we sat down, and then he disappeared under the table.

The number of children diagnosed with autism spectrum disorder, determined usually around the age of nine, has been increasing steadily; today, in the United States, one in fifty-four children receives the diagnosis. The proposed reasons for the increase and the suggested causes of the disorder are controversial.

Beth is currently a vice president at Monterey Bay Aquarium. Naomi is bright, fun to talk with, and talented at math, science, and writing. She is typically at the high-functioning end of the scale, though sometimes she dissolves into quite another state. Which is where the bond she shares with her service dog, Koba, comes in.

"Our bond is hard to explain to people. People say he's your service dog, your buddy, your partner. Well, he's a bit more than that," she said. "We're so bonded I know what he's thinking and feeling, and he knows what I'm thinking and feeling."

When she and her mother first visited Koba and his trainer, Koba started out sitting next to the trainer, but he watched Naomi the whole time, and by the end of the hour, Koba had moved next to her, and that is where he has remained ever since.

When the dog's training was completed, he was delivered to Naomi. The trainer spent three days working with Naomi and Beth to be sure of a good transition into the home. During one of the training days, Naomi, Beth, the trainer, and Koba went to a Costco store as a test. Loud noises, bright lights, and crowds are challenging stimuli. As they walked through the aisles, Beth noticed that Koba kept nudging Naomi's leg with his nose and shoulder, bumping into her, letting her know he was there. "He knew I was being overstimulated, and he thought I was going to flee the store," said Naomi. "He knew it before it started."

At Costco that day, Naomi had a meltdown. But by the time it started, Koba had already begun to do the part of his job that requires the most focus. Naomi had become overstimulated. Hearing voices, she collapsed to the floor, pounding her fists together, flapping her hands, and punching her own leg repetitively—not to hurt herself but to regain focus. Koba, who weighs sixty-five pounds, was already climbing onto her lap to hold her still, all the while nuzzling and licking her. When Naomi's thrashing continued, he used his weight to push her onto her back. He stretched out on top of her, covering her with as much of his body as he could and applying what the trainer called "deep pressure." Minutes passed. The overstimulation decreased. She did not attempt to bolt from the store, and the meltdown subsided. "The voices are gone, Mom. I'm fine now," she reassured Beth. Koba quickly got to his feet, doing a full-body wag.

"At that point, my mom started crying," Naomi recounted, "and I didn't understand."

The trainer told Naomi and Beth that this often happens to parents when they first see a service dog quickly bring a child out of a meltdown.

"I want to clarify about deep pressure," Naomi said. "For some people, another person can apply that and it helps. But that doesn't work for me. When people touch me, I flinch. I would jump away. It wasn't until I was sixteen that I could give my mom a hug."

If Naomi runs away, Koba chases her, pushes in front of her, or jumps up on her to prevent her from running into traffic. If Naomi continues to flee, Koba returns to find Naomi's mother, who knows immediately what has happened. Koba leads Beth to track her, then does what Naomi calls "search and rescue," tracking Naomi's scent.

One time, Beth and Koba were desperately searching for Naomi in the dark. "I couldn't see anything," Beth said. "But suddenly Koba leaped into the air and tackled Naomi. I pulled her out of the street and Koba sat on her."

Until Koba arrived, Beth and her husband spent many nights sleeping on the floor across the entrance to her bedroom door to prevent Naomi from fleeing. Naomi still has episodes, but the last time she fled was four years ago.

Naomi's reaction to overstimulation occurs because of where she is, in that particular moment, on the autism spectrum. But she also has other challenges. When she was thirteen, she was diagnosed with bipolar disorder. Then, in 2017, at age twenty-two, she had a psychotic break and is now diagnosed with schizoaffective disorder, a combination of cyclical symptoms often seen in schizophrenia and bipolar disorder: delusions, hallucinations, depressed episodes, and manic periods of high energy. Naomi hears voices all the time, but sometimes they are louder than others. On many occasions, Koba has brought Naomi back from the land of voices and usually prevents her from bolting.

Each service dog is trained to detect and act on behaviors associated with particular positions on the autism spectrum—the self-stimulating (or "stimming") behaviors, including rocking, pacing in a circle, flapping hands, self-hitting, head banging. "Koba usually lets my rocking slide, but if I start hitting my legs, he'll hop on my lap or take his nose and flip my arm away." Then training is tailored for additional conditions, such as the symptoms that Naomi exhibits when she hears voices. The trainer mimics these behaviors and teaches the dog how to respond with each of them. The training is meticulous and tedious, and most dogs don't make the cut.

The training process seems miraculous, and the results often are. But these dogs are not robots. Vigilance, protectiveness, deep sensitivity, the ability to calm and distract, and to find—all these traits are a part of them, and a part of many other dogs, from the beginning. Beth is convinced that when Naomi's autism schizoaffective disorder presented, Koba trained himself to deal with the new symptoms.

"When the psychosis kicks in, the kitchen appliances start looking at me and conspiring against me," said Naomi. "He knows. He'll jump on me and redirect me and sometimes sit in front of me and bark until I pay attention to him. He works on redirecting my attention away from the voices and to him. He figured that out on his own." In three years, when Koba is ten, he'll retire. Though poodles tend to live much longer, ten years is an accepted limit for service dogs, because, as Naomi explained, "They get tired. This is hard work." She added, "I cried on his birthday." When retirement comes, he will stay with the family, and Beth will take him to senior centers and hospitals to work in short sessions with children on the spectrum. Another service dog will arrive to help Naomi.

Like other traditional service dogs, Kobo underwent strenuous training, preparation, and regulation. That's not generally true for emotional-support animals. Licensed mental health practitioners write letters advocating a person's use of an emotional-support animal. Several online companies sell letters of certification with no real validation. "Presently this area is a free-for-all," Rebecca Johnson, director of the Research Center for Human-Animal Interaction at the University of Missouri College of Veterinary Medicine, told the *Guardian* in 2016. Consequently, the public, generally accepting of highly trained service animals, is confused about other forms of animal-assisted therapy.

Today, the number of emotional-support animals is growing. Therapy dogs comfort college students on test-taking days; at airports, pigs may calm hypernervous travelers. In 2018, United Airlines barred one woman from boarding with her emotional-support peacock. (She did offer to buy an extra seat for the bird.) Some thirty states have adopted stricter laws in recent years.

As part of his work with the Institute for Human-Animal Connection, Philip Tedeschi oversees the University of Denver's emotional-support animal program and agrees that more oversight and regulation is needed. "But in addition to questions about misuse, we should also be really interested in *why* so many people would want to do that," he told me. "These are not sinister people. The bigger story is not about fraud but about people in pain and how animals help them."

One thing that could help is more training programs for people and their vest-wearing emotional-support animals or for anyone who relies on a pet for emotional sustenance. These programs could be modeled after the existing nonprofits that train volunteers and animals to visit schools and assisted-living facilities. Tedeschi contends that the training should not just be for the people utilizing an emotional-support animal or requesting one "but also members of the public who are often misinformed and can demonstrate harsh and insensitive attitudes that violate a person's right to this accommodation."

Still, backlash against emotional-support animals has accelerated, some of it from people with trained service dogs.

"Not very often but sometimes, when Koba's not working and his cape is off, he gets anxious," Naomi said. "Something small upsets him, and I can tell. This sounds weird because dogs, I know, don't talk. He'll get quiet and go curl up on his pillow . . . just something off about him is the best way I can put it. I go over and comfort him. I pull him against me, so he's leaning against me and I rub him. And tell him it's okay. I've also done that after we've been attacked by dogs."

Attacked by dogs?

"Seven times. Five times by fake service dogs, including one time by a 150-pound pit bull mastiff," Beth said. "People can buy these capes on Amazon and put them on their dogs so their dog can go with them to the store. So we've had dogs attack us at Vons and other places. I've had people walk up to me in a store and offer me as much as five hundred dollars for his cape. Some service dogs have been killed. We actually had to send Koba to socialization training to work through his fear of other dogs."

Naomi added, "Koba will look at fake service dogs sometimes, and he doesn't understand their behavior, and he's going like, 'Dude, you've got to straighten up.'"

Clearly, Naomi's relationship with Koba is not one sided. She has begun to use some of the same calming techniques for the dog as Koba uses with her. They have learned from each other, taught each other, co-become.

As our visit ended, I realized I had forgotten that Koba was with us. I looked under the table. He was on his side, perfectly quiet.

"I can read his mind. He's still working, but he's relaxed," said Naomi. "Sometimes when he's applying deep pressure, he'll start snoring in my ear." She laughed.

I asked, "What's he thinking right now?"

"He's thinking he's bored."

Animal-Assisted Self-Care

Despite the problems and abuses that self-prescribed therapy animals can present, their number likely surpasses that of formally trained service animals or program-based therapy animals. And most animal-assisted self-care is informal, not thought of as medicine or therapy.

Just as Alan Rabinowitz overcame stuttering by talking with a jaguar in a zoo, Zayd Jawad found healing with a cat. In 2016, Jawad, a student at Parkland College in Champaign, Illinois, asked to interview me about the impact of nature experiences on people with physical or mental hardships. As we spoke, Jawad shared a bit of his own story. I told him that I hoped he would write to me about his remarkable life, and he did.

When Jawad was five, he was diagnosed with Hunter syndrome, a rare genetic disorder that affects every function of a person's body from growth and development to mental health and longevity. As he matured, his head continued to grow, but his body remained child sized, and his fingers, arms, and legs were stunted and blunt. Like Naomi, Jawad had loving parents and an animal support network.

"Boo, a gray tabby kitten, entered my life at a pivotal point. Boo arrived in a cage. Released, he would gallop around the house in a mad joy of freedom as I was wheeled around in my wheelchair. There were times when I lay on that first-floor bedroom bed for hours, in pain, but he was with me, by my feet or plopped on my head." Boo, being a cat, and Jawad, being a boy, yearned to get outside. "He constantly tried to open the sliding kitchen door, and when he got outside, I watched him roll in the grass and stalk his imaginary prey." The boy noticed that each time Boo came back in, he looked a bit stronger, happier, freer. "As I grew stronger, he grew with me. As I took my first steps on the soft summer's grass, he was with me, inspiring me with his own graceful steps and acrobatics. . . . He showed me by example how to live."

At school, because of his distinctive appearance, Jawad was teased, called names, bullied. "But I realized that even though others saw me as different, and even though I could not excel in sports, I was able to smile brighter than anyone else. I took to being kind to everyone, never judging even those who judged everyone else," he said. Those who had scorned him became his friends. "I jokingly told one super-tall friend, 'You have such big feet.' He told me, 'Zayd, you have such a big heart.'"

By the time Jawad entered high school, he felt rich with friendships. He was succeeding academically. "I felt on top of the world. Then everything changed."

In his freshman year, he endured two spinal fusion surgeries. They were not successful. Previously, he had walked with difficulty, but now he was unable to walk without fear of falling from the pain. Over the years that followed, Jawad devoured books and practiced walking. Sometimes he would fall on his face. Struggling back to his feet, he would imagine himself a lion bounding across the savannah or an eagle in flight. "I once thought that I was caged, that I was never meant to fly through life, and what I realize now is that the door to that cage is not locked." Thinking of his cat, Boo, whom he called his wild brother, who kept him company during the months and years after his spinal fusion surgery, he remembered the moment when he felt fully in the world, when he could run:

> A grand prairie stretched ahead of me, the woods were behind me, and I ran with the wind as my companion. . . . I ran in the direction of a soaring hawk—I knew this one, I had seen him many times before, a red-tail, riding the currents in the same air that we breathed as one. I reached a spot with dappled sunlight, gazed at the creation around me, and raised my hands in awe at the realization of how far I had come and how much I had. . . . My heart leaps as I see clearly a connection to the Quran, the holy book of my own religion. How my soul expands! For I am blessed to see what so many might not— connection. A connection that we find when we look at the world with our hearts.

Today Jawad uses his speaking engagements and writing to help other people find that same connection and bounding freedom, modeled for him first by Boo. Given Jawad's internal resilience, he probably would have done fine without the cat. But Boo became his totem.

One group in particular finds renewed or protected life through animals: the homeless. Annie Petersen is the president and CEO of the Association for Human-Animal Bond Studies, a nonprofit organization that offers animal-assisted therapy and education programs in San Diego and provides financial assistance for diagnostic veterinary care for pet families in need. In 2008, Petersen worked for the San Diego Humane Society as education manager. After the 2008 financial crash, foreclosures emptied out many of the modest homes and mini-mansions that still coat the county's graded hills with beige stucco. Like many other animal welfare agencies, the humane society took in countless animals who had been left behind. Petersen went to work for the Foundation for Animal Care and Education (FACE), a group formed to address the growing tragedy of what it called, chillingly, "economic euthanasia." FACE's challenge is to keep companion animals in their homes, at least when there *is* a home. Raising money from concerned citizens, FACE began to give grants to pet owners on the margins: low-income families, senior citizens, veterans, military families, students, disabled individuals, and other "hard-working families and individuals who struggle to survive paycheck to paycheck." For the homeless and their canine companions, Petersen provides basic pet care supplies and connects them to veterinary services.

Over the years, Petersen's respect for both the homeless and their companion animals has deepened. "Those pets are *soooo* socialized," she told me. In all her years working with the San Diego Humane Society, she has never seen a population of animals that is so friendly. Why? Because these dogs are always with their pack, 24/7. "No one's at work ten hours a day, leaving his dog at home alone. Many homeless people would rather be on the street with their pets than go into shelters without them." Some programs are beginning to allow the homeless to bring their companion animals into the shelters, she added. The mutual loyalty between these animals and their owners is apparent; perhaps more remarkable is the devotion that the larger community of street people extends to these animals, too. She offered this story:

> People tend to hang out together, socialize with each other, watch out for each other—including each other's dogs. I will never forget working with Project Homeless Connect [a one-day resource fair that provides health screenings, flu shots, dental exams, haircuts, legal aid, housing, and counseling]. One couple came up to me with their pit bull. They needed to go inside. They said this was one of the few times they had been separated from their dog. I put it on a leash and

I was walking over to the pet-sitting area, and immediately several homeless people rushed over to me and said, "That's not your dog. *You can't take it.*" The dog recognized them and knew them. They were going to protect that dog. Fortunately, the owners came back. . . . That was a pivotal moment for me. I knew then that this was a great community of animal lovers. They don't just talk the dog—they walk the dog. When they say the dog is part of the family, they *mean it.*

Petersen also helps bring dogs and other animals into schools to be read to by children. And she teaches children how to respect others through their relationships with animals. Through San Diego Health Services, she does the same with victims of sex trafficking. She brings animals to the city's youth emergency shelter mainly as a comfort for the children and young people during a short transition.

Animals give young people a sense of not being judged. That's a basic human need. A dog doesn't care if you were coerced into prostitution at age twelve. This is also a need of just about every single animal, to have someone just be nice to it. Once a child gets that connection, we can introduce other skills, such as grooming. I have a guinea pig with ridiculous hair. It needs haircuts and its nails trimmed. If these kids and young people can relate to the basic care that an animal needs, then they can acknowledge the basic care they need.

Homeless people and homeless dogs have reminded Petersen that our compact with other animals is not only about what they can do for us but also what we can do for them. True healing works in both directions. True connectedness demands reciprocity.

Wildlife, Therapy, and the Pet Effect

Individual therapies and health policies are shaped by cultural context, by professional standards of the time. Decades ago, when one member of a family suffered from mental illness, others in the family were not part of the therapeutic process. Children, in particular, under the guise of protecting them, were often kept completely in the dark about a family member's diagnosis. Over time, therapists moved toward including the patient's family in treatment. Today some practitioners of animal-assisted therapy have taken the next step by considering the family's companion animals as part of the treatment plan.

The next frontier will be to incorporate the influence of wild animals on mental health and treatment. Ecotherapists are leading in that direction by integrating the natural environment into their treatment plans. Some take the view that wild animals as well as pets are members of a client's super-extended family and that a connection to other animals can be encouraged as part of therapy. At the same time, consideration of a client's treatment (good or bad) of pets or wild animals is also considered.

For millennia, humans have drawn solace and cultural and spiritual illumination from wildlife. Nonetheless, the academic world has expressed only glancing interest in the inclusion of wildlife in therapy directly or indirectly. The dangers of wildlife—as attackers, as vectors of disease—are more easily measured than their positive direct or indirect influences on human mental and physical health.

One of the few related studies specific to the therapeutic value of wild animals was conducted by British researchers at the European Centre for Environment and Human Health at the University of Exeter Medical School and the School of Art, Design and Architecture at Plymouth University. Among its findings: (1) When people detected more species in a park, they reported greater psychological well-being; (2) shared wildlife encounters (e.g., feeding ducks) contributed to a sense of family well-being; and (3) people were better able to "lose themselves" and reported what other researchers call "attention restoration"—recovery from cognitive fatigue or stress through "deeper reflection on personal issues or goals." The original research on attention restoration concentrated on green spaces generally, but experiences with wildlife specifically have appeared to produce the same or similar results.

One of the participants in the study, Tara, described how being aware of the gentle movement of the animal life around her garden calmed her at the end of the day: "Sometimes I . . . finish pottering about and I can stand there for twenty minutes and just not do anything. Just listen to the birds, watch the cows walk backwards and forwards eating, you know, and not particularly do anything. Or I might see a fox or, you know, the crows scaring off the kestrels and that. So your mind just wanders, it's just free really of clutter."

As ordinary as this sounds, many of us need to be reminded that wildlife encounters help calm and quiet us long enough to experience, as one researcher puts it, the "healing elements of stopping fast time and being absorbed in nature's slow time." Some of the participants in this study, according to its authors, also reported a "feeling of freedom and a sense of perspective through consciously connecting with wildlife." One woman, after seeing a pair of deer close by while walking her dogs, commented, "I suppose it's because it's free, isn't it? Not free to look at, but as in either running free or flying free." Because the deer were not "cooped up," she also felt liberated. The study reported that other participants agreed that "simple pleasures of wildlife, such as a bird peering through the hedge and a new flower opening up, had provided a sense of comfort and perspective during periods of depression in the past." Observing life cycles, "including the emergence of baby birds and seeing trees and flowers coming into bloom," was also grounding to them. One woman drew parallels between changes in her own life "and the cyclical changes occurring in nature," which she felt had helped her deal with difficult emotions in the past.

Even with all these benefits named, the researchers reported that "only a subset of the participants in this study specifically alluded to the importance of wildlife encounters," with a greater number emphasizing open space and the general "power of nature, the elements and opportunities for social and physical activities." The authors cautioned that different cultures perceive wildlife and nature differently. These findings and others in the report have implications for wildlife managers, park staffs, and public health officials as well as for physicians, psychologists, and other therapists prescribing nature. Should policies be adopted that would encourage more high-quality encounters? Some of the encounters occurred only because people were *conscious of the value* of the experience.

Can people—especially children, through schools, libraries, nature preserves, and places of worship—be persuaded to increase the number and quality of these kinds of experiences in a way that does not damage or disrupt wildlife? Note the difference here between collection of knowledge and personal connection—between, say, seeing a bird, then looking it up on a smartphone application; and, for a transporting moment, joining with that animal in the habitat of the heart.

Ecotherapists are at the forefront of incorporating experiences with wild animals into their mental health work. They encourage their clients to notice the animals in their yards, neighborhoods, and beyond, to tell stories about those encounters, to find meaning in them—much as Zayd Jawad did not only with Boo the cat but also with the free red-tailed hawk riding the currents of air. The field of ecotherapy, like other disciplines that see nature as a partner in therapy, is gaining notice.

Not every scientist agrees about the therapeutic benefits of animals not trained for specific service duties. Some researchers dismiss what they call the "pet effect" as an unsubstantiated hypothesis. A 2017 review of existing research concluded that evidence of pet ownership's positive impact on childhood anxiety and depression was inconclusive, and evidence of impact on behavioral development was unclear "due to a lack of high-quality research." However, the review did find evidence of an association between pet ownership and a wide range of emotional health benefits, including increased self-esteem and social competence, decreased loneliness, wider social networks, "social play behavior," and "educational and cognitive benefits."

A small Tufts University study of second graders revealed that the ones who read aloud to a dog made small gains in their reading ability—gains that were significantly higher than those for children who read to human adults. In fact, a third of the students who were reading to adults dropped out of the program. None of the children who read to dogs dropped out. The researchers suggested that summer reading programs with dogs may help students avoid losing ground in their learning skills over the summer.

Dogs enhance physical health for people of all ages by demanding to be walked. A 2010 study revealed that adults with dogs are more physically active, typically taking about 25 percent more steps per day. The study also found that children from age nine to ten from dog-owning families exercise eleven minutes a day more than their non-dog-owning peers. A study sponsored by the University of Missouri's College of Veterinary Medicine Research Center for Human-Animal Interaction compared a group of seniors walking with shelter dogs to another group of seniors who walked with people. The researchers reported that dogs improved older people's "walking capabilities" by 28 percent in twelve weeks; they walked more confidently and increased their speed. The seniors who walked just with other humans had only a 4 percent increase. The humans were more likely to discourage one another's efforts by complaining about, say, weather conditions. Interestingly, cold weather was less likely to discourage older people who walked their dogs than it did people without dogs.

Any twenty-four-year-old with a dog understands this dynamic: Want a girlfriend? Get a dog. And walk it. The reason? Not just because dogs are people magnets, but because they also help us learn how to be socially competent and to communicate.

Again, although most direct observers give a thumbs-up to animal-assisted therapy, whether it's used in a formal setting or as self-medication, scientific and institutional opinions vary. In 2012, the Department of Veterans Affairs (VA) announced that with respect to service dogs for veterans with posttraumatic stress disorder, "the exclusion of benefits for mental health service dogs [was] not unlawful" and, further, that it would not cover the costs of service dogs owing to "a lack of evidence to support a finding of mental health service dog efficacy." Ironically, the VA does provide veterinary care for some service dogs.

In 2017, Green Chimneys and the Human Animal Bond Research Institute announced publication of a study exploring the effectiveness of animal-assisted social skills intervention for children with autism spectrum disorder. Research was conducted at Green Chimneys, and the findings suggested that incorporating therapy dogs in social skills training helps autistic children engage with peers. "Not only do dogs appear to have a positive effect on children's emotional states, but they can also be motivating factors that encourage social interaction and involvement," according to research associate Joanna Becker, the study's principal investigator. The study's findings demonstrated that the inclusion of dogs in social skills training was more effective than traditional programs that did not use animal therapy. Children also had decreased feelings of isolation and depression.

As animal-assisted therapy becomes more widely known, attracting more publicity and more dollars, constructive scrutiny is needed, including attention to the funding sources. The therapy world is competitive, so everyone has a horse in the race. Pharmaceutical companies and large institutions have the scale to attract major funding. Proponents of animal-assisted therapy generally do not. Another challenge facing researchers is the difficulty controlling for variables. Just as pharmaceuticals or diets work differently with different people, so do animals—and no two animals are alike. Results depend on the person and the pooch. Research on animal-assisted therapy, whether in formal or informal settings, faces the same challenges confronted by researchers who look at the health impacts of the natural world generally. Randomized controlled studies are, in some cases, almost impossible to arrange.

Therapist Philip Tedeschi welcomes the critiques. "These challenges have existed in the field for quite some time. There are so many different ways that animals contribute to our lives that are difficult to measure, so we're looking at methodological approaches and new strategies." Tedeschi recommends a shift to what is called single system research, commonly used in social science research, in which scientists look at changes in individuals over longer periods of time. "I personally don't feel as though we're lacking data," he said. "There's already tremendous evidence that animals are a significant part of people's lives, on a scale of eighty million dogs owned in the United States alone." Then there are all the people who find peace in the presence of a meadowlark. "Looked at it this way, we have millions of people who are deliberately engaging with animals because it improves the quality of their lives."

Tedeschi is right: other animals can improve our health. We already know this through experience, intuition, and history. Explaining exactly how this occurs may be beyond the reach of science. It's like dissecting love.

FOURTEEN

The Replacements: Do We Really Need Animals?

Even as we learn more about the depth of our psychological, physical, and ecological connections to our fellow animals, science and industry are moving to create artificial life, augment living animals with machinery and AI, and blend the genes or parts of humans with those of other animals. This is a co-becoming of a different order.

Peter H. Kahn Jr., director of the Human Interaction with Nature and Technological Systems lab at the University of Washington, is a personable and objective observer and theorist. He and colleagues Rachel Severson and Jolina Ruckert argue that two world trends are reshaping human existence. One "is the degradation and destruction of large parts of the natural world. A second is unprecedented technological development. At the nexus of these two trends lies *technological nature*," which Kahn defines as the creation and use of technologies that "mediate, augment, or simulate the natural world." As an extreme example, he describes a "telehunting" website in which players from anywhere in the world could log on, control and shoot a mounted rifle, and kill a live animal. In Texas, after the kill shot, the animal "would then be gutted and skinned . . . and the meat shipped to [the player's] doorstep." Eventually, Texas outlawed telehunting, but teleshooting continues, in which real animals have been replaced with facsimile targets. Other, more familiar examples of technological nature include television networks such as the Discovery Channel and Animal Planet, which "provide us with mediated digital experiences of nature," and video games like *Zoo Tycoon* (and zoos themselves), which bring "technologies such as webcams into their exhibits so that we can . . . watch the animals in their captive habitat from the leisure of our homes."

To understand how technological nature functions and its impact on human beings, Kahn and his colleagues created a "technological nature window" by installing a high-definition TV camera on the top of a university building and then displaying real-time nature views on fifty-inch plasma screen "windows" in rooms and offices inside the building that did not have real windows. As Kahn reported in *Psychology Today* in 2009, the researchers found that technological nature offers some of the same benefits to psychological health as the real thing. Among their conclusions: technological nature can be better than no nature at all. "Does it matter for the physical and psychological well-being of the human species that actual nature is being replaced with technological nature?" Kahn asks. "I think the answer is yes." But that point of view can be a tough sell. "If you try to explain what we, as humans, are missing in terms of the fullness of the human relations with nature, a well-meaning person can look at you blankly . . . and respond 'but I don't think we're missing much.'" Kahn also diagnoses what he calls "environmental generational amnesia," in which each generation constructs a conception of what is environmentally normal based on the natural world encountered in childhood. As environmental degradation increases, each generation tends to accept that degraded condition as normal. "It is hard enough to solve environmental problems such as global climate change when we are aware of them; it is all the harder when we are not," Kahn argues. "Thus, I believe that the problem of environmental generational amnesia will emerge as one of the central psychological problems of our lifetime."

Technology plays a dual role: it contributes to generational amnesia, but in some cases it can also help us reconnect. German author Alexander Pschera, in his book *Animal Internet*, makes an argument familiar to many who care about the human relationship with other animals—that we have become too distanced from them. With a twist, however, he suggests that some of the ways that we protect nature have actually served to exacerbate that distancing. "A central problem stems from the fact that modern science and its teaching systematically undermine the value of the visible," according to Pschera. "Instead of species identification, teaching now focuses almost exclusively on molecular biology and genetics."

Another example of unintentional distancing is the nature-under-glass or look-but-don't-touch approach to nature. Rules are necessary for protecting endangered species but, depending on the habitat, can be overly burdensome. "Hobbies that were once commonplace and established the very basis of a human interest in nature can now be considered criminal: foraging for mushrooms, picking flowers, catching and observing animals, filling butterfly display cases and curating insect collections," Pschera writes. "This all used to be a self-evident part of a creative way to make nature one's own, a way for humans to immerse themselves in natural space." His suggested solution: an animal internet.

Digital Dog and the Internet of Cows

A variety of websites and apps now encourage citizen naturalists to engage with nature and participate with one another online. The Cornell Lab of Ornithology and Audubon use *eBird*, which makes it easy for thousands of birders around the world to record birds in the field and report them to a global online database of bird records. *Animal Tracker* is an app that allows someone sitting in, say, Germany, to use a smartphone to track animals thousands of miles away. Movements are collected by tiny global positioning system (GPS) tags attached to the animals and stored in a distant databank used by researchers to manage, share, analyze, and archive. The app's creators encourage users to participate in scientific research projects: "Upload your real-life observations and photos of our tagged animals to *Animal Tracker*. Your observations are crucial for our scientists!"

At the same time, agricultural distance monitoring—an "internet of cows," as its sometimes called—is spreading, ranch to farm to table. Wireless communications devices, including Bluetooth ear tags and smart collars fitted to farm animals, monitor their stress, nutrition, and productivity. Proponents argue that using such technology in chicken ranches or dairy farms could not only increase output and efficiency but also sensitize farmers and ranchers to the minute-to-minute welfare of the animals in their control. (That argument is not likely to assuage concern about the unseen cruelties of factory farms.)

Next up, industrial animal augmentation. Melody Jackson, creator and director of the BrainLab at Georgia Tech, researches innovations in human-computer interaction for people with severe disabilities. Observing that dogs can know more than they can say, she designed a computerized vest for service dogs that allows the dog to pull a lever that activates an audio message to report a specific problem to another human being. Among other applications, a rescue dog could pull such a lever on its vest to send out a digital SOS. Meanwhile, at North Carolina State University, a scientist reports progress on a canine smart harness designed to use wireless communication to send information from dog to computer, which interprets and translates data and then sends it to the human on the other end of the leash. The purpose: helping the human understand the dog's mood, whether it's tired or feeling poorly. Further, as *Wired* magazine reports, "Jackson is making sensors that monitor horses and broadcast signs of impending lameness," and other scientists are "crafting cat-human videogames" and devices to help humans and dolphins communicate.*

On the face of it, such technology—and the spending on such research— seems bizarre at best. Here you have two species—dog and human—who have coevolved for thousands of years in order to understand each other in ways that no computer in this century is likely to replicate. Still, there may be special-use canines, including bomb-sniffing dogs, who could benefit by plugging in. Scent is far more important to dogs than how many human words they understand, so the intention would be to interpret what a dog smells. Molecular biologist Adriana Heguy takes such augmentation one step further. She imagines creating an artificial dog nose that "would allow [her] to detect and identify the scents they are capable of detecting."

At that point, I suppose, a real dog is no longer needed. Send in the machine. If machine language can handle everything, why bother with the oldest language?

In one interview, Alexander Pschera spoke about his love of being out-doors: "I am a huge fan of the real wilderness. When I'm out in nature I hate

---

* One company, Backyard Brains, invented animal augmentation devices said to remotely control a cockroach's movements, stimulate a squid to put on a music-induced light show, and enable some plants to transmit signals to other species through what the company calls the Plant SpikerBox. Andrew Gebhart, "Backyard Brains Helps Your Plants Open Up; A Cool New Device Uses Electrodes to Key into a Plant's Behaviors," CNET, October 10, 2017, www.cnet.com/news/watch-these-plants-engage-in-an-interspecies-conversation-backyard-brains/.

people playing around with their stupid smartphones. But when I started talking to park rangers and zoologists who really cared about animals, I gradually understood that the mysterious opacity of nature—which we hold up as a romantic ideal—can actually kill animals, because you can't protect what you do not know." He argues that "analogue and digital must merge in order to create a new space of nature in which the positive, empathic, loving relationship between mankind and creation is the most important condition for the survival of most of the species. And the Internet is the key to this new space."

So which species wins the lottery? Which one will be the breakthrough communicator? Dogs? Prairie dogs? Or perhaps dolphins? Marine mammal behavioral biologist Denise Herzing has studied Atlantic dolphin language for years, recently working with a research team at Georgia Tech on the development of a wearable human-to-dolphin communication device called Cetacean Hearing and Telemetry (with the catchy acronym CHAT). The researchers don't yet know if it will ever be able to connect humans and dolphins in full conversation, but Herzing believes such technologies are coming. When Herzing was asked what animal she would most like to talk with via a computerized translator, she replied, "One on another planet."

Here on Earth, the "interspecies internet" is another example of where the trend is headed, as imagined by cognitive psychologist Diana Reiss; musician Peter Gabriel, who has used electronics to play music with bonobo apes; Vint Cerf, a pioneer of the early internet; and Neil Gershenfeld, a key computer engineer in the development of the "internet of things" (which refers to the embedded capabilities of ordinary physical objects such as refrigerators and cars to connect to the internet). The interspecies internet they propose would theoretically link all intelligent species, presumably equipped with attached or embedded communications devices. Members of multiple species, including *H. sapiens*, would be connected, just as refrigerators, cars, and air conditioners already are, humming along with one another via the cloud.

Powerful animal replacement technology is already scratching at our door. "It might sound surreal for us to have robotic or virtual pets but it could be totally normal for the next generation," writes veterinary medicine professor Jean-Loup Rault in an article titled "Pets in the Digital Age: Live,

Robot or Virtual?" "It's not a question of centuries from now. If 10 billion human beings live on the planet in 2050, as predicted, it's likely to occur sooner than we think."

To Rault, that could be a good thing. Pets are messy. Wild animals are unpredictable. Both bite. And eat. And defecate. "Pet ownership in its current form is likely unsustainable in a growing, urbanized population. Digital technologies have quickly revolutionized human communication and social relationships, and logically could tackle human-animal relationships as well. The question is whether these new technologies actually represent the future of pet ownership, helping tackle its sustainability while solving animal welfare issues."

Robot pets, "such as the iCybie, Tekno, and Poo-Chi" have been "big sellers at Walmart and Target," Peter Kahn reports. At this writing, the Hasbro company offers under its Joy for All Companion Pets brand a robotic golden puppy and three robotic cats—an orange tabby, a silver cat with white mittens, and a black-and-white "tuxedo" cat. Hasbro's pets incorporate technology that mimics purring, barking, and even a heartbeat. They offer companionship but without the mess. The original product description for the company's puppy claims it "has all the love in the world to give but it won't chew up your slipper!" Japanese companies have been turning out robotic pets for years, in part because Japan's population is aging more quickly; by 2030, Japanese citizens sixty-five or older will make up 32 percent of its population. In Japan, grown men carry on relationships with illustrated pillows as ersatz women companions, while robotic pets appear to be particularly popular as companions for people with dementia. In 2005, Sony produced AIBO, a beagle-like robotic dog that uses AI and wireless connections to communicate with people, other devices, and the environment and is capable of learning the owner's likes and dislikes.

This trend is more than the sum of its gadgets. Rault predicts a perceptual shift from animals being valued "for their consumptive value" to being prized as "'reservoirs of human need' such as love and care." He suggests "the dawn of a new era," a digital revolution with "likely effects on pet ownership similar to the industrial revolution which replaced animal power for petrol and electrical engines." His work raises a series of discomfiting questions. If artificial pets can offer us benefits we already obtain from live pets, does that mean the existing human-animal emotional bond is just a projection of our imagination? Could artificial pets so disconnect us from real animals that we'd find it easier to turn a blind eye to human cruelty toward animals? Or is the trend just an extension of an old and very human inclination?

For millennia, people have created replicas for worship, comfort, and play. On a Mississippi bear-hunting trip in 1902, President Theodore Roosevelt refused to shoot a bear that other hunters had captured, declaring their behavior unsportsmanlike. Newspapers around the country picked up the story, illustrated with cartoons of Teddy and the bear. When a Brooklyn shop owner saw the story, he and his wife created the first of what they called teddy bears (with permission from the president), selling them from their shop. Children and adults adopted them immediately and carried them in public, and Roosevelt promoted them as his reelection mascot. For generations, the teddy bear, chief executive among plush stuffed animal toys, comforted children. Since then, the role of stuffed toy animals in child development has inspired hundreds of academic papers about human attachment to animal facsimiles, which likely outnumber dolls in human form.

Artificial animals do provide comfort and, to a degree, companionship, especially for people unable to offer the care and feeding that a live animal would demand. But can they really replace animals in that setting?

A Danish study suggests the limitations of artificial pets. Researchers studied the impact of PARO, the therapeutic, "socially-assistive pet-type robot . . . with an appearance of a baby harp seal . . . equipped with different kinds of sensors, including tactile, light, audition, temperature, and posture." The robot seal could "respond to different stimulations (e.g., striking and holding) given by the users, or recognize the direction of voice from them." After comparing PARO the "carebot" to a real dog and a toy animal used with forty older adults with mild to moderate dementia, the researchers concluded that residents in dementia wards, and presumably other people, lost interest in robot pets. While there "are many concerns with animal-assisted therapy such as allergies, cleanliness, and the unpredictable nature of live animals," they nonetheless have more staying power than robots. Still, just as children can become deeply attached to stuffed animals, children and adults can do the same with robots. "Patients using the PARO robot reported that they 'know it is not real but still love it' and talk to it as if it were a living being. Hence, robots can, without doubt, trigger human emotions," according to Rault. In 2018, the *Japan Times* reported that after Sony closed its "clinics" for AIBO robotic dogs, a new phenomenon emerged: funerals for robot pets. After one service, Bungen Oi, a priest at an ancient Buddhist temple, dismissed "the idea that holding memorials for machines is absurd."

Do robotic wild animals have a future? A wild robot is a contradiction in terms. Still, robots might eventually *go* wild. Technology pioneer Elon Musk and the late theoretical physicist Stephen Hawking have argued for robot regulation, expressing concerns that thinking machines may develop minds of their own, a scenario unlikely to end well.

Robotic wild animals already exist in our imagination and in a few rare real-life settings. In the Hunger Games series, a postapocalyptic world is populated with animals called "muttations," a clever play on the word mutt. These include jabberjays, a spy bird capable of memorizing human conversation; mockingjays, used by the overlords to torture rebels by mimicking the screams of their loved ones; tracker jackers, manufactured wasps with venom that can drive people mad; and wolf mutts, which can balance on their hind legs, have human-like eyes, and four-inch razor claws. Not exactly your therapeutic golden pup.

Meanwhile, robots are infiltrating the worlds of animals and reporting back. To film a 2017 wildlife documentary series *Spy in the Wild*, the BBC used remote-controlled robotic animals equipped with miniature cameras to record some of the most intimate animal behaviors and apparent emotions, including a camera disguised as a prairie dog that recorded the "kissing" and "jump-yipping" of a real prairie dog family bonding. John Downer, the executive producer, told the *Guardian*, "We began to see that the cameras were not only recording, they were sometimes *eliciting* behavior. You were having that connection between the spy creature and the animal that you never get with any kind of filming, and so things would develop that you didn't expect." In another documentary, a robot camera made to resemble a young monkey recorded live old-world monkeys at a temple in Rajasthan. The troop appears to come to believe that the immobile robot is a monkey who has died. As the *Guardian* reported, "The langurs are seen gathering en masse to surround the motionless 'baby,' hushing their chatter and hugging each other as if collectively grieving."

Escape from Uncanny Valley

In the early 2000s, at the Center for Robot-Assisted Search and Rescue at the University of South Florida, researchers developed "shape-shifting, marsupial robots," search-and-rescue (and possibly firefighting) machines that carry smaller robots with them and change configuration to fit their surroundings, becoming serpentine, for example, to allow access to confined spaces. Other institutions have their own achievements: a similar snake bot (Carnegie Mellon); "Cassie," a bipedal robot that mimics the long, rolling strides of an ostrich (Oregon State University); a four-legged robot that can run and jump like a cheetah (Massachusetts Institute of Technology [MIT]); and a faster cheetah bot that races at twenty-nine miles per hour (Boston Dynamics). Interestingly, MIT's cheetah bot can only run five miles an hour, but it is still better than the Boston Dynamics version at leaping over hurdles dropped in its path.

Some of the potential uses are intriguing. For example, think of combining the abilities of animals and machines into early-warning systems for natural disasters—or for war. The Legged Squad Support System was developed by Boston Dynamics for the military and started trials in 2012. The "Cow," as U.S. Marines testing it in Hawaii call it, can carry four hundred pounds of gear and walk twenty miles in twenty-four hours, barring terrain difficulties.

In 2017, a high school in Bengaluru, India, organized a "robotic animal show"; also in that city, a mini-zoo attracts visitors to its animatronic African elephants, zebra, moose, Chinese panda, rhinos, shark, white tigers, and dolphins. Used to give these animals a spark of ersatz life, future zoos could theoretically be populated mainly by robotic creatures, which would please many who object to the caging of real animals.

Someday AI may provide animal robots with enough data and discretion to provide more interaction than a real animal can offer. This could occur in parallel with environmental generational amnesia. As time goes by, each generation might also accept the gradual transfer of attachment from real pets, or even wild animals, to AI-powered critters.

When AI is combined with cell culture, genetics, and biomechanics, scientists can produce the "living" robot—or a "biohybrid," as Kevin Kit Parker calls his creation. An applied physicist at Harvard University, he was inspired when, during a visit to the New England Aquarium in Boston, a jellyfish's pumping actions reminded him of a heart, which he thought could prove an important contribution to the creation of an artificial heart. His team grew heart muscle cells in silicone film molded into the shape of a jellyfish with flaps. Electric pulses activated the cells and flaps, and the biohybrid "medusoid" then "swam" through a sugar and salt solution. On another visit to the aquarium, he observed the movement as his daughter reached down into a petting tank and touched a stingray. He told a reporter for *Science*, "Maybe there is something similar with how the stingray changes direction and heart flow."

Using optogenetics, which involves light-responsive molecules that trigger pulsing action, Parker placed heart cells from rat embryos into a manufactured gold skeleton held between silicone layers. He then built a fleet of these swimming machines, which could navigate underwater obstacle courses. The "creatures," controlled by an operator flashing colored lights, are more drone than robot, and the technology is a long way from being used in an artificial heart, but the swimming medusoid, as *Science* reports, takes us a few strokes closer to a fusion of engineered humans and self-propelled artificial life-forms that think.

Looking to the long term, will animals remain purely animal? Chinese designers are already working to genetically engineer super-muscular dogs and tiny pet pigs. CRISPR (clustered regularly interspaced short palindromic repeats) offers the ability to edit any genome of humans, other animals, or crops. "Just as anthropologists can no longer find so-called primitive cultures, because these people have all been exposed to outsiders, we may be entering a time when biologists can no longer find any so-called primitive animal species—that is, animals that have been unadulterated by human tampering," according to Larry Hinman, founder of the Values Institute at the University of San Diego and a leading voice on ethical issues in science. Hinman has studied the implications of CRISPR and the human-robot connection. Darwin, he points out, broke down the barrier between animals and humans, revealing that we are all animals. Next up: the literal blending of animals and machines. In a decade, Hinman predicts, scientists will be commercially producing hybrids of humans and other species, noting, "As editing the genomes of humans and other species becomes less expensive, the pace of production will accelerate."

To get further insight into artificial life, I called Andrew McCulloch, professor of bioengineering and medicine at the University of California–San Diego and principal investigator of the National Biomedical Computation Resource and the Cardiac Atlas Project, a worldwide project to create "a structural and functional atlas of the heart." He and his team work in the field of synthetic biology, which focuses on reducing single-cell organisms to their simplest components and then rebuilding them from their genome up. "This is a bottom-up biologists' approach to artificial life," McCulloch said. Practical applications include engineering microbes to make or sense a chemical or to convert one chemical into another. "Our descendants are more likely to play with virtual pets than physical robots," he said. A virtual pet, sometimes called a digital pet or pet simulation, is an avatar of a real or fantasy animal available on the web or through software—an app on your smartphone, for example. The purpose of some virtual pets is to become a companion; the "owner" keeps it alive by feeding, grooming, playing with it—getting to know it and encouraging it to know her. "Potentially," McCulloch suggested, "you could have a stronger bond with a virtual pet because it would know you better, through an unlimited ability to gather, record, and apply your behavioral data."

McCulloch isn't worried about digital pet simulators and robots posing a threat to real animals. Decline in ecological diversity is a far larger challenge and not at all virtual. "When I go to Africa and I see a rhino, and know that rhinos might be extinct by the time my kids are grown, that is a distressing thing—the idea of eons of evolutionary history being wiped out." He believes that the new sciences of artificial life could help save the planet's biodiversity, that innovative biology could be an alternative to the scourges of industrialization. "Modern synthetic biology can harness life in ways that are less harmful." And if we make things out of *living* (and therefore renewable) resources, that would be better, he contends, than making them out of finite nonliving resources. "For example, if we can engineer living resources that can make a material that is as strong as steel without digging up iron ore, then potentially we would have a more sustainable material with less environmental impact."

One emerging application of science may be just what the vegetarian—and others of us—ordered: "smart meat," laboratory-grown meat produced by using some of the tissue-growing methods used by regenerative medicine. Still much too expensive for supermarket shoppers, lab-grown, or cultured, meat can be produced without the nasty growth-promoting hormones or antibiotics currently pumped into factory-farmed cattle, chicken, and other animals. Cultured meat would also require fewer added nitrates currently used in food preservation. And, according to one study, lab-grown meat could cut the amount of land and water consumed by on-the-hoof meat production, as well as greenhouse-gas-producing methane—flatulence—of pigs, chickens, turkeys, and cattle. (Pointing to the cow, humans divert blame.) Assuming the smart meat tastes good, has no life-threatening or disabling side effects, and is affordable, it could permanently alter our culture. A potential happy side benefit of cellular agriculture would be that farmland, no longer needed for edible livestock, could be returned to natural spaces for wild animals. With smart planning, a diffusion of small villages across that land could place humans in more direct contact with the wild world.

McCulloch believes that, overall, "the informed use of biologically driven technology is more positive than negative." He admires Kevin Kit Parker's medusoid. "It does not have a nervous system," he noted. "But it could respond to light, which provides the energy for it to contract cardiac muscle cells." Was Parker's artificial stingray alive? "Depends on how you define 'life,'" he said. "Some people define life primarily as the ability to reproduce. Others say a living thing needs to be able to move on its own or consume energy."

A plant is an autotroph, he explained. It lives by using the energy from sunlight to produce organic compounds from its surroundings. A heterotroph must consume organic compounds—carbohydrates, fats, proteins. All animals, fungi, and protozoans and most bacteria are heterotrophs. They eat other organisms. "If I were looking at where the field of artificial life might be going," he said, "I would say engineering synthetic organisms that actually eat other organisms, probably plants, a biomass that is readily available. And plants don't escape easily."

Wait a minute, I said—would that mean that someday artificial life-forms, assembled from bolts, breath, bodily fluids, and the spice of AI, could be roaming the neighborhood eating grass and an available cat or two? Maybe, he said. But you'd have to start small, with, say, programmed nematodes (worms) or altered insects.

Looking further into the future, McCullough can imagine scaling up the size and effectiveness of such synthetic animals. In the lab, it's already possible to manufacture cells that create nerve networks. One could generate worms to act autonomously as part of a group or create other forms of artificial life capable of swarming and more complex social activities.

It was time to zero in on this question: So these creatures, part animal, part robot, and infused with AI, would *know* how to get around, how to graze, maybe how to stalk and eat old-fashioned flesh-and-blood animals?

"'Know' is a funny word," he said. "It's hard to know what 'know' is."

A moment of silence ensued.

"So, tell me, is this something that scientists are working on, or did you just imagine the possibility now?" I asked.

He laughed. "I think I just made it up now."

An Alternative Universe

When our children or grandchildren pick out their next pet, it might not be a living dog as we currently know dogs. Maybe it will be a live but fluorescent dog or a digitized dog or robotic cat with a decent Chinese vocabulary. And perhaps their own grandchildren will one morning wake to the calls of jabberjays or the grunts of grazing robots in the dying forest. Like it or not, a "transhumanist" or "postbiological" vision of the future is close to realization.

Elan Leibner, chair of the council that guides educational development of Waldorf schools nationwide, deeply admires Rudolf Steiner, the Austrian philosopher, social reformer, and architect whose thinking inspired the Waldorf system of childhood education. That system is based on close contact with the natural world. In a note he sent to me in 2016, Leibner said that before his death in 1925, Steiner was deeply concerned that through the development of technology, humanity was creating what Steiner called "sub-nature." Leibner interpreted sub-nature as a "world of logical ideas that, despite their coherence, lack the wisdom that created the natural world and are, in fact, leaving human beings susceptible to . . . the technological addictions of today." Steiner's writing by then was targeted at longtime students of his esoteric work, so Leibner offered this interpretation of some of Steiner's final thinking: "Steiner believed that the counterforce for balancing the influence of technology is not simply nature, although that in itself is certainly a good influence, but the development of a level of consciousness that rises as far *above* nature as technology descends below it."

For the human animal, that's a tall order. Though some creators of technological nature will argue, like Descartes, that animals (including the human animal) are no more than sophisticated machines, the question of soul remains. Currently, we have no scientific proof that either living beings or machines have souls. We do, however, have faith, whether or not we're religious. Most people, regardless of background, tend to speak of nature using spiritual terminology. That seldom occurs when we speak of robots, and when it does, it translates as irony and unease.

In the 1970s, Japanese professor Masahiro Mori suggested that people tend to consider a robot's presence in much the same way they do a person's *if* the robot physically resembles a human. But if the robot's behavior approaches but does not quite match human behavior, our feelings veer from empathy to revulsion. He called this psychological habitat the "uncanny valley." We do not feel that way as long as robots are clearly robots. Similarly, we do not enter the uncanny valley when we interact with stuffed animals, which clearly live only in our minds. And with domestic or wild animals, we enter the valley of wonder. No imaginable machine or augmented reality can take us there. At least not yet.

As technological nature spreads, already-difficult ethical and moral questions will become more baffling. Just as science fiction imagines a Borg world in which people gradually become machines, classic sci-fi novelists like Andre Norton conjure other worlds in which reality is shaped by a deep and soulful connection between humans and other animals. There humans depend on animals for knowledge they cannot gain on their own. On those planets, technology is advanced, but humans live in empathetic balance with other animals. For many of us, this is a more appealing vision of the future than one in which our gadgets so subsume us that we can no longer hear the whisper of life.

In a brief video made a year before his death in 2009, Bob Randall, Yankunytjatjara elder of Uluru, or Ayer's Rock, sits on his porch in front of an image of a winding snake. He explains his people's way of understanding what he knows as the vast family: "The land owns us. The land grows all of us up. No human is older than the land, no marsupial is as old as the land. Everything's been and gone, the life in the flesh has died, but the land is still here." Each generation, following the oldest law, takes responsibility for the land, cares for it. Randall continues:

> You feel that . . . when you include everything that is alive in that space . . . and you grow up knowing these are all your family. You can never feel lonely in that situation, you know, you just can't. How can you when all around you is family members from this ground up to all the trees around you to the clouds hanging up around you, the birds flying by, the animals and reptiles that are just hidden in the shrub there . . . for now, and that can come out if they want and hunt for their little food, and then they can become food for us as well. It is a beautiful way of being. It doesn't push anybody out and it brings everybody in. . . . And I wouldn't exchange it for anything.

Do They Love Us Back?

One day, my younger son asked me this question: *Do they love us back?* By "they," he meant live animals. The answer seemed obvious at first. The mamba, probably not; a poodle, of course!

Takefumi Kikusui, an animal behaviorist at Azabu University in Sagamihara, Japan, studies oxytocin, the hormone that plays a role in maternal bonding, trust, and altruism. He describes a positive feedback loop between mothers and babies, in which oxytocin is released in the mother, whose gaze releases the baby's oxytocin, and the loop continues. Kikusui demonstrated that the same feedback loop seen between humans and infants is present between humans and dogs. Some researchers question the cause of the oxytocin spike, suggesting that mutual gazing between people and dogs may, on the dog's part, occur because the dog associates the gaze itself with food, and the food triggers the surge. While oxytocin and other so-called love chemicals are present in the brains of many animals, we know less about what those chemicals accomplish in most of them than we do in dogs. This is a route to explore further.

I raised my son's "Do they love us back?" question with wildlife biologist Mollie Matteson. It's a "fabulous question, but I don't think you'll find the answer," she responded, then suggested rewording the question: "Do they see us?" In one sense, she meant that metaphysically: Do they *see* us? As fellow beings. But she also threw in a caution: "When you're talking about another species and talking love, you may be implying more; you may be out on a limb. For another thing, they have every reason to not love us." Therapist Philip Tedeschi answered the question affirmatively but also with careful wording: "My opinion is that animals can develop significant relationships with people. Whether we choose to call it love might depend on whether we are willing to attribute our human understanding of love to another animal."

In his television work, Tedeschi once met a person who kept a Bengal tiger as a pet. The human was feeding the animal on a regular basis, so it's understandable that the tiger would, at the least, exhibit something like friendliness with that person—but that doesn't mean the tiger loved the human. So, similarly, could the love of a house cat or dog whom we feed be questioned or discounted? Tedeschi didn't make that leap. Reciprocity, of course, exists in every close relationship. "Would our own human relationships change," he asked, "if we didn't get things from them that are important, like nourishment or protection or shelter? If someone we cared for didn't offer that support, the relationship would change, wouldn't it?" This also can be deduced: once you start feeding your Bengal tiger, don't stop.

Whether animals are capable of love as we know it (though most of us believe they are), animals do bring us into contact with other people. They act as anti-rumination agents. They pull us out of ourselves and bring us into ourselves. They lead us home.

Anne Pearse Hocker

PART FOUR

The Age of Connectedness

Creating a Home for All Creatures

Maybe it's animalness that will make the world right again: the wisdom of elephants, the enthusiasm of canines, the grace of snakes, the mildness of anteaters. Perhaps being human needs some diluting.

—CAROL EMSHWILLER, *"Carmen Dog"*

FIFTEEN

New Ways to Live Together

J ames Garcia grew up in a one-bedroom home in inner-city Denver in the
1970s, where wild animals were rarely seen. Going outside represented
escape sometimes, but mainly it meant work. "Tenemos que mantener la
yarda limpia," his mother would say. "We need to keep the yard clean." He
understands that he was blessed with a mother who loved and protected
him. But nature angered him. "When I was outside, spiders were something I stomped on; birds were something that just flew away."

One day, James traded some of his toys for a friend's BB gun, spotted a
bird in a tree, and pulled the trigger. The bird fell to his feet and quivered.
"I had never experienced death before, but I knew how pain felt and I knew
this bird was in pain. I handed my friend the gun, and I went inside to cry."

Later, when James was sixteen, he would hang out at a nearby park,
skipping rocks across the pond water as he had seen people do on TV. Once,
out of the corner of his eye he noticed a white bird sitting at the water's edge.
He moved closer, assuming it would fly away. He noticed the white feathers,
the sharp, long beak, "and the feathers sticking straight up out of its head."
He moved closer. He hoped that the bird would fly to show him its wings. It
stood up, then just flopped side to side. When James was within an arm's
distance, he realized the reason for the bird's trouble.

Fishing line went from his mouth into the water. I took a deep
breath and I grabbed the bird's head, and I tucked the bird under
my arm like a football. The bird thrashed under my arm and against
my body, but I held tight. I held his head steady and looked into his

mouth, and I noticed a fishing hook down in his throat. I knew if I pulled the line from his mouth, it would injure him more. With the bird still under my arm I tried to pull the line out of the water. The line wouldn't budge. I put the bird down and with all my strength tried to pull the line apart hoping it would snap. The line cut deep into both my hands. I watched the blood fill my palms. Looking up from my hands, I watched the bird pull at the line trying to get loose. I didn't want the bird to keep pulling on the line, and I couldn't watch him struggle anymore. I got up and walked away.

He looked past the bird and saw a plastic bag in the water and a tire, a can, and cardboard. He could smell the dirty water. He scanned the landscape and noticed trash on the grass, even with a trash can nearby. He looked beyond the park to the graffiti and the junk in nearby yards. "I was angry. The people in my community didn't care. *There's a bird dying because of the trash you people left and nobody cares. My family works hard to keep our yard nice and clean, and you people don't care about the trash and filth that fill the neighborhood.* I stormed off and as I walked home I kept repeating to myself, 'As soon as I get a good job I'm out of this place . . . I'm out of this place!'"

He wanted to leave his neighborhood and not look back. He told himself he was better than the people there and even the human race itself. Years went by. Now and then that bird would pop into his mind, and he envisioned how he should have saved it instead of walking away. "I felt the bird was calling me." Garcia came to learn about environmental justice and the economic forces that push people in every kind of neighborhood to lose connection with the animals and plants and landscapes around them. Over time, the hate he felt for his community turned to understanding. If you're holding down multiple jobs, caring about nature is low on the list of priorities. And yet there were those people in his neighborhood who were, and still are, knowledgeable about the urban animal life around them—the fox or the coyote disappearing around a corner at dusk, the raptor on the ledge, the songbirds and the pigeons. Though small in number, those people live everywhere. James had not thought about such things as a boy, but on that day in the park, a single animal gave James his life direction.

Today, as the bilingual outreach educator for the Denver Zoological Foundation, he teaches in the classrooms of that same neighborhood. He ends his presentations by asking his students for three favors: "Can you be nice to animals? Can you be nice to plants? And the most important and hardest favor . . . can you be nice to one another?"

Wishful thinking, perhaps. Answering Garcia's questions affirmatively and then following through requires uncustomary humility, patience, and forgiveness to those who fall short, including ourselves. The humility part, in particular, requires reinforcement. If human beings are to skip the Anthropocene and enter ecotheologian Thomas Berry's Ecozoic era or Australian ecophilosopher Glenn Albrecht's Symbiocene—where we advance through a shared sense of deep connection with other living things—the outcome will depend not only on improved energy efficiency or a reduction of carbon emissions but also on supportive urban design. Political change is required, but entering the age of connectedness will happen mainly in the human heart, expressed through the acts of people like James Garcia, whose motto reflects real-world wisdom: "If I'm able to change one child's life, then I haven't done enough."

Notes from the Animal Underground

Considering the mounting bad news about the health of the planet, it's easy to lose heart. But hope lives at the end of the block, beyond it in the trees, or at the edge of an urban pond.

Earlier I mentioned the concept of beautiful acts—Norwegian ecophilosopher Arne Naess's phrase for caring for the beings around us not because we should but because we want to. The children's TV host Fred Rogers often recounted the story of what his mother would tell him about dangerous or disastrous times. "My mother would say to me, 'Look for the helpers. You will always find people who are helping.' To this day, especially in times of disaster, I remember my mother's words, and I am always comforted by realizing that there are still so many helpers—so many caring people in this world." If you live in a neighborhood of animals, acting on those concepts may make life better, or at least offer some hope, particularly if you know other members of the animal underground.

Patty Andersen, a mother of two teenagers, described an early experience she had while growing up in British Columbia. When she was five years old, she ventured out from her family home to watch the first snowfall of the season. "I found myself a mere block away from my house, but at that age it may as well have been ten miles," she said. During this trek through the snow, she came upon a cat shoulder-deep in the snow, looking to Patty as though she was in desperate need of rescuing. "Having had few experiences with cats or animals in general at that age, this beautiful marmalade-colored creature was, to me, the most exotic four-legged beast I had ever laid eyes on," she recalled. "So without a thought that I might actually be making the cat's situation worse by changing her geographic location, I lugged all eight or nine pounds of her through the snow, down the block, and to my home where I unceremoniously plunked her on my kitchen floor. 'Look Mom,' I exclaimed, 'I found a cat who doesn't have a home. She's sooo cold. Can we keep her?'"

Patty's mother was mortified, believing that her daughter had stolen a cat and requested that Patty immediately return the cat to where she had found it. "Despite my buckets of tears, I did as I was asked and returned that cat to its yard and cried all the way home." But that aborted rescue began Patty's love affair with animals, which continues to this day.

A generation later, Patty's daughter, Miranda, had a similar experience, but with a wild animal. Miranda is a precocious and charming fifteen-year-old whose achievements include creating a film and a TEDx speech about nature-deficit disorder, winning the 2015 Nature Inspiration award, and being named one of the Top 30 under 30 Honorees by the North American Association of Environmental Education. Miranda sent me a story that expanded on her mother's experience. "In our neighborhood in Vancouver," she wrote, "there is something of a wildlife underground of people who, like us, find the company of animals preferable to certain humans, and we network together to do what we can for nature." One day Miranda found a raccoon by the side of the road. It had been hit by a car whose driver didn't bother to stop. She pulled a blanket from the back of the family car and awkwardly attempted to capture the struggling raccoon so that she could take it to an animal hospital. But as cars backed up in either direction, not a single individual was willing to take up the cause. She cried in frustration not only at the difficulty of helping the animal but also from her "utter disappointment in humanity." But then "a heroine appeared."

She came silently from a home, bent down to speak with the raccoon (I'm not kidding), wrapped him in a blanket, and scooped him up and put him in a cat carrier in her nearby garage. Unlike what I had experienced, our heroine was not growled at, clawed at, or generally maligned verbally by said raccoon. Rather, the raccoon remained docile. As fate would have it, our heroine had been coexisting with raccoon families in her yard and under her house for many years. Each year's new kits would come to know and love her voice as they grew up in her yard. After capturing the raccoon, she insisted on making the ninety-minute-car ride to a wildlife care facility. She gave me her number and told me to call her for updates on the raccoon's condition later that day. I came to refer to her as the raccoon whisperer.

Over time, Miranda met other members of the wildlife underground who cared for wild animals. They did not feed wildlife or radically alter the animals' daily patterns, but they did step in when other humans or animals hurt a member of their shared nature culture.

Eva Van Dyke, an assistant teacher at an Austin, Texas, elementary school, told me a similar story about a rescued swan that became part of her family. In this case, the animal's life was altered but not forever. She told me how her mother was raised in the Bavarian Forest with chickens always nearby. When Eva's mother grew up, she became a veterinarian and filled her own daughter's life with rabbits, a guinea pig, a cat, a horse, and turtles. Today Eva continues the tradition with her own daughter. Her family created a backyard wildlife habitat frequented by mighty owls and humble toads and snails. She shared this story:

When I was six, my mom and I moved back to the Bavarian Forest where she had grown up. We lived in my grandmother's big house by a river with beautiful white swans. I loved this river and played by it every day. One day, we found a young swan that had been cast out by its family. My mom made some kind of soupy food for it, which I would take to it a few times a day. The other swans attacked our little swan, so we took it to a small branch of the river that ran behind our house. I'd visit the swan every day after school, and it grew bigger and bigger. Pretty soon it was a large, impressive bird and was my friend. I couldn't have been prouder. It's possible I may be romanticizing that swan, but I've always remembered the day that three older boys came down to the river where I was petting it. They started to bully me, threatened to beat me. When they came closer, my swan rose out of the water, spread its wings wide, and charged. I laughed so hard to see the bullies run! My swan returned to me, tail wagging.

The story had a happy ending. The swan learned to fly and found a new swan family farther up the river. One day, it flew over and saw my mom's car waiting at a red light. So it flew down and landed in the middle of the intersection. My mom got out, put the swan in the car, and drove it back to the river and its new family.

Such beautiful acts will have their critics. Some will dismiss Eva's story as a fanciful projection of her own values onto the swan. But it's hard to see how the interaction hurt the swan or how it would not help shape Eva in a good way. A wildlife advocate or two might criticize Miranda and her "heroine," too, for interfering with the natural course of things, but the purely natural life in their neighborhoods had already been breached—in this case by a car.

Given the gathering speed of urbanization, humans must find a way to coexist with other animals in densely populated areas. Eva and Miranda are, in a sense, ahead of the curve. As you'll read in chapter 18, conservationists and wildlife biologists today are moving populations of wild animals to locations far from their traditional homes. What is sometimes called "bucket biology," often by well-meaning but usually ill-informed amateurs planting trout in troutless streams, is now, in the hands of professionals, called "assisted migration." Across long distances or in the neighborhood, the new rules and beautiful acts are works in progress.

In our relations with animals—particularly wild animals—one challenge is to know how to connect with them without hurting them or ourselves. How do we become closer to them? When is being close too close? When does need become transgression?

The poet Rainer Maria Rilke writes, "I hold this to be the highest task of a bond between two people: that each should stand guard over the solitude of the other." Wild animals, for their solitude or independence, stay a respectable distance from us. How might we do the same for them? How can we protect the spaces in which other animals live and still watch them, connect with them, be with them? The point is not just to fulfill our human need for connectedness but to mindfully replace our destructive interactions—as individuals, as a society. In our relations with some species, that will require us to avoid as much contact as we can. With others, we may still interact, but with respectful, even loving connection.

Caring for the welfare of animals and conservation will require both caution and connection. If we do not come closer to them, how will we know how close we can be? If we do not learn to connect with them, who will care enough to turn away the road graders and strip miners? If we do not walk along the stream, who will report the oil that appears on its surface? And if we do not learn to care for them at a respectful distance, love and stand guard over their solitude, we will lose them. In the other-than-human world, robots will be our final companions.

Fortunately, good people are working on a new contract between humans and other animals.

Can't We All Live Together?

Physician Howard Frumkin is director of Our Planet, Our Health, an international program of London's Wellcome Trust, and one of the world's leading experts on climate change, biodiversity collapse, and the future relationship between humans and other species. Like many scientists, policy makers, and laypeople, Frumkin struggles with the terminology. He prefers *global environmental change* or *planetary change.* "We'd need a field of planetary health even if there were no climate change, due to the many other transformations in land use, river systems, coastal morphology, nitrogen and phosphorus cycling, and artificial chemical contamination." By any name, such human nest fouling is undermining long-held assumptions about human-animal interaction.

"The most worrisome news I've heard recently concerns insect die-offs," Frumkin told me in a recent email. "One study showed a more than 75 percent decline in insect biomass in German nature reserves between 1989 and 2016. That's right, in *protected areas* that presumably feature less exposure to toxic chemicals than elsewhere!" What happens to the food chain for all animals, including us, if that continues?

Simultaneously soft spoken and ebullient, Frumkin does despair on some days. But he's no Cassandra. As the former head for the U.S. government's Center for Environmental Health and later dean of the University of Washington School of Public Health, Frumkin was an early champion of international efforts to connect children to nature and a longtime supporter of the use of design and public health policies that support the health of all species. For him, hope comes from the cities around the world that are stepping up and confronting the climate emergency. The cost of solar energy and wind power grows cheaper every year. Young people in wealthy nations are alive to the challenge and are choosing less resource-intensive lives—going vegetarian and not owning cars. While believing that human beings must do all they can to radically reduce carbon emissions, he argues that planetary change may move people into tighter communities, where they would theoretically be more likely to discover friends and closer social bonds. That may be cold comfort in a warming world, especially in the least affluent neighborhoods and countries.

Here's an additional possibility: As climate change and urbanization continue to move wild animals out of traditional habitats and into cities, multiple species will come into closer contact. If our species can devise new rules for living peacefully with other animals, and create additional natural habitat in cities, urban biodiversity will increase and our species loneliness may be reduced. Creating that new compact will be key to our survival, beginning with our mental health.

In 2014, Joanne Silberner, a freelance multimedia reporter and former NPR correspondent who is married to Frumkin, produced a groundbreaking series of radio reports and articles on what climate change is already doing to human mental health. Her reporting focused on Australia, the continent likely to be hit hardest by climate change. Among the people she interviewed was Helen Berry (no relation to Thomas Berry), psychiatric epidemiologist at the University of Canberra who has studied the effects on Aboriginal communities. "When you think about what climate change does, it basically increases the risk of weather-related disasters of one sort or another," said Berry. "What happens from a psychological point of view is people get knocked down.

Whenever people are knocked down, they have to get up again and start over. And the more that happens, the more difficult it is to keep getting up." In Queensland, her colleagues' research has identified children with low levels of connectedness to family, school, or other groups and found they are at high risk of being traumatized by extreme weather events associated with climate change. Silberner also interviewed elders from several Aboriginal communities "who all told of a general sense of unease. All have noticed something—the absence of snow in the winter, the disappearance of rivers."

Solastalgia is the word coined by ecophilosopher Glenn Albrecht for the intense and painful sense of loss when the natural environment around us is damaged or destroyed. Think of it as the wistful longing for one's own home as it disappears. Such despair will increase a thousandfold as climate change progresses. Like many of us, he believes the true antidote to such despair is for countries, communities, and individuals to work in every way they can to shift toward a more symbiotic relationship with nature. The Aboriginal people interviewed by Silberner think in a similar way. To her surprise, she detected more frustration than anger among them. Berry's research corroborated this sense of despair, but it also pointed to an intense enthusiasm for people's desire to reconnect with the land. For example, one Aboriginal woman found solace working in her garden, suggesting that the best cure for the despondency of solastalgia might be found in working to care for and repair the natural world.

I encountered Albrecht, one of the most important ecological thinkers, a few years ago in Perth, Western Australia. When I met him, he was a professor of sustainability at Murdoch University. He had already added a host of new words to the environmental lexicon, including *soliphilia*, a state of mind that encourages people to work together to repair the world and themselves. Since then, Albrecht has left a full-time career in academia to write books—and to practice what he preaches. Even before he struck out on his own, he had begun to restore a wetland in Newcastle, New South Wales. His goal was to allow the wealth of plant and animal life to return. He began this restoration work as a hands-on way to overcome the factional and political divisions that are rife even within the conservation world. "You have to love something before the motivation to protect it becomes paramount, and that love overrides political affiliations," he explained.

He now calls himself a "farmosopher." He lives fifty minutes by car from Newcastle, on a small-plot acreage. "We call it Wallaby Farm because it is the home of many red-necked wallabies (we thought of calling the place 'Red Neck,' but . . .), and they are wild and free in our area. These wallabies are about the height of female eastern gray kangaroos. We do not 'farm' the wallabies but provide them with a peaceful and safe place to lead their lives. They mow our grass for nothing and play out their intricate lives right in front of us." At Wallaby Farm, he also grows fruit and vegetables and provides a refuge for a huge range of plants, animals, and insects. He keeps a small flock of chickens for eggs and manure. The acreage, with hundreds of trees, is also what he calls "an oxygen 'farm,'" sensibly equipped with solar power, a large energy-storage battery, and an on-site sewage and water-recycling treatment center.

"I have needed to be here for my own mental health. Wallaby Farm enables me to write and work at my desk without the 'administrivia' of a university hanging over me all the working day. This place is fecund and fertile. It promotes creativity." In recent correspondence with me, he described his personal contract with the world:

> What I am always trying to do is hold back the retreat of the animals. By providing places of refuge for animals, I am also providing a degree of refuge for those who feel the emotional scarring of seeing an aspect of the world they love in the act of disappearing. *Silent Spring!* Every place that is conserved/preserved/protected, no matter how small, is a way of saying that we must share this world with others and live together.
>
> That I have protected wetlands and other types of habitat for birds (my first love) also means that I am ipso facto protecting habitat for all kinds of beings. That is very good for my own mental health in an era when the sixth great global extinction is taking place and I live on a continent where, in the last two hundred years, we have lost more mammals than any other. I feel ethically and spiritually compelled to work by myself and with others to fight the current era in our history as a species. That is why I want the Anthropocene to be replaced by the Symbiocene. I want to work with others to change the path we are on. Nothing else is more important.

What Albrecht, Frumkin, and the Aboriginal people interviewed by Joanne Silberner are describing—and James, Miranda, and Eva, too—is a way of life that recognizes the threat of the climate crisis and biodiversity collapse but refuses to give in to the global psychological depression. Not able to heal the entire world, they are choosing to live lives of caring and reciprocity. In communion with the natural world, they are conducting beautiful acts not out of (or at least not solely from) guilt or obligation but from their heartfelt inclinations—their desire for personal healing and for reassurance that hope survives. Not only for their own sake but also for the family of all animals.

A New Contract for Cohabitation

To find out how Western civilization's ethical rules are changing, I turned to philosopher Larry Hinman. In Western culture, he explained, there are two philosophical conceptions of nature. One is mathematical—describing the natural world in terms of physical laws and statistical probabilities. The second is experiential and, in a way, magical—though Hinman usually avoids that word. These streams of thought are converging into a third approach, which is relational, offering a counterpoint to technological nature. For example, Alfred North Whitehead, a mathematical logician whose work helped shape a variety of disciplines, from ecology and biology to psychology and physics, argues that we need to stop thinking in terms of *things* and instead think in terms of processes that are ongoing—that is, *relationships.*

The philosophical voices of Martin Buber, Thomas Berry, and most recently Albrecht and environmental philosopher David Abram fit within this tradition, which holds that science can give us an incomplete and misleading objectification of what's real, what's not, and what's in between. Truth, or what we see as our day-to-day reality, can be found not only in things or even in individual lives but also in the connections and relationships among them—in the reality of communion.

Let's return to Thomas Berry and his interpretation of communion, which I first touched on in chapter 2. In 2000, Berry's friend Carolyn Toben founded what is now the Center for Education, Imagination and the Natural World, a North Carolina organization inspired by Berry that offers children and teachers a way to understand the human-Earth relationship. For years, she, codirector Peggy Whalen-Levitt, and the current staff have invited countless children and their families to her land to learn about and, more important, to experience the natural world. Berry, whom I met three years before he died at ninety-five, was a gentle, soft-spoken man who always seemed to be smiling. He had a profound effect on most people who knew him. For ten years, Carolyn recorded her conversations with him, exploring what he called the "human-earth-divine relationship." She published those discussions in *Recovering a Sense of the Sacred*. I contacted her one day to ask her to elaborate on how ecotheologian Berry viewed the human-animal bond.

She began her reply by correcting me. "First of all, Thomas never wanted to be called a 'theologian,' as he was always intent on shifting us into the huge universe of spiritual heart-mind thinking." She said that when he talked of "communion," for example, he was using it as a metaphor for bringing all living things into an interdependent relationship, a "communion of subjects, not a collection of objects." Carolyn said that one evening at dinner she asked Berry about his role as a theologian, to which he responded that he was not a theologian but rather a cultural historian.

With grief in his voice, Berry told her, "We have had little attraction toward a shared communion existence within the greater world of living forms. We hardly think of ourselves within a multi-species community." He was, despite the sadness, brimming with hope. He believed that humans were approaching a breakthrough, a readiness to join the communion of lives, "because of the desperation of our situation, the loss of animals and plants and aspects of the universe." He continued: "The epic of evolution calls for a new sense of relationships. . . .We are in the third age of relationships in our human evolution. The first was the human-divine relationship, the second was the human-human relationship, and now the third must be the human-earth-divine relationship as we discover our bond of intimacy with all living forms and recognize the companionship of the abiding numinous presence." He went on to describe the new alignment he saw coming. In his view, we would someday move from our separation—our loneliness as a species—to identifying ourselves as subjects, not objects, of the whole and sacred universe, a vision (as interpreted by Toben) of "a single coherent community with all elements in total interdependence with one another," each animal, plant, and star unique, "each with its place within the whole."

She added that Berry also believed that if "we could learn to hold this vision for ourselves, the deep separation between the human and the non-human could be healed."

When I first met Carolyn, we spent an afternoon wandering the paths of her beloved family land, Timberlake Earth Sanctuary in Whitsett, North Carolina. We stopped to watch a box turtle slowly cross our path. A child in a wheelchair watched it with us. I thought of that moment, so still in time, when I spoke to her on the phone. Now in her later years, she continues to invite groups of children and families to her land to touch and be touched by nature. When they arrive, she meets them at the edge of the forest and suggests they begin at the beginning: "I ask them to think this thought when coming upon an animal: 'The same spirit that abides in you abides in me.'"

SIXTEEN

The Betweens

Mike Pelton, one of the world's foremost experts on bears, has been giving a lot of thought to the disappearing borders among the domestic, the wild, and the weird. He and his wife, Tamra Willis, a professor at Mary Baldwin University, in Staunton, Virginia, live on a farm in the Shenandoah Valley. The week before I arrived, Mike and Tamra had left the farm for a couple of days. They came back to discover that their bird feeder was gone.

"We haven't found it. Probably a bear," said Tamra from behind the steering wheel. She was driving down a winding mountain highway to the Charlottesville airport. I had stayed at their farm that weekend, in a room over an old springhouse. Mike's office was up there, too. Its floor, desk, and shelves were piled with books and papers about biology, natural history, human history, and bears. Now Mike was sitting in the front seat talking about his lifelong fascination with bears, his deep respect for them, and his awe of their intelligence and adaptability as they move into more densely populated human settlements.

"Don't forget to tell him about the Jacuzzis," said Tamra.

One of Pelton's former students had reported a call from a Virginian who lived on a cul-de-sac adjacent to Shenandoah National Park. "Guy called in to report that a bear was sitting in his Jacuzzi. It had ripped the top off and was soaking in his hot tub." It may not have been turned on, but the water was still warm and the bear was kicking back. No alcoholic beverage was involved. Animals also strive for comfort. Raccoons are known to be attracted to the hot tub lifestyle; rats and other rodents come for the warmth and stay to nest in insulation and wiring.

Until he retired ten years ago, Mike directed the longest bear study ever done. The fiftieth anniversary of this research, done in the Great Smoky Mountains National Park, took place in 2018. But, as Tamra put it, "Mike's still active in all things bear." His specialty is the North American black bear, but he and his graduate students have also studied brown bears, Asiatic black bears, rabbits, muskrats, river otters, raccoons, woodchucks, wild hogs, white-tailed deer, elks, opossums, skunks, foxes, coyotes, red wolves—and humans.

Bears are among the animals that Pelton and other wildlife biologists call neophiles, because they're attracted to the novel. "Any kind of strange or new object or odor, they will respond to. They're like raccoons. They will test anything that they see that smells a little different, looks a little different," he said. "And they're quick to pick up on negative or positive reinforcements." Crows, for example, first express caution or even fear when they encounter some new and unfamiliar object in their territory, but then they test it, challenge it, and finally adjust to it. But they don't flee. The same is true of coyotes. Bold animals—the risk takers, the ones attracted to new challenges—are the ones, like coyotes, who tend to move into cities. (Some young technophiles in Silicon Valley and Seattle refer to themselves, with pride, as "neophiliacs"—because they adjust rapidly to change, reject the routine or traditional, become bored easily, and exhibit a need to create novelty or stir up social unrest.* In other words, your basic raccoon with computer-programming skills. All of which raises the interesting possibility that high-tech cities may be attracting people and animals who share the same traits. Crows of a feather flock together.)

Tamra steered the car along a steep drop, down the winding mountain highway through forests of oak, ash, and hickory and patches of trillium.

Mike looked out at the long valley and described the growing bear diaspora. In recent years, North Carolina biologists and conservation officers

---

* The term was first used by Christopher Booker in *The Neophiliacs: Revolution in English Life in the Fifties and Sixties* (Boston: Harvard Common Press, 1970), and it was later popularized by writer Robert Anton Wilson.

captured bears long enough to place GPS collars on them. Researchers were trying to figure out the dynamics of these bears in the presence of higher human densities. Very quickly they discovered that bears were coming into Asheville's subdivisions at night to forage.

"When we moved here to Virginia in 2000, there were no records of any wild bears that the Virginia game commission had tagged ever crossing the Shenandoah Valley from the Blue Ridge to the Allegheny or vice versa," said Mike. "Except there were some nuisance bears already in the valley who had been captured and dumped in more remote areas, and those bears would occasionally migrate back home," he added. "Now there are resident bears located across the valley."

Relaxed beside Tamra, he talked about bear magic, not a term he would use in the company of scientists, but on this drive he did. He described bears as "silent shadows" that travel through the human imagination just as they move across the landscape of forest, meadows, and prairie, and now to the edge of town.

"There's always a bear clan. Bear icons, bear totems, bear dances, everything," he said, echoing one of his heroes, the late author and environmental philosophy professor Paul Shepard, who argued that people, ancient or modern, worship bears because they worship themselves. "Their molars look like human molars. They have a huge braincase. They have a form of color vision like ours, which is unusual in carnivores. Their digestive system is like ours. In grunts and squeals, they communicate in something like their own language, including 'jaw-popping,' which they do when irritated, as warning."

Pelton's first bear encounter was when he was a boy, camping in the Smokies. One night, a bear wandered into camp, then dissolved into the dark woods. Pelton and a buddy decided to hide, wait for it to return, watch it for a while, and then scare it away.

"In the old Boy Scout handbook, it taught you how to build a deadfall trap," he said, turning in his seat. "You'd prop a big log up on a couple sticks. We found a baby-food jar and we pushed peanut butter down into it and placed the bait beneath the propped-up log, so when the bear came in and tried to get the peanut butter this log would fall on the bear and scare it away."

They watched until late at night. Their eyelids were heavy when they became aware of the shadow. "We could see it put its head down under the log and then walk away. We checked the trap. The jar had not been moved, but it was empty. He just took his tongue and went *shloop*." The boys baited it again, and the bear came back and did it again. And again. This routine went on until the bear had had enough peanut butter and wandered off for the last time.

That was the moment when Pelton first fell under the spell of bears. To Pelton, the real bear magic is its ability to adapt and survive. During hibernation (the preferred scientific term is *carnivore lethargy*) the females don't eat, drink, defecate, or urinate for months. They live off their existing fat, burning three thousand to four thousand calories a day just in the den. "You can look at their urinary bladders after three months and it's empty; they're actually recycling water through their kidney system." Their heart rate drops radically, but they have no trouble with blood clots. "During our field research, we see bears in their dens with severe lacerations, even broken bones. When you catch the bears the next year for retagging, you can hardly tell they had even been injured. It's remarkable to witness." When Pelton first started observing bears in their dens, he noticed shivering and assumed that they were either cold or afraid. "Can you imagine lying in bed, as a bear does, for three months without moving and coming out with no calcium loss? No bedsores? Bears only lose a small percentage of muscle mass." He thinks one of the reasons may be the shivering.

So does NASA. Scientists studying how humans adjust to weightlessness learned that astronauts who slept on vibrating platforms were healthier. Scientists are now studying carnivore lethargy for potential application to suspended animation for long-distance space travel and for treatment applications for kidney disease, obesity, osteoporosis, anorexia nervosa, and severe burns. Other abilities also help bears survive and thrive in human settlements. A bear's sense of smell is seven times better than a bloodhound's and over two thousand times better than a human's. Though bears are often described as "lumbering," Pelton has watched them literally run down the trunk of vertical trees, like raccoons, though they are ten to twenty times the weight. They have dexterous paws, movable lips, rounded ears that can both flatten and raise, and almost prehensile tongues (great for extracting peanut butter from baby-food jars). "One recent study tested how quickly different animals were able to figure out how to liberate food from a container, and black bears were ranked number one," said Pelton.

One myth about bears is that they cannot see well. But they can still see as well as we do. Like us, they have binocular vision. When shown charts on a touch-screen monitor covered with dots, bear participants in one study could tell when just a few dots had been moved. In the complicated exercise, bears motivated by the potential for food were able to "count." This and other new research suggests that bear intelligence may be on par with primates. "They're particularly good at seeing close-up stuff, which makes sense because they spend so much of their time picking berries—it takes a lot of berries to fill a bear," said Pelton. The assumption about poor bear vision, he added, probably stems from the fact that bears do stand up to get their bearings and wave their heads around as if confused; in reality, they're using their remarkable noses during those moments more than their eyes. "They're plantigrade; like us, they walk on the soles of their feet. And on occasion, they become bipedal and walk upright, like humans."

This brings to mind the viral home videos of a black bear often seen eerily walking upright, like an awkward man, through suburban New Jersey neighborhoods. "Pedals," as he was named online, was funny until people learned the probable reason for his upright gait: at some point in his life, his front paws had been badly burned in a fire. He wandered, walking, for years and became famous, even beloved. Some people wanted to capture him and place him in a wildlife sanctuary; others pointed out that he was doing just fine. In 2016, the walking bear was reportedly killed in the state's first sanctioned bow-and-arrow hunt in decades. *Après Pedals, le deluge.* The number of bear sightings in human neighborhoods is increasing.

In urban living, are bears the new raccoons? "Yes," said Pelton. "I never would have thought it. Never in my career did I ever dream that we'd be dealing with so many bears in our backyards. I really haven't heard anyone talk about it that much yet, but yes, I think that's what's happening."

Arrival of the Neophiles

For the most part, the wild animals that live among us stay to themselves, hidden in secret pockets, little parallel neighborhoods of their own. Then, unexpectedly, they emerge. Some, like Pedals, capture our imagination. New Yorkers become enthralled and fiercely protective of raptors that nest on high building ledges. The fox who found its way up a London fire escape to a rooftop near Finsbury Park earned its own hashtag, #rooffox. Photos of the rooftop fox were shared tens of thousands of times, prompting one Brit to tweet, "Bring him some tea. Where are your manners?" More dramatically, the daredevil raccoon of St. Paul, Minnesota, became a media fixation when it climbed a vertical concrete wall twenty-three stories, cheered on by anxious followers around the world, who also fretted for its safety. At least one saw religious significance in its ascent, asking, "Has anyone noticed that, in one photo, the wall and windows make the shape of a cross?"

Over the past decade, Americans have grown more appreciative of wolves, but they remain ambivalent about raccoons—possibly because they're becoming more common in urban areas, which makes them seem more mundane (like squirrels and pigeons), and because some do carry diseases, invade attics and basements, and outwit us so easily. Originally residents of the tropics, raccoons have been following rivers and streams north, probably for centuries. In North America, their range now extends to Alaska. Thanks to their fearlessness, the availability of human food, and hunting and trapping restrictions in urban areas, raccoon hegemony has come to nearly every city in North America.

In 2016, Veronica Pacini-Ketchabaw and Fikile Nxumalo, researchers from Canada and the United States, wrote a fascinating article about the "nature/culture divides" that occur when raccoons, children, and "troubled education" cross paths daily. Raccoons' "unruliness" has long been a challenge to the humans who, as they write, have "colonized" raccoon territory. Raccoons are considered "disorderly," in part because they confuse scientists: "In the 18th century, scientists spent decades debating where to place the animal in the natural order. The raccoon's intelligence, curiosity, acute sense of touch, and mischievousness presented much taxonomic confusion as to whether the raccoon was a wild animal, vermin, or companion." In the early 1900s, some people even declared the raccoon to be an ideal pet "because of its 'charm' and ability to live with humans." But the raccoon's "comfort around humans and constant pushing of human-nonhuman boundaries (e.g., opening doors, stealing food, escaping homes, eluding capture) quickly drove scientists to warn the public that raccoons "could never truly be granted their full 'liberty' like other pets, such as cats and dogs."

Raccoons' "unruly intelligence," write Pacini-Ketchabaw and Nxumalo, "was the topic of heated debate in American psychology at the turn of the 20th century." As they point out, some psychologists even asserted then that, as one put it, "Raccoons possessed ideas, a form of thinking more analogous to that of humans and other mammals." The density of neurons in their cerebral cortex is comparable to primates. They can hear earthworms beneath the surface of the ground. Their brains are geared to forepaw sensation; specialized hairs—whiskers—at the tips of their digits can identify objects before the paw even reaches them. When they seem to be washing their food, they're not; they're washing their paws to better feel what they eat. They can rotate their hind feet to point backward, allowing them to race down the trunks of trees. They can open complex locks and remember how they did it for three years. Raccoons' faces, eyebrows, playfulness, inquisitiveness, and sense of entitlement are uncannily human. Pacini-Ketchabaw and Nxumalo report:

> Captivated by the raccoons' humanlike behaviours, a group of children and two educators watch this charming raccoon family through the classroom window. All of a sudden, the mother raccoon turns her head toward the window as if she is letting these curious humans know she is aware of them. Responding to this motion, one of the children places his hand on the window to gesture hello. The mother raccoon leaves her youngsters and approaches the window. Without hesitation, she raises her paw to meet the child's hand through the glass. Silently, the child and the raccoon gaze into each other's eyes. The other children and the educators look at each other with surprised expressions. No one moves until the raccoon walks away from the window and joins her youngsters.

These cohabitating children, raccoons, and teachers are "fraught with frictions around perceived human binaries that separate nature from culture," continue Pacini-Ketchabaw and Nxumalo. "Day after day at these childcare centres, raccoons cross boundaries, and day after day educators diligently labour to keep the boundaries intact and teach children to enact them." It's an old story on new terrain: The raccoon shows up in First Nations and Native American children's stories and creation stories, like coyotes playing the role of the Trickster. These stories teach "about respect, cooperation, honesty, hard work, and humans and animals as relations." Along with other scholars in the environmental and Indigenous humanities, Pacini-Ketchabaw and Nxumalo urge us to stop thinking of animals and humans as autonomous communities and start thinking in terms of "naturecultures"—a term coined by Donna Haraway, a professor in the history of consciousness, to describe how, in some communities, nature and culture are interwoven to the point that they can no longer be separated into "nature" and "culture." Some are traditional cultures, others are communities in which new combinations of wild animals, pets and livestock, and human beings choose or are forced by climate or changing development patterns to live together.

Indeed, the success of urban neophiles may mark a transformational moment, one in which humans come to recognize the need to create natureculture zones for wild animals, domestic animals, and themselves, in which all can live together in relative peace. Whatever animal control methods are used, the ultimate determinate is cultural carrying capacity—how much association with wild animals a community wants or can abide. The growing number of neophiles in urban areas will require more public education and more flexible wildlife management—including methods not yet invented— because these animals are capable of learning and adjusting at a rapid rate.

As I write these words, in fact, I hear galloping on the roof above me. A mother raccoon and her kits have just arrived on their nightly visitation. Sometimes, in the late hours, I step out on the front porch and stare up at the corner of the roof. I allow my eyes to adjust, and I think I can see their masked eyes peeking over the edge, staring at me. Then I'll hear a light "Grrrr." So I respond in kind: "Grrrr." I always try to have the last "Grrrr." I'm beginning to think we understand each other.

Later I'll check the back deck, where Kathy leaves water for them. Water, not food. As the California drought drags on, it seems the humane thing to do. The mother raccoon may see me watching her. She stands up on her hind legs, then approaches the house as if to challenge me. I stand my ground, behind the glass. After a while, she just lies down, tired. Maybe she's getting old. She flattens herself on the boards as the wrestling kits pummel her. All she wants to do, it seems, is go to sleep. I like her.

How Coyotes Conquered America

While studying conservation and ecology in college in the late 1990s, Seth Magle became fascinated with the black-tailed prairie dogs living in the grassy areas along the sidewalks near his home in Boulder, Colorado. He wondered how and why these small social mammals had settled so easily into life in a city.

Today Magle is director of the Urban Wildlife Institute at Lincoln Park Zoo in Chicago, where he has launched a major study of a different animal—urban coyotes, which cause both fear and delight among city dwellers. Since 2010, the institute has studied Chicago's urban ecosystem, planting motion-detecting cameras and acoustic monitors in neighborhoods to track the behavior and movements of coyotes, birds, bats—and humans. Currently, research partners in Madison; Indianapolis; Austin; Fort Collins; Denver; Los Angeles; and Manhattan, Kansas, use the institute's wildlife-monitoring protocols. Magle is setting up a nationwide—potentially worldwide—Urban Wildlife Information Network whose mission is to reduce human-wildlife conflict in cities and to champion nearby urban nature as an essential component of worldwide conservation of biodiversity.

Coyotes are among the most successful "Betweens," as I call those wild animals who have claimed urban areas as part of their territory, whether they have chosen or been forced to live among humans. They populate urban centers from San Diego to New York City. In New York, they are seen in Stuyvesant Town, the Bronx, Queens, and Central Park from the Great Hill and the Pool to the North End. In 2013, coyotes discovered the Hamptons. They first began to breach the suburbs of Chicago in the 1990s. And now, the Cook County Coyote Project (also called the Urban Coyote Research Project) is studying coyotes in the city. Its method: live-capture, attach radio collar (or "crittercam") to record video images from the coyote's point of view, release, and follow via GPS. The purpose is to find out how the species is interacting with humans, domestic animals, and other wildlife. "Originally known as the ghosts of the plains, coyotes have become ghosts of the cities, occasionally heard but less often seen," according to the project's online profile. "Though a relatively recent phenomenon, coyotes are the top carnivores in an increasing number of metropolitan areas across North America." The Chicago project is mildly controversial. Some critics contend that its focus should be solely on the "problem coyotes." But by paying attention to all types of urban coyotes, the project offers a framework "to manage both cases of conflict and those without."

Its findings, so far, are revealing and sometimes counterintuitive. In 2000, the project began tracking thirteen radio-collared coyotes (of the two thousand coyotes estimated to roam Chicago and its suburbs). Today the project tracks as many as one hundred coyotes per year. And these coyotes are telling a new story about city living. Stan Gehrt, principal investigator with the Cook County Coyote Project, expected urban coyotes to be less healthy and their mortality rates higher than the suburban dwellers. Not true. They hide their dens in unlikely places, including on a parking garage roof and near Soldier Field, and one coyote managed to raise her pups *without* a den—or at least not one that the project could find. They successfully hide just feet from where hundreds of human pedestrians pass by. (In Portland, Oregon, a coyote was photographed riding on a seat on the light rail system.)

In Chicago, Gehrt is most impressed by how coyotes have learned to cross multilane highways. Many are able to safely cross six-lane expressways in heavy traffic by slipping through the gaps between cars or waiting for a traffic signal to turn red. Far more of them should be hit by cars, considering their numbers. But coyotes have taught themselves how to look both ways before crossing streets and highways. A truly urban coyote has a range of 6.6 square miles, compared to only 1.5 square miles for the suburban coyote; the city coyote travels longer distances in less time.

When Gehrt and his team started their project in 2000, coyotes were still relatively new to the city, and the public consensus was that they didn't belong there. If one was seen too often or in the wrong place, it would be removed to assuage residents' fears. "No one wanted it in their backyard," Gehrt said. "We had to do our work in a very secretive way. People said they wanted to kill them." Today, partly because of that work, people are more accepting of coyotes in their neighborhoods. "In the early years, our biggest conflict was with cat owners. Now we seldom hear that complaint. Almost zero portion of [the coyote's] diet is cats. One reason could be that people, now more aware of urban coyotes, keep their cats indoors, although Gehrt offered a more likely explanation: "What we find is that cats aren't stupid. Especially the feral cats. They know where the coyotes are, and they don't go there." Though coyotes are flexible enough to do well in the city, they prefer their traditional diet of rodents, including voles and rabbits, which "is important because rodents harbor more diseases than any other group of wildlife." The project, however, has yet to document coyotes eating urban rats, who may, like cats, be too cagey. Small dogs are easier targets than cats, but fewer of them are eaten by coyotes than many people think. Coyotes also help control the urban white-tailed deer population.

None of this means that pets and people do not come into conflict or that coyotes are docile. Taylor Mitchell, a young musician, was killed by large coyotes in 2009 while hiking on Cape Breton Highlands National Park's Skyline Trail in Nova Scotia. She was mauled and died of blood loss.

If a coyote encounter with a pet takes place when a human is nearby—say, on the other end of a leash—things also can get ugly. Even so, the Cook County Coyote Project notes that no coyote bite or attack has been reported on humans in northeastern Illinois. Media reports of coyote bites (a forty-nine-year-old man in Aurora, a suburb of Chicago, and a three-year-old child in Columbus Park on the West Side of the city) "were later proven instead to have been the result of domestic dogs," according to a report by the Cook County Coyote Project. In fact, domestic dog bites are far more common than bites by coyotes or any wild animals. To keep everyone safe, the project distributes and posts online a six-step guide to avoiding conflicts with coyotes.

A few people, eager to make a personal connection, continue to feed wild animals. But as coyotes come to expect to be fed, they are more likely to become aggressive with people, which doesn't usually work out well for either party. Feeding aside, I asked Gehrt if people do develop relationships with the coyotes. "There are definitely those who appreciate and understand their important functions," he said. "The problem with coyotes is they're so secretive. It's difficult for people to watch them like they can with birds and squirrels. Some of them do relate to coyotes, though."

Still, given a choice, most people prefer not to have a coyote living next door. "But we grow used to them," Gehrt continued. "The same response has been documented elsewhere for larger predators like wolves, bears, mountain lions. In Europe, as wolves, bears, and lynx started to recover, the communities were initially extremely resistant, but over time as they lived with these predators, people became habituated to them, just as wildlife become habituated with people."

Animal control agencies have, for the most part, also changed their approach. As with raccoons, killing or relocating coyotes is ineffective to the point of futility, as it creates smarter, warier, more resilient animals. Also, coyotes regulate their own population size. When their numbers shrink, more food is available for mother coyotes, who then produce healthier pups. Hormonal changes, stemming from dropping coyote numbers, also stimulate larger litters. And when population drops, young females become sexually mature earlier. Some animal control agents, seeing the numbers on the wall, have retrenched and now capture or kill only coyotes that exhibit more aggressive behavior.

One other factor is at play. In the Midwest and the East, coyotes are devoid of predators. The traditional coyote range was once restricted to the western plains of North America, but as hunters and ranchers exterminated wolves in much of the West, coyotes moved into their fellow canids' domains. Without natural predators other than humans, coyotes are still growing in numbers, with a twist: When wolves were reintroduced to some areas in the Northwest, they reclaimed some of their former turf. A few wolves have moved east along the U.S.-Canadian border; short on potential wolf mates, they *may* occasionally hook up with coyotes, producing hybrid coywolves, larger than standard-issue coyotes.

When I took this up with Seth Magle, he challenged that claim, explaining that the small amount of wolf DNA found in eastern coyotes is "primarily because of historic breeding rather than current breeding." Just as most people today carry a trace of Neanderthal genes, most coyotes today carry between 2 and 10 percent of ancient wolf genes. To complicate matters further, some researchers argue that the eastern coyote is a four-in-one hybrid, a mixture of coyote, western gray wolf, eastern wolf, and domestic dog. The addition of dog genes may have helped the eastern hybrids adjust to more human-developed habitats. None of this proves the creation of a new coywolf species, but it does suggest that the strict classification of different predators, based on genetics and behavior, is a moving target, as are our attitudes. Coyotes' strong response to a decrease in numbers was an important aspect of their survival five hundred thousand years ago, prior to the Pleistocene. Coyotes faced predators who were larger and scarier than humans. After the waves of Pleistocene extinctions, coyotes emerged primed for long-term, against-the-odds survival.

"It may now be that coyotes have greased the skids," Magle said.

Greased the skids?

"Yes, for the larger predators, who will have a chance to get a foothold because of people's experience with coyotes. Not that the larger predators will be as successful in cities."

But they're coming just the same.

That'll Be a Caramel Macchiato for Me and an Espresso for the Bear

Bears, raccoons, and coyotes are not hanging out at Starbucks yet, but *Wired* magazine suggests an intriguing possibility: "If humans can keep civilization intact long enough, will urban animal populations eventually become their own distinct species—bold, relaxed, and clever, with a store of learned information about our habits, and perhaps a few other traits that arise by chance?"

In response to urban expansion, and the movement of some wild animals into cities, animal brains appear to be changing. This may be happening not only for neophiles attracted to human settlements—and for the animals who couldn't care less about us, even if they, like pigeons (cliff-dwelling rock doves), do appreciate our architecture—but for others as well. For example, the brains of the white-footed mouse and the meadow vole from cities or suburbs are about 6 percent bigger than the brains of the same species found in farms or other rural areas. Brain size is not necessarily associated with intelligence, but such rapid change in brain size when other body parts stay the same size does suggest that moving into human settlements requires neurological as well as behavioral adaptations.

Once the challenge is met and colonization is complete, the brains of some of the descendants of the pioneering generations tend to gradually revert to close to their original size—presumably because they've mastered the system, until the next challenge, which, because of the increasing population of wild animals in cities, will be sooner than later.

As human-animal interaction with the Betweens increases, *some* animals not only become cagier and smarter, but they change physically and become gentler. Russian biologists bred foxes for a more desirable demeanor. After fifteen to twenty generations, a small percentage of the foxes became friendlier to humans. The chemical makeup of their stress hormones changed, and their fear responses softened. A small percentage of the foxes developed floppy ears and rolled, shorter tails, and their fur began to emerge in more varied colors (apparently changes in the foxes' adrenaline levels affected melanin, responsible for pigment in fur). They were, in a sense, becoming dogs over the course of a mere fifty years. In addition, their muzzle shapes began to change. These and more were the unintentional domesticating results of intentional breeding for temperament or, at times, evolution itself. Consider bonobo apes, who diverged from their cousins, the generally cranky and even warlike chimpanzees, and evolved to become more social, more affectionate, than chimps. In an apparent strategy to defuse social tensions, they make love not war—literally and everywhere, without regard for gender, at the drop of a leaf. "Normally you think of domestication as something that happens at the hands of humans," according to Brian Hare, an evolutionary anthropologist at Duke University and coauthor of a research review on "self-domestication" published in the journal *Animal Behaviour*. "The idea that a species domesticated itself is a bit crazy, but there are some species that outcompeted others by becoming nicer." Others are simply smarter.

For some urban newcomers, life does get darker. Literally. Researchers in Tanzania and California have discovered that wild mammals in urban areas who usually hunt and travel during the day are becoming nocturnal, which is one reason that there aren't more dangerous encounters with humans. In Nepal, tigers in farming areas have shifted to nighttime hunting. So have coyotes in the Santa Cruz Mountains of California. Daytime animals become creatures of the dark not only for hunting purposes but also, surprisingly, because of hikers and other nonlethal intrusions that expose the animals to new risks and new predators. So, in the short run, we will coexist and co-become in unexpected ways. The upside is that these animals may become better adjusted to us, which means they'll know better how to avoid us (as long as we don't feed them) and be less aggressive when we do encounter them. One difference between bears and, say, mountain lions (also called cougars, pumas, or panthers) is that mountain lions are introverts. They're not neophiles. They hunt mainly when humans are sleeping. That's their default mode, and good news for people. However, as urban deer become more accustomed to people, mountain lions may adjust their work hours. Bears forage at all hours (when they're not hibernating), which makes a human-bear encounter more likely than a cougar-human meet-up. Still, the odds are low that an average suburbanite or exurbanite is likely to meet a bear or any other-than-human apex predator on the way to Whole Foods.

Just as animals may tend to become gentler in our presence, we may, with intent, become gentler in theirs. When we interact with animals, the neurochemicals and hormones associated with our social bonding are elevated. People who spend time in more natural environments in cities tend to nurture closer relationships with fellow human beings and to value community. The widely used term *social capital* refers to how well people look out for one another and the sense of belonging that comes with that. Therefore, when we consider the social capital of a community, we should include more than one species. Natural places and biodiversity can help us maintain a sense of peace, place, and purpose. And who knows, we might coevolve into smarter animals.

Moving among us, the Betweens do bring risks. They also bring an unfamiliar enchantment to cities.

When Kathy and I lived in San Diego, we often saw coyotes trotting along the streets, disappearing as we approached. One afternoon, Kathy called me to our window. A thin, ragged coyote stood in the backyard looking at the turned dirt before sitting on a rock wall for a while. The coyote, a female, gave us a searching look through the glass, then stared at the ground. "She looks like she's hungry," Kathy said. As Kathy struggled against her inclination to put food outside the sliding door, the coyote continued to stare at the dirt until she finally decided to move on. We both felt moved by her visit.

Growing up on the suburban edge of Kansas City, I would have given just about anything to see a coyote, a bobcat, or a bear. When a neighbor thought she saw a bobcat from her kitchen window, my twelve-year-old head all but exploded. That bobcat became the most fantastical beast in my imagination. And now . . . in that very county, lions pass by. In recent years, mountain lions have been moving from the Northwest down the Missouri River and its tributaries, including the Kansas River near where I grew up. The lions follow in reverse the very route taken by Lewis and Clark. Trailing resurgent deer, they have crossed through Kansas and Missouri all the way to St. Louis and east of there, too. Surely, when lions pass, magic, wonder, and a little chaos follow. And, though rarely, tragedy.

I have never seen a mountain lion, and the odds that I ever will are small, but I have since seen several bobcats. One encounter was at a lake far out in the rougher edges of the county, not far from the Mexican border. It is a desolate but not deserted place. On occasion, while drifting along the shore, fishermen will see a single line of quiet men, women, and children walking north on a worn path along the water's edge, carrying their water jugs and blankets and plastic bags stuffed with clothes. Sometimes fishermen will steer their boats to the shore and hand these people their catch, and then the people move on, always silent. At dusk one evening on that lake, my younger son, Matthew, and I saw what we thought was a small deer across a cove; on closer scrutiny, we realized that it was a large bobcat with surprisingly long legs. We drifted toward it, and it watched us. Then it stepped from rock to rock down to the water. There the bobcat reached out a paw and delicately patted the surface of the water. It lifted its paw a couple inches, patted the water again, barely touching the surface. Then it swiped at something in the water. The bobcat was fishing, using its paw as bait.

Back in the city, I was out walking late one night and decided to head to the small lake ten blocks from our home. I didn't often walk there in the dark alone. This time, I stepped through the locked gate and made my way up a hill to the water. I loved standing there, watching the moonlight dance.

I walked down a boat ramp toward a little dock where ducks and geese and coots congregate under a dim security light. Five feet before I reached the dock, an orange blur shot out from under the dock and flew across my path as my heart jumped. The bobcat stopped a few feet away. It turned and looked straight at me—just as Alan Rabinowitz's jungle jaguar had scrutinized him and the black Kodiak fox had once held me in its gaze.

The bobcat stared, unmoving. Its eyes caught the dim light. I stepped forward. It stepped back. In this halting way, I followed the cat up the hill until it disappeared through an opening in a hedge to its other world, surrounded by the city.

SEVENTEEN

Welcome to Symbiocene City

Anyone who has floated down the Potomac River as it winds through the Washington, DC, region and then into the heart of the capital, is astonished by the river's almost primordial nature. Along the river, beavers, otters, foxes, osprey, herons, and owls live and thrive. Drifting past logs layered with basking turtles, you might see the rising antlers of a buck.

Eric Dinerstein knows the Potomac well. "Amazing, of all the capitals of the world, only two have a wilder river than the Potomac," he says. Miles of dense riverbank vegetation hide the big-box stores and town houses. "It's a great example for the future. On the river, I've seen wild turkeys, and we now have hibernating black bears in Montgomery County, though I'm not sure they're along the river." As director of biodiversity and wildlife solutions at RESOLVE, and previously lead scientist and vice president for conservation science at the World Wildlife Fund, Dinerstein understands that the most biodiverse habitats are usually deep in the interior lands with less disturbance. But a wealth of biodiversity can also find its way at the between places, the borderlands and waters that join mountains and plains, coast and sea, urban and rural zones; and at the edges of parks, where soccer fields give way to rocks, and wild grasses, and shadows. Cities are all edges.

As more wild animals move into cities, the main question isn't whether they can adapt to us but whether we can adjust to them—and do it in a way that protects and improves human well-being and their own. Conservation of the wild urban places is essential. But the greatest challenge will be to create new sanctuaries for animals and humans. Pursuing this next stage of human settlement, farsighted people are laying the groundwork for a new kind of city, one that serves as an incubator of biodiversity.

Designing for Peaceful Coexistence

Creating nature-friendly cities is becoming an international movement. One of its leaders is Tim Beatley of the University of Virginia. Applying E. O. Wilson's biophilia hypothesis to urban life, Beatley directs the Biophilic Cities Project. Its purpose is to create a worldwide network of cities planning for a greener urban future—cities creating new spaces for native animals and plants to thrive alongside people. A biophilic city, as he defines it, is "a city that makes room." Beatley points to Singapore as an emerging model. Singapore has changed its motto from "The Garden City" to "A City in a Garden."

To the delight of visitors to Singapore's Gardens by the Bay, river otters are returning to the river that runs beneath a skyway that floats between eighteen immense sculptures called Supertrees. Up to nearly one hundred feet high, these Supertrees use photovoltaics to generate solar power. Their steel frameworks form a vertical garden of tropical flowers and ferns. Their canopies moderate the surrounding air temperature, absorb and disperse heat, and provide shelter for human and other life below.

Some cities are realizing and expanding already-existing natural gifts. In Angers, a city in western France, a green island urban park located at the confluence of three rivers is linked to northern Angers by a towpath. It's the home of some twenty thousand birds and is part of an environmentally protected area for thirty species. The island continues to be used for ancient and sustainable methods of grazing and hunting. The park attracts more than five hundred thousand visitors per year and offers four-star camping, water sports, and a House for Environment, an organic garden open to schools and the general public.

In London, a movement is afoot to transform the entire city into a national park. Daniel Raven-Ellison, founder of the Greater London National Park campaign, points out that an impressive 47 percent of London is already green space, including gardens and the world's largest urban forest. He and his allies want to make that concept a central and larger part of London's identity. "There is enormous potential for London to become an even better environment for wildlife," he writes. "A Greater London National Park would be a new kind of park: a 'national park city,' one that could be replicated elsewhere in the UK and the world." His purpose is to inspire a massive effort to increase the city's biodiversity "250 years after the industrial revolution prompted the first wave of national park sites," placing London "at the forefront of a series of global campaigns to bring nature back into the city."

Specific to the United States, the National League of Cities (which includes some nineteen thousand mayors and other municipal leaders) and the Children and Nature Network are partnering to define what it means for a city to be good for both families and nature; these organizations include in their plan how to design urban places for multiple species, how to measure the benefits to humans and other animals and plants over time, and how to train future mayors and other municipal leaders to make their urban regions nature rich in the future. In recent decades, pioneering "new urbanists" have worked to bring front porches, sidewalk cafes, and walkability back to neighborhoods. Some new urbanists have resisted bringing more nature into cities, possibly because of the association of nature with what some designers consider the failed suburbs of the past. But a new guard is emerging, which could hasten the next great wave of the new urbanism—*biophilic urbanism*—by which I mean the creation of a new layer of natural habitat across entire cities, on green roofs and street dividers, in backyards, and on corporate grounds—all contributing to a stronger food chain, more natural habitat, greater biodiversity, and improved human health. These cities will be places where people are more bonded not only with other species but with fellow humans, too.

Among other hopeful trends is the movement to create agrihoods—in new or existing urban, suburban, or exurban neighborhoods where the typical covenants and restrictions are turned on their heads. Usually residents of planned communities are prevented from planting vegetable or even flower gardens in their front yards, but in agrihoods residents are encouraged to plant vegetable and herb gardens and native plants. Urban and suburban locavores are already transforming their own homes and neighborhoods. Some cities have reversed old ordinances that excluded even small numbers of chickens and goats from urban land. One unanswered question is, what new rules should be applied to backyard livestock given the fact that wild predators are moving into some cities? If walking a small dog increases the chance for an unpleasant encounter with a predator, what will an urban or suburban backyard populated by chickens, ducks, or goats invite? Needed soon: innovations in coop design and human behavior. Some chicken raisers invite the whole neighborhood to participate. "Toss your scraps over the fence," says our neighbor, whose chickens live in a side yard. A sign on the fence says: "I dream of a world where chickens can cross the road without having their motives questioned."

A different but complementary approach, which I have written about and promoted since the 2011 publication of *The Nature Principle*, offers a way for individuals and families to move ahead without waiting for city governments to act. They could begin to "terraform" (a popular term for greening Mars) urban life now, through a grassroots, possibly crowd-funded creation of a "Homegrown National Park." Doug Tallamy, a botanist and entomologist at the University of Delaware, who first suggested the idea, argues that if we really care about biodiversity collapse, we should plant native species and other pollinator plants around our homes, churchyards, schoolyards, and on the green roofs in cities. These natives will hopefully help restore populations of insects—including native bees—which feed other wild animals, potentially reviving bird migration routes. Because of climate change, the species of plants we choose will change over time, and that will take an added commitment. Such a park, comprising tens of thousands of miles of backyards, would serve as a new kind of wildlife corridor, one that would eventually lace throughout our cities and stretch around the world, becoming a "Worldwide Homegrown Park."

In recent years, the term *wilding* has grown popular among conservationists, who argue for bringing more nature into urban places. The word gives some people pause, because it sounds dangerous. And it can be. Wilding calls for an acceptance that risk comes with the territory and a belief that the benefits will outweigh the risks. Risk assessment and management for both people and wildlife is necessary.

When designing for species coexistence, the basics are evident: wildlife corridors, green roofs, wildlife bridges over roadways, and wildlife tunnels beneath freeways. But when we look to the future, there's a lot we don't know. Wildlife ecology is complex as it is, but cities are a relatively new frontier. As part of his work at Chicago's Urban Wildlife Institute, Seth Magle asks, What *is* happening to the intelligence of, say, raccoons when they take up residence in cities? "Is a raccoon a raccoon a raccoon," or does it become, in a sense, a different animal in urban areas? How do wild species in cities decide where to shelter, where to look for food, and where to find mates? How can humans and other animals, wild and domestic, cohabitate in cities? To find the answers to these and other questions, Magle's institute is partnering with urban planners, landscape architects, and public health officials to create what he calls "biodiversity-monitoring franchises" in other cities.

To make policy recommendations, biologists and planners must establish new rules based on science, not sentiment. These rules will likely differ among bioregions and over time because development and climate change are ongoing.

The Nature Conservancy reports that only 2 percent of natural lands on the U.S. East Coast are connected in such a way as to allow animals to move through cities. Blockages occur on roads and farms and in commercial developments. Only 41 percent of natural lands across the United States are connected in ways that allow animals to move through them as their populations continue to migrate. As Brad McRae, a landscape ecologist at the Nature Conservancy before he passed away in 2017, succinctly stated, "The bottom line is that species will need to move or adapt, or die." The Nature Conservancy is exploring ways to create new physical habitat tailored to wildlife migrants, including underpasses, overpasses, green roofs, and other solutions to help animals move through an urban region.

The good news is that building wildlife corridors is no longer an exotic idea in urban design, and there is growing interest in biophilic architecture. Workplaces created or retrofitted through biophilic design show improvements in worker health and productivity, improved product quality, and greater customer satisfaction. Through nature-rich urban design, entire cities could offer similar benefits—and create new habitat for wild creatures at the same time.*

---

* Increasingly, architects and urban designers look to nature for design tips, applying them in ways that stretch the imagination. In *CityLab*, Amanda Kolson Hurley reports that,

Doglandia

Meanwhile, humans have been practicing peaceful species coexistence in close quarters for tens of thousands of years. Especially with dogs. Over time, the civic role of dogs has changed considerably, at least in most developed countries.

"Many things have changed in the ways of dog ownership since I was growing up in Houston in the '50s and '60s," says Leigh Fenley, a former San Diego newspaper editor. "The whole world then was one big dog shelter. They moved about with relative abandon, driven by their noses and winning friends with their tails in motion." In that America, dogs visited other families in the neighborhood and were sometimes semiadopted by them. In some cases, they protected other dogs and people. One way or another, they were an integral part of the community. Not everyone has sanguine memories of dogs on the block. They also chased cars, nipping at tire treads. They fought, sometimes violently, and occasionally bit people.

Today, with leash laws and a more vigilant public, the number of free-range dogs has dropped significantly. Even as more people own dogs, especially in densely populated neighborhoods, the number of dog attacks is growing. One reason is the unintended consequences of dog overbreeding. Another reason, ironically, is the constriction of canine social life, according to Marc Bekoff, professor emeritus of ecology and evolutionary biology at the University of Colorado–Boulder. As people become more isolated and fearful, so do dogs. The central problem has never been whether dogs are free, though restrictions are inevitable, but whether people are responsible.

---

in 2017, researchers announced the discovery of what quickly became dubbed "Octlantis," an octopus community off eastern Australia, confirming that octopuses, though generally loners, had created a complex colony with clustered shelters that began as piles of shells before being sculpted by the octopuses into dens, "making these octopuses true environmental engineers," according to one of the researchers. Kolson Hurley writes that because octopuses "think" and "see" with their tentacles, rich in photons and neurons, they navigate their mini-cities (and everywhere else) in ways that could someday be emulated as full-sensory urban design. She adds, "Neuroscience reveals that humans experience urban places through the movement of our bodies as much as [through] our conscious thoughts. . . . Why not an octopus-inspired building, or city, one day?" Amanda Kolson Hurley, "Octopuses Are Urbanists, Too," CityLab, September 20, 2017, www.citylab.com/design/2017/09/octopuses-are-urbanists-too/540384.

Dogs have been straddling the line between civilization and wildness for thousands of years. But not all dogs lean our way. Of the approximately one billion dogs that are alive today, only about a quarter of them are companion animals. The rest are strays, scavengers that survive and procreate at the edge of human existence—not all that different, in fact, from the wolves who once hung out at the edge of human encampments. In fact, in much of the world, unlike the United States, some dog populations are becoming wilder. *National Geographic* reports that in 2014 the Indian government claimed there were some thirty million stray dogs in India, with at least one hundred thousand of them living in Mumbai. (Killing dogs is illegal in India, so a sterilization program is under way.) The government report also included this nugget about what happens when Spot meets spots: leopards kill approximately fifteen hundred dogs annually in Mumbai's massive urban Sanjay National Park, which as a side effect prevents one thousand dog bites of people and possibly ninety rabies cases each year—thus saving the government about U.S.$18,000 each year. One of the study authors called that "an ecosystem service we don't think about."

Stray dogs also share some traits with the urban coyotes who have learned to cross freeways. Mother Nature Network's Laura Moss reports that Moscow's resourceful thirty-five thousand stray dogs have "been observed obeying traffic lights, and witnesses say they're notorious for the 'bark-and-grab,' a ploy that involves startling people into dropping their snacks. They also ride the subway. After a day of scavenging on the streets, the dogs board the train—choosing the quiet carriages at the front and back—and return to the suburbs. Experts say the canines have learned to judge the length of time to spend on the train and even work together to make sure they get off at the right stop." Seattle, not to be outdone, boasts one free-range dog who learned how to take a city bus to a nearby park.

Though admirable exceptions are emerging, most subdivisions built in the last three decades tend to discourage socializing among humans as well as dogs. The two-career family creates the keyless latch-key dog. Home alone all day, dogs can become lonely, undisciplined, and brimming with pent-up longing or rage.

In my neighborhood, one neighbor's mammoth dog named Bill—a rescue dog of indeterminate origin—learned how to open the front door by pulling down on the lever. He would then happily take himself for a walk. When the door handle was replaced with one without a lever, Bill escaped by chewing through the wall. In San Diego, an animal control officer advises pet owners to "spend more quality time with their dogs, just like they should with their kids." More walking. More talking. Playdates with the neighbor dogs? Why not? Some dog owners, recognizing their dogs' social needs, drop them off at doggy day care centers, a trend that started in California and spread to the East Coast. In Orlando, Florida, for example, there's Dog Day Afternoon (an unfortunate name, given the movie by the same title about a lethal hostage situation) and Miss Emily's Bed and Biscuit. Miss Emily's has what the owner calls a "mosh pit" for repressed dogs who need to release their inner puppy. Teena Patel, who owns and operates the University of Doglando, a dog-and-people training program and pet day care center in Orlando, advocates for more off-leash areas for dogs and, better yet, not just dog-friendly places but also a dog-friendly lifestyle. She offered these suggestions: natural petscapes using tree trunks, sand pits, splash pads, and hay bales switched out frequently to keep the animals interested and the area clean. Now here's Patel's radical idea: rather than dedicating only certain parks and beaches to dogs, she suggests signage that announces certain hours in a neighborhood or city when dogs are allowed to run free, just like their ancestors in 1958. Cats beware.

Animal rescue organizations and the Ecology Global Network estimate that there are more than sixty million feral cats in the United States and one hundred million or more globally. Along with free-range domestic cats, feral cats are hard on songbird populations, killing more than a billion each year in the United States and a million a day in Australia, studies indicate, yet feral cats have their fiercely protective fan base. Catlandia? Better indoors than out. Opinions will vary.

Two related trends are of note. One is the advent of air-conditioned dog houses—including coin-operated ones outside restaurants. The other is the outdoor cat enclosure, usually attached to the house by a window. At least one version allows a semi-free-range cat to travel from the house through a tunnel to a domed structure made of wire mesh where it can be outdoors without hurting birds.

Texting Pachyderms and the Bats of Bendigo

The boldest wild species, as bear biologist Mike Pelton has pointed out, are as curious as house cats, as probing as dogs. Neophiles are the animals most likely to lose their fear of humans, and that lack of fear can pose real dangers to both humans and the wild.

In 2012, Jim Sterba, formerly with the *Wall Street Journal*, wrote a foreshadowing book about this issue, *Nature Wars*. While the book does a good job describing the changing reality, its war-focused title is emblematic of an older view of our relationship with other species, as enemies in a wild to be conquered. In 2017, a two-hour Animal Planet television special, luridly titled *The Uprising*, presented cases of recent wild animal attacks on humans, asking: "Are these dangerous and deadly attacks random events or part of an emerging pattern? Could something more significant and more calculated be going on? . . . Is the animal kingdom out for blood? . . . Is it possible that these outbursts are deliberate acts of retribution against mankind?"

Well, no. Animal violence against humans does exist, but these acts do not occur in the numbers that most people believe—either in the wild or in cities.* And they must be weighed against the benefits that exposure to wild animals offers people.

Still, the threat and the possibilities remain. Long before bears and mountain lions started showing up in modern cities in the United States, people at the urban fringes of India and in African countries were threatened and killed by wild animals, including lions and tigers. That continues. In Israel, jackals move into the perimeters of cities; hyenas enter to forage in urban regions of Africa and Asia. "I'm headed to Australia today," Stan Gehrt, the coyote investigator from Chicago, told me when we talked. "I'll be curious to see to what extent dingoes [the wild dogs of that continent] are colonizing cities and what the human response is to that." In African countries and India, traditional and high-tech responses to danger from wild

---

* Stanford University researchers report that the most lethal animals, to Americans at least, are farm animals (mainly horses and cattle), then stinging insects (hornets, bees, and wasps), and finally dogs. Children under the age of four are most likely to be killed by a dog. The study reported 1,610 animal-related deaths from 2008 to 2015 in the United States. Jared A. Forrester, Thomas G. Weiser, and Joseph D. Forrester, "An Update on Fatalities Due to Venomous and Nonvenomous Animals in the United States (2008–2015)," *Wilderness and Environmental Medicine* 29, no. 1 (March 2018), 36–44, doi.org/10.1016/j.wem.2017.10.004.

animals are widespread. Electrified human-shaped dummies discourage subsequent attacks on real people. Some Indian farmers make use of solar-powered electric fences while others mount automatic strobe lights, activated by light and motion sensors, which beam light randomly. More natural solutions include beehive fences, because elephants, known to attack humans and ravage food crops, are terrified of bees. Because tigers (as well as North American mountain lions) usually attack from behind, going for the neck, in India, some rural people prevent attacks by wearing masks of human faces on the backs of their heads. It's difficult to imagine protective backward-facing masks catching on in most parts of the urban world (except, perhaps, at corporate meetings). In any case, tigers soon caught on to the ruse.

Expanding the idea of an animal internet, as described in chapter 14, one of the more ingenious new approaches is texting. "While the elephants themselves don't send texts, their radio collars containing SMS chips do. Imagine getting a text message from a wild elephant," writes Orion McCarthy in *Conserve*. "In the Western Ghats of India, a new conservation initiative has utilized texting as an early-warning system to prevent human-elephant encounters. Elephant tracking collars embedded with SMS chips automatically text nearby residents, warning them of recent elephant movements." As McCarthy points out, not knowing where elephants were played a role in 75 percent of elephant-attributed human deaths in the region. After the texting-based warning system was installed, the number of fatal elephant attacks on people dropped by 50 percent. Such a system might work in the cell-phone-saturated United States, although driving down a highway and suddenly receiving a text from a bear would create its own problems. The use of GPS tracking collars does allow biologists to identify particularly vulnerable junctions of human and other-than-human life, including deer and predators. With the use of these collars, scientists and animal control officers can be more proactive and funding more targeted.

As the Chicago researchers and animal control officers learned with coyotes, seemingly sensible approaches, such as trapping and relocation, don't always work. Wildlife managers in Alaska use Tasers on nuisance bears. But once you've tased a bear, what do you do with it? Relocated nuisance bears often return to where they were nabbed, or they become problems in their new location. Sometimes the animals die from the stress of handling. They may have difficulty locating food sources or adequate denning sites. In the new location, dominant bears may kill them.

When a region—especially an urban region—exceeds its biological carrying capacity for any animal, that animal begins to displace native animals and plants. In part because of that issue, some urban regions allow bow hunting within city limits. But hunting can backfire and not only because of public controversy. Virginia hunters traditionally hold "dog-training season," when, unarmed, they practice running their dogs, According to bear researcher Pelton, "Once bears have been run by dogs two or three times, after that when they hear the pickup truck doors slam and hear a dog bark, they're gone. So I call it bear-training season."

Animals as disease vectors are more of a problem than bears with borderline issues, though they can also protect human health in surprising ways.

One evening, during a visit to Bendigo in Victoria, Australia, Kathy and I were warned by a hotel clerk not to look up at the sky. We walked outside and soon did, of course, and saw a gathering cloud of wings swirling from the horizon and then darkening the sky above us. Fruit bats. Flying foxes. Megabats. With wingspans, as we learned later, that can stretch beyond three feet. The reason we were warned not to look up is because these megabats let loose bombs of megascat. Evidence of that was at our feet—applesized gray balls of splat. The bats, we were told, were not regular residents in Bendigo; they had migrated hundreds of miles from the north and had roosted—thousands of them—in the city park. That night, the weight of bats brought down power lines, causing a blackout in Bendigo. Not long afterward, I learned about a recent theory of how the Ebola virus spread. Fruit bats carry the virus, and the bats are on the move because of climate change.

When I told climate and health expert Howard Frumkin about the bats of Bendigo and mentioned the potential health risks from wild animals in the city, he said, "The appropriate level of caution or fear-mongering will vary a lot with location and circumstances. The Tasmanian devil is in the details. The risk-benefit calculus is very different in the Ugandan bush than in rural Connecticut."

Any ecological space can careen wildly out of balance. Too many deer in an urban space can destroy habitat for other species, including endangered ones, cause sickness and starvation in the deer population, and lead to highway deaths of both deer and humans. Too much of a good thing, and the animal in question more readily becomes a disease vector. At some point on that spectrum, deer popularity drops to the level of vermin. This fact points to the need for sophisticated training and solid support for those undertaking careers in urban ecology and animal control so that the wildlife population is balanced and managed in a way that maximizes its benefits and reduces its threats.

Frumkin is a leading proponent of the One Health Initiative in public health. As described by the Centers for Disease Control and Prevention (CDC), "One Health recognizes that the health of people is connected to the health of animals and the environment." The goal of One Health is to increase collaboration among multiple disciplines, across regional and national borders "to monitor and control public health threats and to learn about how diseases spread among people, animals, and the environment." One Health goes by other names as well. In 2013, Barbara Natterson-Horowitz, a cardiology professor at the David Geffen School of Medicine at UCLA who also serves on the medical advisory board of the Los Angeles Zoo, and science writer Kathryn Bowers, dubbed this approach to medicine "zoobiquity." In their book of the same name, they write, "Zoobiquity springs from a simple but revelatory fact: Animals and humans get the same diseases, yet physicians and veterinarians rarely consult with one another." A few samples from their long list of the diseases shared by people and other animals: Golden retrievers, jaguars, kangaroos, and beluga whales all get breast cancer. "Siamese cats and Dobermans get obsessive-compulsive disorder. Many are on Prozac. Canaries, and fish, and even Yorkie dogs faint when they're stressed out. Mares can become nymphomaniacs. Koalas catch chlamydia infection. . . . Reindeer seek out [psychic] escape in hallucinogenic mushrooms. Gorillas experience clinical depression and eating disorders." Bowers recommends that health professionals who work with humans do more to tap the experience and knowledge of veterinarians and wildlife biologists.

Just as canaries were once used to detect fatal gas or lack of oxygen in mine shafts, the health of other animals can serve as early-warning systems of diseases also threatening to humans. For example, the CDC determined that the health of local animals (in this particular case, disappearing ducks in Nigeria) could serve as an early-warning system for lead poisoning of children. The agency also solved what it called "the mystery of poisoned sea otters." In 2007, eleven dead or dying sea otters were discovered around Monterey Bay in California. Their gums were yellow and their livers were swollen. Scientists and veterinarians discovered that the otters had died of a microcystin toxin given off by blue-green algae. The toxin, which can be dangerous to humans, had originated in a freshwater lake that drained into a creek that flowed into a river and then to the bay. Also, the West Nile virus often kills birds before it infects people. "Reporting and testing of dead birds is one way to check for the presence of West Nile virus in the environment," according to the CDC. "Some surveillance programs rely on citizens to report dead bird sightings to local authorities."

One Health also promotes the personal and public health benefits of human relationships with other animals, domestic or wild. The challenge, particularly when it comes to humans and wild animals, is to promote relatively peaceful coexistence.

The Raccoons Next Door

When people move into a new neighborhood with different customs and expectations or enter into a marriage, they may feel comfortable with the neighbors or in-laws, or they may not. Either way, they're wise to establish boundaries and learn how to get along despite differences on child rearing, race, money, politics, or lawn care. Compared to dealing with humans, does getting along with the raccoons next door really seem so difficult? Yes, it does, insist urban ecologists, conservationists, and wildlife management professionals. In his office above the barn, Mike Pelton keeps a stack of photos of people feeding bears at parks, even putting honey on children's hands so a bear can lick it off. The biggest problem is not animal behavior, but human nature.

Feeding wild animals is not helpful, especially in cities. At our best, we want to nourish living creatures around us. But there are better ways to do that, such as protecting and creating wild spaces for animals in the cities and planting native species that reboot the food chain of insects, birds, and beyond. By providing this kind of nourishment, we are nourished by the company of other animals.

Chicago's Seth Magle is often asked to estimate the benefits of interaction with other species, especially cost benefits. "Listening to songbirds, seeing a rabbit that makes you smile. That's hard to measure. So is the sense of awe," he says. He and his colleagues at Lincoln Park Zoo feel so strongly about the value of wonder that they held a "storytelling slam" in August 2017, inviting people to come to the zoo to tell their stories about "the coyote in the yard, the unexpected encounters with nature, the indescribable feeling." That sense of wonder, he says, is the most important gift that the presence of wildlife can offer. "We need to hold a place in the city for that to happen." He likes to point out that each of us lives in an ecosystem that is "every bit as complex . . . as the Amazon or Outback of Australia. It's just more familiar to us." Magle considers that fact inspiring. He argues for more funding for innovative, flexible animal control methods and for the ongoing training needed to keep up with the rate of change and increased wiliness and intelligence of the incoming animals.

The best approach will be to build human knowledge of the animals in our neighborhoods and beyond. This approach will, in fact, require more human contact with the wild animals but at a respectful, cautious distance. And public education will require more than biologists.

As we strive for interconnection in "Symbiocene City," schools, service groups, and conservation organizations could teach people how to prevent aggression from wild animals: by not harassing the animals (especially the ones with big teeth or horns) and by learning the rules of encounter with specific species (e.g., should you play dead, run, or make yourself look large and threatening?). And also by spreading the word: Do not feed wildlife. Feed your pets indoors. Take down bird feeders at the end of winter. Reduce serious loss of songbird populations by keeping cats indoors. Fence your vegetable garden. On a more positive note, keep those binoculars and digital cameras available for when a deer or eagle or rare ring-tailed cat happens by. In Symbiocene City, you may feel an urge to become a wildlife artist, or keep a nature journal next to your guides of wild mammals and birds in your bioregion, or create a wildlife sanctuary in your yard. What a joy it could be to work with others to restore urban wetlands and plant native species.

Just as communities create Neighborhood Watch groups to prevent human crime, we could launch Neighborhood Wildlife Watch groups. Even in the most populated urban neighborhoods, members of such groups could track the influx of Betweens, prevent dangerous encounters, and record the exit of animal refugees from climate disruption. They might volunteer at urban wildlife rehabilitation and pet rescue centers. Places of worship and schools, too, could create Wildlife Watch clubs; these could educate students through biology and other natural history education courses about the bioregion in which they live. Young people could learn about the risks and opportunities that come with nature-rich cities. They might explore together the ways that different cultures interact with animals and the range of mythology and folktales and medicinal practices that different cultures bring to the city. They could be seedbeds of citizen science, launching future biologists and veterinarians and animal-assisted therapists. Through such groups, students and adults could explore how a city might build a stronger sense of identity, attract ecotourism, and identify the potential for new jobs and careers in public health, urban ecology, urban design, and architecture. In addition to reducing harm to wild animals, domestic pets, and human beings, Neighborhood Wildlife Watch campaigns could work for equitable access to nature. They could give people a greater investment in their regional and personal identity and the psychological well-being and confidence that comes with that.

In these ways and more, building human-nature social capital will reduce species loneliness and increase hope. As Bob Randall, the Yankunytjatjara elder, expressed it, this "would be a beautiful way of being that doesn't push anybody out" but "brings everybody in." In this context, people could share their animal stories around a twenty-first-century campfire, real or virtual, and in these stories find joy and renewal.

EIGHTEEN

The New Noahs

Jeff Williamson entered the inner sanctum of an insane elephant, if that was a fair diagnosis. The elephant stared at us from behind the bars, her eyes dark, dull and unsettling. She began to sway in syncopated rhythm.

"This behavior is stereotypical, a sign of anxiety," said Williamson, a compact man in his sixties with thick eyeglasses and a soft, deeply compassionate voice. At the time, he was director of the Phoenix Zoo, the largest privately owned nonprofit zoo in the United States. He does not like borders and he does not like walls. In fact, he is known as the zookeeper who hates zoos.

"This is a rogue elephant," he explained. "She killed a trainer at another zoo."

It's not easy to be a rogue elephant. As Cynthia Moss, who studied elephants in Kenya's Amboseli National Park, writes in *Elephant Memories*, "At times it was actually difficult for an elephant not to step on or run over someone but they always swerved or backed quickly to avoid doing so." Is this just pachyderm politeness? Probably not. First, as herbivores, they never needed to subdue and eat us. But the dominating atmosphere of zoos grates on them, and they do hold grudges.

Under Williamson's leadership, the Phoenix Zoo made it a practice to accept animals rejected by other zoos. This is the second man-killing elephant the zoo had accepted. This one was segregated from the other elephants because she was violent toward them, too. We watched the elephant for a few moments as she swayed and bobbed and stared. These were not comforting moments, for the elephant or for us. Then we walked out into the glaring desert sunshine. As shared and managed human-animal habitat, Williamson sees zoos as both metaphor and laboratory for the cities that contain them. While he was at the helm of the Arizona Zoological Society/ Phoenix Zoo, Williamson was determined to help the animals live as natural lives as possible—or at least as comfortable as possible. As we walked, we saw play-enrichment toys—balls to roll, ropes to pull, boxes to rearrange and climb. Such toys are there to keep the animals from dying of boredom. Within human play spaces, these are called loose-parts toys, based on a theory that the more loose parts available, the more creative the play. Loose parts are "something we should see more of in suburban neighborhoods for children," he said.

Williamson believes that "zoos should go away." That's what he told Andrew Ross, the author of *Bird on Fire*, a book focused on the Phoenix urban region. Williamson calls zoos an extension of the "European and Asian culturally elite model of wildlife as a form of recreational amuse- ment." This model, he says, is outdated and ecologically damaging. He describes Phoenix as an organism that has chosen a kind of behavior that is alien to living systems. Zoos, he argues, are part of that irrationality. Even so, he made his zoo into a refuge for the outcasts. He set up a program that invites people of all ages to come to the zoo to care for injured animals and form relationships with them, to, in essence, love them. The zoo also established programs that connect kids and families to the wider natural world, including a family nature club through which multiple families could hike or join other outdoor adventures in the Phoenix area. Like most of us, Williamson is an inconsistent human. He may dislike the basic idea of zoos, but he loves the animals within them. He has more ambivalence about his own species.

Zoos have changed considerably since the days when they displayed as many critters as possible in rows of sterile cages. Some of the change is illusion. Literally. At the famous San Diego Zoo, little African klipspringer antelopes live in a mountain scene enclosure of a facsimile rock outcrop- ping. These rocks are made of concrete formed over metal framing. Tubes snake up through the rocks to pop-up irrigation heads. On these rocks, the klipspringers, with hooves pointed down like the toes of ballerinas, can jump ten to fifteen feet straight up. Gorillas that once sat on bare concrete surrounded by feces and fences now live in a large similarly naturalized enclosure. They blend in and do what comes naturally—and, as a result, are less likely to throw pieces of their environment at visitors.

At newer displays, sprayers create the illusion of fog; nondirectional recordings simulate the sounds of insects and birdcalls, as zoos manipulate temperature, rainfall, humidity. The ultimate high-tech zoo employs invisible barriers throughout. This has already been accomplished with snakes at some zoos by restricting them to their areas with refrigerated barrier strips that the cold-blooded critters are not inclined to slither over. A few years ago, a zoo horticulturalist shared his vision: instead of routing buses through the entire zoo, create a river like Disneyland's Jungle Cruise so that people could ride boats down the river where real, not robotic, crocodiles would rise from the waters—separated from the visitors by invisible sonic barriers. I wonder: Are these sonic barriers and other invisible border walls really any more humane for the *animals*? Or do they simply make the humans feel better about seeing animals in captivity? In any case, bit by bit, zoos are being transformed into biospheres. Someone trapped in a zoo could survive for a time on fruiting bananas, gorilla grass, figs, wild celery—all edible to animals.

Zoos also practice human mood control. For example, the increase in negative ions released by those fog sprayers on the San Diego Zoo's Tiger River are mood enhancing. The air is more oxygenated than in most of the surrounding city. Most people also find the winding "river" mood enhancing. Malaysian tapirs, milky storks, and other animals live along the waterway on grassy hillsides next to waterfalls, pools, and boulders. As artificial as such approaches are, they're better than the cages they replaced.

Zoos will always have principled critics who maintain that no matter how effective zoo-sponsored conservation programs are, zoos as institutions will remain fundamentally flawed, because they keep, breed, and use animals for profit-based entertainment.

Nkrumah Frazier, a friend who grew up on a farm in rural Mississippi, does see value in zoos. Nkrumah has worked with Outdoor Afro, an organization devoted to increasing outdoor recreation among African Americans, and also founded two nonprofit organizations to connect young people to nature: Hikes Across America! and the South Mississippi Family Nature Club. I once asked him about the origins of his love of nature.

"When I was a boy, we always had at least one dog and as many as one hundred head of cattle," he said. "We hunted and fished on a regular basis but only for subsistence, never for sport. I learned to respect animals during that time in my life, but I saw our domestic animals as property and wild animals as resources to be used." Nkrumah said that, as a college biology student and later, working as a biologist in ocean conservation, he had been taught that animals act mechanistically, based on instinct and to manage their energy and resources. "It wasn't until I started working as an animal keeper at a zoo that I developed a deeper respect for animals."

For six years, he worked at the small Hattiesburg Zoo in Hattiesburg, Mississippi. There he was surprised by the intelligence of many of the animals, and how every animal had its "own distinct personality and mood swings similar to humans." He noticed that some animals appeared glad to see him return after an absence of days or weeks, and this response seemed to have nothing to do with food or shelter. "The only reason I could come up with was that the animals were lonely and wanted companionship." Today he argues for zoos as a way to strengthen the human-animal bond particularly for children and young people in urban neighborhoods.

What's next for zoos? Joanne Vining, at the Human Nature Research Laboratory, points to a new zoo practice of featuring the care of animals during visiting hours in order to model caregiving behavior. She writes, "The design of a new children's exhibit at the Brookfield Zoo in Chicago . . . specifically focuses on different ways for young children to care about animals and plants." At the San Diego Zoo, a new children's zoo will move away from the old petting zoo model to encourage children to connect to animals in the animals' own backyards. Made possible by a thirty-million-dollar gift, the new Sanford Children's Zoo will replace one that has existed for decades. Favoring a nonintrusive approach, petting and feeding wild animals will be out. The experience will be designed "to help children empathize with wildlife," said Mark Stuart, president of the Foundation of San Diego Zoo Global. The children's zoo will include a walk-in beehive, a tree house next to a spider monkey exhibit, and a stream and waterfall where kids "can get wet and semi-wild as they learn to feel compassion and better identify with nature," according to the *San Diego Union-Tribune*.

Zoos and similar institutions can also become hubs of bioregional awareness—the spinners of great webs of connection between people and the life around them, including exotic animals and the animals next door. Seattle's Woodland Park Zoo has set a goal to become a focal point for a growing network of the state's environmental education programs. At this writing, institutions such as the Minnesota Zoo and the Vancouver Aquarium Marine Science Centre are beginning to revise their missions, to reverse the inward focus to outreach. In fact, zoos across North America have recently begun to promote family nature clubs, like the one Jeff Williamson established in Phoenix. The Minnesota Zoo in Apple Valley offers a two-hour monthly family program that introduces families to nature exploration at the zoo proper, in the more than two hundred acres of surrounding property, and offsite.

Much more can be done. Zoos, aquariums, nature centers, natural history museums, arboretums, and other botanical parks could expand their public education efforts to offer courses in nature connection, critical anthropomorphism, and local natural history. They could expand their roles as centers of bioregional awareness and knowledge through regional satellites such as primary and secondary schools, university libraries, camps, nature centers, and others. Zoos could, in short, escape their own walls. "We are not well served by our separation from the ecology we are a part of, on which we depend," Williamson told me. In the open desert or in cities, all species "share common goods, services, and we form a community; we should be modest in our assumption that we are the central reason for community existing. We play a role in forming a spence of community with the rest of life."

Notice Williamson's use of "spence," an archaic term for larder, a room or large cupboard for storing food. The spence is the keeper of sustenance and therefore of life.

As urban leaders work to green their cities and accommodate wildlife, they could learn from the history of zoos and their adaptations. Certainly, zoos have struggled to maintain harmony between humans and other animals in tight quarters at an artificial distance and to create environments that feel more natural to animals (from our perspective, anyway) and to humans. "Disneyfication" is a pejorative sometimes deserved, though Disneyland's Main Street—with its nostalgic, human-scale design—has often exerted a beneficial influence on urban architecture and design. In an urbanizing world, zoos could play a similar role as more people share space with other animals. Some practices adapted from zoos could improve the lives of multiple urban species; others could lead to unintended negative consequences.

Zealandia

The sky was crystalline blue over Wellington. During a visit to New Zealand in 2014, I stood on the crest of a hill overlooking the capital city as Charles Daugherty pointed at what he believes will be the future of the human-animal connection: a green gap in the mountains on the other side of the city. "That's Zealandia," he said. An urban nature sanctuary, Zealandia is one element of a massive plan to restore New Zealand's native biodiversity and return parts of New Zealand, a country of islands, to its prehuman habitat.

Daugherty, former chair of biological sciences, professor of ecology, and assistant vice-chancellor at Victoria University of Wellington, and one of the foremost zoologists in the country, worked for years to bring the kiwi and the tuatara back from the edge of extinction. Daugherty has a particularly soft spot for the tuatara, a reptile that looks like a lizard or a dinosaur but is neither. Among animals, they represent the unique order, Rhynchocephalia, separate from but alongside crocodiles, turtles, snakes, and lizards. And only in New Zealand. Greenish brown, a tuatara can measure up to thirty-one inches from head to the tip of its tail and weigh up to three pounds. It has a spiny crest along its back, a pronounced overbite, and a third eye in hatchlings—a barely visible photoreceptive spot between its more identifiable eyes. Its spine is closer to fish vertebra and some amphibians than to other reptiles. Tuatara can live to at least one hundred and may be able to live much longer than a century.

Daugherty, American born, is an amiable man, passionate about returning his adopted country to an earlier state of grace. Years ago, when he first began his work on some of the smaller, isolated offshore islands he was stunned by their primordial nature. Some eighty-five million years ago, New Zealand split away from the supercontinent Gondwana before predatory mammals had evolved. As a result, the islands of New Zealand were a paradise for birds especially. Some, including the giant moas and the kiwis, with no need to escape predators, gave up flight. The first human settlers brought stowaway house mice and three species of rats; then, later, ferrets and short-tailed weasels (called stoats in New Zealand) were brought to control rabbits, which reached plague proportions after their introduction in the mid 1800s. Other species that have proven disastrous for New Zealand native habitats include deer and feral goats and pigs. These invaders destroyed forest habitat and feasted on the birds and their eggs; over time, more than forty species of birds were wiped out. Others remain threatened, including New Zealand's iconic kiwi. The introduced predators continue to kill twenty-five million native birds every year and prey on native species of lizards, and large insects. As beautiful and verdant as they appear to visitors, the two largest islands of the country remain biological ghosts. Daugherty described his first experience on one offshore island, where native species had actually survived:

I was immersed in a world that had been here at least eighty-five million years. Going to the islands is like time travel. At night, the seabirds are so abundant they're literally bouncing off you. The noise is deafening. The ground is bare because of so much animal life. And the tuatara are all around. Absolutely prehistoric. That experience changed me, made me think harder about ecological restoration. I realized there are places where you can tell what the world was like without humans, and we cannot only preserve that but re-create it. That's what's happening here. We are restoring nature. Even the seabirds can come back. There was no single moment that was transformative for me, but that experience of being immersed in my senses, with tuatara everywhere, birds and large insects—several inches long!—everywhere, and life is everywhere, and diffuse, and it *takes you out of yourself.* Those experiences turned me into a missionary, to go beyond just studying animals, to taking responsibility for them and for the future.

The tuatara's days were numbered as Daugherty and others began their work restoring habitat on offshore islands, which included removing predators. From the crest of the hill, he pointed across a distant blue expanse. Now there are forty islands where tuatara live, he said, "including that island you see out there." Describing the intimidating-looking tuatara, Daugherty's eyes softened with affection. They are, he assured me, gentle animals — albeit with powerful teeth designed to hold on. When he needs to, he grabs them around the neck and they calm down quickly. They'll sit quietly on his arm. "They're endlessly patient in their way of life. They burrow and live in an area the size of a large tabletop. They spend years not going much beyond that." Their diet consists mostly of insects and earthworms and, seasonally, baby seabirds and lizards. Their ancestry goes back 250 million years, and they are closely related to the animals that preceded or appeared around the same time as dinosaurs.

To Daugherty, the preservation and restoration of the tuatara and the other original inhabitants of the islands, including the large North and South Islands of New Zealand, is neither an abstraction nor a scientific experiment. To him, it's personal.

Around the world, men and women like Daugherty are going to unprecedented lengths to counter the extremes of climate change and biodiversity collapse, which began long before the first predictions of global warming. As a trustee of Predator Free New Zealand and former trustee for Zealandia Sanctuary, Daugherty is also one of the leaders in a growing movement to make all of New Zealand predator-free. Only in the planning stages during my visit, the blueprint was officially launched two years later. In July 2016, then prime minister John Key and other ministers announced the formal adoption of the target to eradicate seven species of the invasive "pests," as they are casually referred to in New Zealand. The plan met some criticism—such as, what about feral cats? (Their turn would come.) Some skeptics considered the goal unreachable; the funding is inadequate, they said, and they pointed out that the plan calls for technology yet to be developed. Nonetheless, new methods are already in place, such as GPS-linked traplines, which are an estimated one-seventeenth of the cost to maintain than they were just a few years ago. Other new baits and genetic tricks are designed to interfere with the fertility of specific predators. This effort could make New Zealand the world leader in conservation technology.

And then there's the poison, which brings us back to Zealandia, the world's first fully fenced urban nature sanctuary. The 556-acre "ark" has allowed species absent from the mainland for over a century to come home. To kill rats and the other predatory invaders, conservationists first enclose the land, then use helicopters to drop sodium fluoroacetate in a processed form known as Compound 1080 or the anticoagulant brodifacoum, killing nearly all mammals in the fenced-in area. Animals that manage to survive are then trapped or shot. Later, the native species are reintroduced and soon flourish.

In Wellington's Zealandia Sanctuary, the mammals killed have been replaced by more than twenty-five species of native birds, plus many other species of lizards and invertebrate and plant species, all thriving in their recovering mainland habitat, making the preserve the most biologically rich square mile in New Zealand. Conservationists are already creating similar wildlife sanctuaries in or near many of New Zealand's cities. New Zealand's approach is analogous to marine sanctuaries. "In marine sanctuaries, you protect a defined region, and you hope for the 'halo effect,' that the protected fish will spread out from the sanctuary," Daugherty explained. On the not-so-bright side, some New Zealand residents are "horrified that kakas [large raucous native parrots reseeded in Zealandia] are starting to show up in their yards." As kakas jump the fence and head out into Wellington and beyond, other species will follow. "That's a sign of success. A kaka in every yard! That should be our goal."

The use of poison remains controversial. "People accept it to varying degrees, but some people are adamantly opposed to use of any poisons, even when the unwanted effects are minimal." The long term effects are not known, Daugherty admitted, noting that researchers are working urgently to find new eradication methods to replace the use of poisons. Skeptics include some of the Indigenous Maori people. "One asked me what a Ph.D. is worth," said Daugherty. "After all, it's just a piece of paper. If you stand on it, you're not any taller. He had a point." Nonetheless, Daugherty noted that New Zealanders have a phrase, "Just get on with it," and that, he said, "is the spirit of conservation here." The New Zealand government has committed to meet the goal of a Predator Free New Zealand by 2050 for the seven target species. In theory, this will allow the meek to inherit that part of the Earth.

Mammoth Thoughts

Other conservationists are most focused on wild animals beyond cities. One of the methods, already in process, is the movement of whole populations and even species in response to the threats of climate change and biodiversity collapse. "Translocation is coming," according to Courtney White, former director of the Quivira Coalition, which brings ranchers and environmentalists together across the western United States to use land trusts and other methods to protect open land and ranching culture. "Some species are already on the move, but others will need to be picked up and moved over obstacles like railroads and highways—or hundreds of miles away." Also called assisted migration, assisted colonization (or managed relocation), whether done or encouraged by government, translocation as a management strategy is not new, and its results are not guaranteed. One of the most egregious examples came at the end of the nineteenth century, when the U.S. Department of Agriculture encouraged farmers to plant an import from Japan called kudzu. The goal was to repress soil erosion. Farmers and gardeners have cursed the highly invasive, crop-destroying, tree- and shrub-killing vine ever since. Today's opponents to translocation predict similar consequences, such as native species extinctions. They argue that conservation biologists have not yet developed sufficient knowledge to make wise decisions. However, proponents of assisted migration believe that drastic climatic times call for drastic conservation methods.

An estimated one thousand species have already been relocated because of climate change, poaching, and displacement by humans, according to Axel Moehrenschlager, chair of the International Union for Conservation of Nature (IUCN) reintroduction specialist group. Some species are moved to higher elevations in a nearby location; others must travel longer distances. Examples include the relocation of Indian tigers to Cambodia, the airlifting of South African rhinos to Australia, and the assisted migration of other animals into their historic ranges, such as the gray wolf in the United States and the Arabian oryx in the United Arab Emirates. In a 2016 interview, Moehrenschlager explained that "species are under increasing threat around the world, but the science is maturing about how to bring them back....This is not a new tool—it's gone on for more than 100 years—but it's definitely escalating in terms of frequency and geographical spread, not just for an individual species but for entire ecosystems."

The approach, while still controversial among biologists, is gaining currency. Ron Swaisgood, with the San Diego Zoo, is one of those biologists who at one time would have found it unimaginable to intercede in nature to this extent. Asked about his view now, he said, "I think it's inevitable, and our thinking on this issue has evolved. In a fragmented landscape, we will need to move species around if they have limited dispersal ability, otherwise they will be stuck on reserves that no longer contain suitable habitat." The ability of wildlife biologists to translocate species has improved in the last twenty years, he said. The IUCN reports about 58 percent of translocations to be fully successful and 95 percent to be at least partially successful.

Meanwhile, Eric Dinerstein and others are already racing to create a massive park for megafauna—big animals. Mammoth big, far beyond the confines of cities. In addition to his other roles in conservation, Dinerstein is the author of *The Kingdom of Rarities* and *The Return of the Unicorns*, among others. In 1984, he led a recovery group to save the greater one-horned rhinoceros in the Royal Chitwan National Park in Nepal, where the population had once declined to as few as one hundred rhinos. Dinerstein also serves on the National Council for the American Prairie Reserve, a Montana-based nonprofit creating what it hopes will be the largest nature reserve in the continental United States. Among its goals is to bring back free-roaming bison herds the likes of which, outside of Yellowstone, Americans have not seen since the 1840s. "Imagine the effects vast herds of bison must have had on the American Prairie Reserve and surrounding areas back when bison roamed widely and in great numbers," said Dinerstein in a 2013 interview. "I'll bet the prairie looked much different [from] today if you looked close up: more wallows, more bare spots, unevenly grazed areas, mineral-rich soils where bison carcasses may have accumulated. . . . [T]he large numbers of bison would have attracted some formidable predators and large numbers of scavengers. It was a different world, but if we can picture it, maybe we can restore it, at least in part." In the 1830s, there was more wild ungulate biomass—bison, deer, elk, pronghorn, mountain sheep—in North America than on the Serengeti today. Dinerstein wants to know if we can get some of that back.

Across the Pacific, in northern Siberia, an even more ambitious experiment is being conducted by the North-East Science Station and Pleistocene Park. Both are scientific organizations located a few miles from the town of Chersky. The North-East Science Station, dating to 1977, is a major Arctic research post. Pleistocene Park itself, where animal reintroductions began experimentally in 1988, is slowly evolving. Scientists are attempting to reach back some twelve thousand years to restore the mammoth steppe ecosystem of the late Pleistocene. Currently the park is an enclosed area of more than seven square miles. In the April 2017 issue of the *Atlantic*, Ross Andersen reported that its director, Nikita Zimov, would like to see it "spread across Arctic Siberia and into North America." The Pleistocene Park dream envisions the same grassy plains that were a significant feature at the end of the last Ice Age. The park, founded in 1996, has been stocked with a number of hardy herbivores, including bison, musk oxen, moose, Yakutian horses, reindeer, and yaks.

As with the creators of Zealandia, the makers of Pleistocene Park hope that the halo effect will cause populations of the big animals to disperse beyond the park's borders. Scientists are also working to bring extinct animals "back from the underworld of geological layers," as Andersen put it so elegantly. The plan is to "import the large herbivores of the Pleistocene . . . from far-off lands, two by two, as though filling an ark." But to transform the park into a biome that stretches from Siberia to the North American Arctic will also require the recruitment of millions more animals that might have been at home in the Ice Age. The park team hopes that soil compaction from these hoofed megafauna—as well as a new version of mammoth—and a concurrent diminishment of trees and expansion of grasslands will help slow thawing of the Arctic permafrost and reduce the release of methane gas from decaying soil organisms. The plan assumes that the benefits of mega-fauna soil compaction will be greater than the drawbacks of their methane-producing digestive systems. One expression of technological nature—some call it de-extinction science, or synthetic or resurrection biology—could play a role in reviving megafauna. Harvard geneticist George Church and a team of scientists have attracted wide media coverage as they attempt to use the genome-editing technology CRISPR to produce a synthetic mammoth (followed by, the thought is, many more). The concept is exciting. If, somehow, viable genetic material from deep-frozen mammoth carcasses can be found and pulled from permafrost and then combined with the genes of Asian elephants, a mammoth-esque creature might result. A perfect mammoth replica is not required. In 2017, Church and his team made a forecast that the first hybrid woolly mammoth could roll off the genetically engineered assembly line within two years. As with new models of Toyotas and Chevrolets, production delays and a recall policy may be the reality.

People are drawn to the *idea* of bringing creatures back from the dead, of encountering them someday just as we might encounter Sasquatch. The same yearning for connection with the primal and the primeval is at work here, and it produces a queasy excitement. Ironically, the return of these magnificent animals, ravaged by early people during an earlier change in climate, could offer added mitigation against today's human-created climate change.

Lost World Found

Dinerstein views such efforts as part of a far larger idea: set aside half of the terrestrial area on Earth for wildness, protected from humans. This vast area, not always contiguous, would preserve not only habitat for megafauna but also for plants and millions of invertebrate animals and microorganisms on which the planet's ecosystems depend. The idea was first proposed by conservation biologist Reed Moss and conservationist, writer, and photographer Harvey Locke, and it was fleshed out in the article "An Ecoregion-Based Approach to Protecting Half the Terrestrial Realm," coauthored by Dinerstein and nearly fifty other scientists from around the world and published in the journal *BioScience.* E. O. Wilson champions the proposal in his book *Half-Earth.* He reports that a biogeographic scan of the planet's habitable areas shows that "the vast majority of its species can be saved within half the planet's surface." Reach the one-half mark or above, and Earth enters a safe zone where life can stabilize. He first makes the biological argument. In summary:

> The ongoing mass extinction of species, and with it the extinction of genes and ecosystems, ranks with pandemics, world war, and climate change as among the deadliest threats that humanity has imposed on itself. To those who feel content to let the Anthropocene evolve toward whatever destiny it mindlessly drifts to, I say, please take time to reconsider. To those who are steering the growth of nature reserves worldwide, let me make an earnest request: Don't stop. Just aim a lot higher.

Wilson then makes a psychological and political case for protecting half the biological Earth:

> Half-Earth is a goal—and people understand and appreciate goals. They need a victory, not just news that progress is being made. It is human nature to yearn for finality, something achieved by which their anxieties and fears are put to rest. We stay afraid if the enemy is still at the gate, if bankruptcy is still possible, if more cancer tests may yet prove positive. It is our nature to choose large goals that, while difficult, are potentially game changing and universal in benefit. To strive against odds on behalf of all of life would be humanity at its most noble.

Regarding such an extreme proposal, there are good reasons for caution, which can be summarized in four words: the Great Leap Forward. China's most draconian period, from 1958 to 1962. Under communist rule, people of that vast nation were sent by the millions out of the cities to create a wave of rural industrialization. The result was widespread famine, misery, and tens of millions of deaths. Associating Wilson's proposal with China's great mistake is, on its face, unfair. But questions do arise. For example, would humanity retain visiting rights?

Kim Stanley Robinson, the science fiction writer best known for his trilogy imagining the human habitation of Mars, prefers Earth as our destination. A supporter of Wilson's Half-Earth goal, he contends that humans would not need to exit many of the regions to be included in such a massive preserve. Worldwide, people are *already* leaving rural areas and moving to cities. Large regions of the planet "are emptier of humans than they were a century ago, and getting emptier still," he writes in the *Guardian*. As young people leave to get work, villages are shrinking and combining with other villages. "So emptying half the Earth of its humans wouldn't have to be imposed: it's happening anyway. It would be more a matter of managing how we made the move, and what kind of arrangement we left behind." Within the depopulated regions, some land would be "given over to new kinds of agriculture and pasturage, kinds that include habitat corridors where our fellow creatures can get around without being stopped by fences or killed by trains." People there would have jobs in regenerative farming, permaculture, wildlife biology, and other work restoring balance.

When Noah set off in his ark, his assignment was to save not only other animals of the Earth, two by two, but to do the same for his fellow humans. The China comparison may be an apt warning, suggesting that the new ark be built to accommodate humans comfortably and that all of us play a role in its creation. If preservation of biodiversity is to stand a chance, the process must create jobs and a better life for people most impacted.

As radical as the Half-Earth concept may seem, successful smaller-scale examples do exist. One of them is the vast Adirondack Park in upstate New York. In the nineteenth century, the mountains there were stripped of life by loggers. In the early twentieth century, farmers, scientists, conservationists, and the state's voters established five hundred thousand acres to be "forever wild." Then, through land trusts, conservation easements, and other methods, the park grew to three million acres—20 percent of the state. From the beginning, wise planning included people who would live in strategically placed and contained towns and hamlets. The basic idea was to take an ecologically destroyed area and revive it by bringing people to it in sustainable ways. Today Adirondack Park is thriving, both for people and for wildlife. It serves as an economic and ecological model for similar preserves that could be created around the world.

In New Zealand, Charles Daugherty reports that in addition to the plan to restore native populations in Zealandia and similar preserves, major regional initiatives are now in progress. "The vision that may emerge is much like that of the Adirondacks, which is explicitly intended to encompass human activities while also supporting sustainable nature," he told me recently.

Both in new human-nature preserves and existing urban centers, a surge of jobs and potential careers could emerge, especially if the definition of green jobs expands to include not only work focused on energy efficiency and carbon reduction but also to employment opportunities connecting people to nature (and to one another). Many such jobs already exist, and others could be created through entrepreneurs, investment capital, and institutions that would support them: urban wildlife managers; professional "wildscapers" who help homeowners and businesses replace traditional lawns with bird-attracting native vegetation; nature therapists and green-exercise trainers; biophilic architects and urban planners; and developers and builders who create nature-friendly residential developments. Some of these jobs might be avocations; most would be paying careers. The true greening of America, and the world, will regenerate urban areas to accommodate both wildlife and people and, at the same time, create vast protected preserves dedicated to restoring life. Some of these preserves would, like Adirondack Park, accommodate human settlements. Others, like Zealandia, would be dedicated only to other-than-human species. Because of the "halo effect," as described by Charles Daugherty, revived wildlife populations in the preserves would naturally flow out into the surrounding areas, seeding new generations. Eventually, in the Symbiocene, populations of wild animals both within and beyond urban borders might well stabilize. And perhaps some of them, the Betweens, will awaken one morning to find their way beyond the cities, drawn outward to their ancestral homes—by the call of the wild.

PART FIVE

Wild Souls

Love, Humility, and the Principle of Reciprocity

Suppose God came back from wherever it is he's been and asked us smilingly if we'd figured it out yet. Suppose he wanted to know if it had finally occurred to us to ask the whale. And then he sort of looked around and he said: "By the way, where are the whales?"

—CORMAC MCCARTHY, *Whales and Men*

NINETEEN

Dreaming Animals

At the Wildlife Society's North American annual conference in 2015, I met Ovide Mercredi, a poet and former national chief of the Assembly of First Nations. At that time, he was also president of the New Democratic Party in Manitoba. Mercredi grew up in a Cree community that had been isolated from the majority population until the 1960s. He became a national leader for Indigenous people's rights, adopting the nonviolent path of civil disobedience. At the conference, attended by several hundred wildlife biologists and others, he challenged the members to broaden their view of their connection to other animals, if they had not done so already.

"What you call wildlife, we call relatives," he told them. "We did not see wildlife as assets, but we were deeply connected to them for clothing and food." But in his culture, the consumption of other animals is not isolated from the sacred, and this ethic was communicated to each generation through storytelling and by example as part of everyday life. For example, when he and his family camped along Limestone Bay on northern Lake Winnipeg, not far from where his father was born in a railroad caboose, they would search for gull eggs for breakfast.

> The lesson was, take only as much as we needed and don't take all the eggs from one nest. When we did that, I think the seagulls thanked us for that, because we allowed them to continue with their own life on this planet. Then, in the late summer, we'd be canoeing along lakes and creeks and we would see all these young ducks running around on the water and our parents would say, "Do not

hunt them until they are grown," and then we would hunt them not for sport but for food. Showing respect to animals. Within our Cree understanding of what is right and what is wrong, there is what in Cree we called "pastahowin," which is not sin but worse, because what you do will come back to you. My mother used to tell the story of this old man who enjoyed inflicting pain on rabbits he would catch. When time came for him to die at old age, he did not die easily but over a long period of time. When he died, he died with the image of a rabbit before him.

This idea of sacredness, that animals are not just wild but sacred, was explained to me by a bird that comes early in the spring, the red robin. We are told as young hunters that killing that sacred bird is prohibited, and if we do, someone in our family will die. It may seem strange to you that these stories are told to people so very young, but it is important when you hunt there are no red robins around.

As he spoke, I remembered the spring robins that came when the long winters of the Midwest began to retreat. Gripped by the restlessness of spring fever, I perceived robins as special, especially the *first* robin I saw as it hopped across shrinking islands of snow.

Avatars, Symbols, and Messengers

Today a growing number of religious or spiritual people are opening their arms to other-than-human animals. Many religious leaders of all faiths, and nonbelievers as well, no matter their political persuasion, have supported the growing movement to connect children to the natural world. Some of them say they recognize that all spiritual life begins with sense of wonder and that experiences with nature provide one of the first windows into wonder.

This openness goes deeper, and has existed longer, than many of us might suppose. An MIT study in the 1960s showed that people from a variety of spiritual backgrounds tend to speak of nature using spiritual terminology. So do atheists. Some refer to this inclination as animism (from *anima*, the Latin word for "breath" or "soul"). Whatever one calls it, this is the belief or sense that animals, objects, and places, to one degree or another, have a spirit form, an inner *something*. In Shinto, Buddhist, Hindu, Wiccan, and

Indigenous cultures, that something is recognized in radically different ways. This belief is supported by the revival of Native American religious traditions—or at least the perceived revival. Though wounded by oppression, these traditions have remained vital for centuries.

Early in these pages, I mentioned wildlife biologist Mollie Matteson, who finds herself mildly put off by some people who talk about their spiritual encounters with other animals, as if their profound experience were the central story, separate from the realm of other animals. Matteson said the animals-as-spirit-guides approach is embarrassing to some people, especially when it feels—or is—exploitative. As a down-to-earth biologist and conservationist, she also resists crude anthropomorphism, which might, depending on the story, dress an animal up as, well, God. And yet she had her own story.

Her encounter occurred during an excursion sponsored by the Animus Valley Institute of Durango, Colorado. The institute, founded by Bill Plotkin, facilitates deep nature connection. Plotkin, trained as a psychotherapist, is the author of *Soulcraft*. "Some people call the process a vision quest," explained Matteson, noting that others reject that term as a cultural appropriation of Native American ceremony. The institute's approach, steeped in ecopsychology, encourages participants to seek their own meaning in a natural world experience and then share it—not only as a personal expression but as part of a commitment to a larger shift in humanity's relationship with nature. "It's important to go somewhere you can be immersed. Denali National Park, Yellowstone, someplace animals aren't being shot at all the time," she said. In other words, go someplace with a strong signal. Here is her story:

I was in Death Valley. I was on a solo quest. Two and a half days into a fast, I was just out in the desert sitting, hunched, squatting, looking at the ground. Something caught my eye. It was scat. I'm examining it and I see something that is unusual. At first, I thought it was a bird wing. Then I realized it was a bat wing. I continued to fast, spending most of my time sitting in a circle of stones where I was supposed to contemplate my purpose and to invite a vision to come to me. I stared for hours at the desert, in particular at what looked like a grimacing face in the rock and shadows of an eroded cliff across the wash.

My last night of the solo, I sat up all night in my circle. I was freezing. It was a very long night, very uncomfortable. After a while, I thought, "Okay, where's my vision?" I screamed aloud, *"Give me a vision!"* Then I saw two eyes above me. And then everywhere, the sky was full of eyes, all of them looking back at me. My vision was of the eyes, seeing me in the dark.

For two years, Matteson was unable to tell anyone the full story of her desert quest that night. Life moved on. She accepted a job with the Center for Biological Diversity, which uses science, law, and media to protect natural habitat for threatened species. Matteson helped the Tucson-based center to establish its first northeastern office, in Vermont.

A couple months after she took the job, scientists began to report a disturbing trend in nearby New York State: bats were mysteriously flying out of caves in the middle of winter and dying. What soon became known as white-nose syndrome proceeded to wipe out large populations of bats in the Northeast and continued to spread across the country, decimating colonies. Matteson became a bat advocate, and she has worked for years to protect bat species endangered by both the disease and threats to their habitat. "In different ways, bats kept showing up in my life. That first year of the white-nose syndrome, I found a bat on the ground next to my parked car. Another bat flew through my backyard in the middle of February and landed on my house. I continue to encounter them in ways that just don't seem like coincidence."

She said she now understands the truth of the bones of the bats, the scowling face on the cliff, and the eyes in the night sky. "We're at a time in history when so much life is being lost," she says. "There was something there that night, something about being called to witness."

Did she really see eyes above the desert? Were they simply stars? And were the eyes really looking at her? "Who knows," she said. "What probably matters more is whether I remain willing to let in what I don't understand, and to be guided by it."

Animals have always played a role in the human spiritual quest, as avatars, messengers, and symbols. This is particularly true within Indigenous cultures, of course, but also as part of other religious traditions.

Jay Griffiths's book *Kith* was first published in the United Kingdom, and in 2015 it was issued in the States as *A Country Called Childhood*. A prize-winning author, she has given long and deep consideration to the intersection of spirit, community, and nature. A quest, she writes, is "an impulse in the human spirit to go further, to move beyond"—that is, a rite of passage, "most famously understood in the Native American Vision Quest, but European fairy tales honor the same principles." Griffiths examines the folktales about young people, especially, heading into a wilderness, "beheading trolls along the way, perhaps, or seeking the castle East of the Sun and West of the Moon." The hunger for *further* is never quite satiated. "Young people must undertake this alone," she writes. "They must use their own intelligence and, crucially, must use their inter-intelligence within the natural world, listening to the voices of birds or other animals, noticing the wind, the moon, and the trees. Fairy tales are full of animal-helpers, teeming with the vivacity of all of nature speaking itself and being heard, in turn."

Mollie Matteson saw her future in the bones of a bat. Several of the stories that were told or sent to me (to be sure, an unscientific sampling) suggested that animals had carried deliberate messages—if only symbolically, because of the meaning that the storytellers projected onto the messengers. A majority of these stories that focused on spiritual issues involved birds.

I mentioned that to ecopsychologist Patricia Hasbach. She wasn't surprised. "Over the years I have heard many people talk about birds in spiritual terms—most often related to a bird visitation after the death of a loved one," she said. "They will describe a sense of connection and love for the deceased person, and this is often accompanied by tears. Clients will also describe birds in their dreams "as creatures that whisk them away.... Birds take flight, they move beyond human grasp across fences, boundaries, etcetera, and they travel between the earth and the sky." Carl Jung, the Swiss psychiatrist and psychoanalyst who founded analytical psychology, explained the collective unconscious as a container for instinctual structures or archetypes common to all of us. No accident, then, that Jung identified birds as archetypal symbols of the spirit, mediating between the physical world and the spiritual world. "He reminds us," said Hasbach, "that the Christian Holy Spirit is symbolized as a dove and that birds have symbolic significance across cultures throughout human history." When she listens to her clients relate their dreams and stories through this filter, she detects birds symbolizing "transcendence (death, rebirth, renewal), fear, courage, wisdom, peace, and fertility."

Christopher Moreman, chair of the Department of Philosophy and Religious Studies at California State University–East Bay, has studied the relationships between birds and the spirits of the dead, or at least how humans have perceived those spirits. The visitations of birds, he writes, are "routinely seen as portents of impending calamity and death." Or they steal spirits of the dead. "In China, the owl is heard to cry, 'wā, wā!' (dig, dig!), urging that a grave will soon be needed." In some traditions, the owl is synonymous with wisdom. There are naturalistic reasons: its luminous eyes and ability to see in the dark, and that owls are stunned wide-eyed by sudden light. In older Anglo-American folklore, a swallow flying down your chimney or a whip-poor-will on the roof can predict a death. Moreman continues:

> In parts of England, a cock crowing at night can signal an imminent death. A Scottish variant specifies that the caregiver must feel the rooster's feet—if they are cold, then a death is indeed predicted, but if they are warm, then there would instead be good news. Many Native American legends attest to ambivalence toward nocturnal birds. By way of explanation, the ornithologist Edward Armstrong suggested that the cries of nocturnal birds are generally eerier than the more musical sounds of songbirds—as if the dark of night was not enough. A pre-Islamic tradition that has survived in some parts of the Arab world explains that a murder victim will return as a white owl, screeching for vengeance. . . . Islamic martyrs are described as becoming flocks of green birds.

Birds are also associated with fertility, life, and longevity in some cultures. Storks, deliverers of babies in both European and Lakota folklore, are connected to fertility possibly because their migratory pattern indicates the return of spring. Birds are also thought to carry spirits. In Russian legends, "dead children return as swallows in spring to console their parents," according to Moreman. "As a form of Jungian archetype, birds reflect a fundamental aspect of human nature—the denial of death as finality through a desire for renewal, transformation, and rebirth."

Then there are crows.

The Man with the Crow Tattoo

When I first shook Claude Stephens's hand, I was startled to see a crow peeking over the second button of his shirt. It was a life-sized tattoo of a crow. Stephens is man with an impish grin and contrarian seriousness. He is facilitator of outreach and regenerative design at Bernheim Arboretum and Research Forest, a sprawling swath of 16,137 acres near Clermont, Kentucky. Most of the preserve was bought and protected by Isaac Wolfe Bernheim, who formed a foundation in 1929 to manage it as "a place where all people could find peace, understanding and common interest in nature, regardless of race, creed or economic status." Before then, the land was heavily logged, so today the hillsides are approaching old-growth status, and more than 250,000 people visit every year.

Stephens calls the Bernheim Foundation an "ignorance-based organization." He told me this with pride, noting that he begins every staff meeting and even meetings with potential funders by reviewing "what we don't know rather than what we know." Meetings, he believes, are more productive when he uses that approach, one that he associates with crows.

Like coyotes and raccoons, crows are tricksters. "I approach my work as a trickster," he said as we walked on a path through the woods surrounding the arboretum's headquarters. He sees himself as the "person who uses surprise, humor, doing the unexpected thing." He pointed to the tattoo of the crow under his shirt. "Intentional placement. Crows are mischievous and that seemed like a mischievous type of location." He continued, "My Instagram name is Crow Hollister. 'Crow' because when I was ten, my grandfather, a very smart agriculturalist, told me that after he died he was going to come back and look after me and that he would take the form of a crow."

And why did he pick the crow?

"As a farmer, he had a love-hate relationship with crows. They could ruin a crop. But overall, he liked 'em." And, he said, his grandfather knew that crows are a common animal; they live on every continent, except Antarctica. "He assumed that after he died, that no matter where I went, there would be a crow somewhere nearby. Like, he could have picked a blue whale, right? But that would have meant I'd never see him again. So he picked a crow."

Where did "Hollister" come from?

"Do you remember *The Andy Griffith Show*? There was a moonshiner on the show and his name is Rafe Hollister. So my alias is Crow Hollister. You know," he went on, "once somebody tells you they'll be watching out for you after they die, as a crow, then from that point on, every crow you see, every crow you hear . . . I'll be talking to someone, and I'll go, 'Wait a minute,' and they'll say, 'What? What are you doing?' And I'll say, 'I just heard a crow, I was listening.'" Stephens's stepdaughter, eight, is a crow listener, too. "Her favorite animal is the crow because she knows that story about my grandfather. I've passed it on to her." She also likes the tattoo of the crow on his chest. "I can make it move for her." When they're outdoors together, if she finds a crow feather, she picks it up. The inside of Stephens's truck is decorated with the feathers of crows the two have found. "She's always reminding me that she has more than me."

To Stephens, the crow also represents the land in which he is deeply rooted and in which his grandfather is buried. He's a seventh-generation Kentuckian. His family lives on land that's been in his family for all that time, and his brother lives in the house his family built in the 1780s. "So my stake is in the ground."

After his grandfather died, Stephens's interest in crows expanded. They're among the smartest animals, with good memories. Recent research has found that corvids—including crows, ravens, and jays—can remember events and physical objects that please them. They have what appears to be a wicked sense of humor. Sometimes Stephens attempts to trick the tricksters:

> With a group of kids, I'll set a stuffed owl in a field. We'll withdraw to a hundred yards away and sit down very still. A crow will fly over and see that owl, not realizing it's a stuffed owl, and make another pass or two, then settle in a tree above it and do an alarm call, which is three caws. Responses to that call will come from other crows in the woods. Then several crows will show up, staying at a distance from the stuffed owl. Then a few more. Just like us, crows are drawn to novelty and will try to figure it out, understand it. That's what

they're doing. When there's a critical mass of them, one of them will dive-bomb the owl, and then another one will say, "Oh, I should do that, too." And then suddenly they all start dive-bombing this owl. But it doesn't take them long to realize, "Aw, that's just a stuffed owl. That owl is not responding like a live owl would respond. We've been tricked." And off they go. They don't care about it anymore.

What Stephens admires most about crows, even more than their intelligence, is their social life. A crow's universe revolves around its tight-knit family and then around its very large clan. They roost in great numbers both for protection from red-tailed hawks and great-horned owls and, apparently, because they like one another's company.

In *Ravensong*, author Catherine Feher-Elston writes about "crows surrounding injured clan members to protect them from intruders and murmuring mournful cries when a family member has been badly injured." She describes how crows play not just among their own but with other species, too, particularly dogs and wolves. They'll wait until a wolf is asleep, then swoop down and pull its tail or ears; they seem to enjoy this, and so, sometimes, do the wolves. "Crows, coyotes, and wolves," she writes, "have been known to develop unique symbiotic relationships. Navajos, Hopis, Koyukon, and other Indigenous American peoples say that crows and these members of the dog family help each other hunt. Crows and ravens have been observed leading coyotes and wolves to prey, and then share in the meat." (Curiously, corvids fear thunder and hailstorms. During thunderstorms, groups of ravens sometimes huddle together "in low-lying tree branches, close to the trunks, crying piteously, heads shaking with fear; 'heart attacks' have been known to occur at these times.")

Crows mate for life. They breed cooperatively; other crows aid in the nesting and the feeding of chicks and help protect the group territory. Chicks remain with their parents for as many as three seasons and help raise the new juveniles. Crows also exhibit what might be considered ethics or codes of conduct. Lawrence Kilham, one of the world's experts on corvids, reports that when crows scatter to forage and one crow finds something interesting, then they all fly over to see what it is. If it's, say, a frog, the crow who found it gets to keep it. The other crows, says Kilham, "will all stand around and look at the crow with the frog; it may look like they will attack and try to take it from him, but they never do. The thing is, they respect the one who has found food—the attitude seems to be 'finders keepers,' so even if you are one of the lowest members of the hierarchy, what you find is yours."

Crows don't rob from members of their own family or clan. However, crows may punish offenses by other crows or attack approaching crows from other families, and yet they have also been observed coming to the assistance of crows from outside their own family circle. I once saw dozens of crows cawing, calling, and barking; they were making an unnerving racket. Like dark leaves, they filled and weighted the branches of a single tree. They were looking at the ground. On the grass was a dead crow. As crows often do, they were responding to the death of one of their own, and they did that for a long time.

Knowing crows feeds Stephens's spirit and reinforces the way of life he has chosen, which is focused on intelligence and playfulness but mainly on loyalty to family and nature. Most mornings on the way to work, Stephens will stop his truck to take a photo of two trees on his familial land to record how they change and grow through the seasons and over the years. "Sometimes, right then, a murder of crows will fill the trees."

Here he paused and asked if I knew that term, a "murder of crows." We have other group names for animals: a parliament of owls, an ostentation of peacocks, a skulk of foxes, a knot of frogs. "A large group of crows is called a murder of crows because they were often seen that way on battlefields, feeding on the dead. And so they were associated with murder." Other theories about the origin of the term are no less macabre. Crows are said to circle in large numbers when a human or other animal is expected to die; likely, they're waiting to feed or, just possibly, to pay tribute or to mourn.

As for their harsh calls and racket, more is going on here than meets the ear. Crows use at least 250 different calls to communicate with other crows and with other species. "A local crow," Stephens told me, "developed an entire routine of barks imitating neighborhood dogs; he barked like the dog next door, imitated the sound of barks from a long distance, whimpered like a small puppy, and whined like a dog begging for food."

As I got up to leave Bernheim, I asked the man with the crow tattoo if, over time, he had learned rudimentary crow language or at least their vocal patterns. "There's this guttural growl and clicks, and there are patterns of caws," he began. Then suddenly he remembered something that had happened long ago:

> I was away at scout camp when my grandfather passed away. It was expected; he was in poor health. . . . But I was away at Rough Rivers Scout Camp, not far from here. It was toward the end of a week of camp, and my parents and the camp operators decided not to tell me immediately but to wait until camp was over.
>
> My parents told me when they picked me up. We then headed to our old home. When we got there, I was told to get ready for the funeral, to put on my good clothes. I did, and then I went out and sat on the back porch. A crow flew down out of the walnut tree and landed on the railing of the porch. It did what birds, especially crows, do. It looked at me with one eye and turned its head and looked at me with the other eye. It was switching back and forth as if the different eyes would give it different information, sizing me up. And I didn't move. I just sat there. And then it cawed three times. Then it flew away. And it was like, "Dang, that had never happened before." Since my grandfather had told me he was going to watch after me as a crow, I thought, "I guess he was right." That moment cemented into my psyche. That connection. It was like, "All right, it's on, he's doing it."

The Spirit of the Brahminy Kite

We are a dreaming animal but not the only dreaming animal. What do crows dream about, or cows? Other mammals share with us the same neural structures necessary for dreaming. Research conducted at MIT revealed that rats will dream about previously running a maze. These facts stimulate admittedly fanciful questions, ones that in a different culture might not seem strange at all: Can humans and other animals inhabit the same dreamscape? To adapt writer Philip K. Dick's phrase, will robot dogs someday dream of electric sheep?

When she was nineteen, Janani Eswar cofounded Growing in Nature, an Indian organization based in Bengaluru that connects children to nature. She was concerned about the disconnection even in rural areas around the world. Her motivation was also rooted in her own experience with animals. When she was eighteen, an animal encounter gave direction to her life. She shared this story with me:

> My grandmother and I were sitting side by side, sipping our morning *kashayam*—an herbal drink—when it happened. A fleeting alarm from the sunbirds, a *chip-chip* of warning from the flower peckers, and a dash of burnt sienna in the corner of my eye. I ran to the balcony railing, calling my grandmother to come as well. Just as I reached the railing, I caught another glimpse of a bird of prey called the brahminy kite as it soared around a building and vanished from view. Growing up, I was told stories about brahminy kite, which is said to be a representation of Garuda [the sacred bird of Vishnu], a Hindu deity. These stories often talk about valor, vigor, and quiet strength.
>
> I am also normally skeptical about dreams. I mean, a dream could just mean an upset stomach, right? But that night, I dreamt about that bird. It was a very simple dream. This time, as it flew past the balcony, it looked into my eyes. And I saw a clear picture of it flying around that corner. I felt a deep sense of being supported and recognized. I also felt a twofold warning: one, to pay attention to my impact on this world, to watch for any alarm calls I create by being; and, two, to be ready to change my plans when the situation calls for it. To this day, when I see a brahminy kite, I remember these lessons. I feel greatly loved and I send up a thought of gratitude to it for being.

A few years ago, through our shared work connecting children and families to the natural world, I met Daniela Benavides, a remarkable woman in her late twenties who lives in Peru and travels around the world as an environmental and feminist activist. She works with communities damaged by political atrocities and environmental degradation. Responding to these hardships, she cofounded and continues to direct ConCiencia, a Peruvian nongovernmental organization that builds environmental literacy and community empowerment in poor and vulnerable communities. In later correspondence with me, Benavides described her native country as a country of deserts: "The desert that surrounded my childhood echoed the impalpable atmosphere of fear that our lives floated in. Terror, kidnappings, telephone threats, car bombs, curfews, and blown-up electric towers cast shadows on the walls of our evenings."

Even so, Benavides loves the stillness of the desert, where life is amplified: "A hawk's cries rivet through the skies, through the dust, into the rock and through the soles of the feet" of a wandering and wondering ten-year-old. One overcast Sunday afternoon, she decided to follow a trail up over the rugged mountains of Chaclacayo. She would have preferred to go with a friend, but no playmate was available that day. As she walked, her face became flushed with fear, and her throat constricted. She wondered if she was lost. She was farther up the mountain than she had gone before. She imagined herself alone among the *apukuna*—the protective spirits of the mountains that her father liked to tell her about. In Benavides's childhood community, the *apukuna* dated from the Inca Empire. They can be found in rocks and caves and perhaps in the animals that inhabit the high desert and mountains. Though the *apukuna* are there to protect people, Daniela feared them.

"Suddenly, *it* caught my eye," she said. "It was black and mean looking, coiled on a rock, chest up in the air. The first snake I'd ever seen, and bigger than any wild animal I'd encountered in my backyard adventures. I was afraid. Then angry at it for being scared. Then curious. I threw a rock next to it—I wanted it to react. It *winced*. Just like I would. 'She's just like me,' I thought, 'curious, afraid, and maybe now angry, too.'" As she slowly approached the snake on its flank, it rotated to face her. "At a prudent distance, I sat on a rock. We held the silence. I realized then that all life is equal, that we all just want to eat and sleep, go on adventures, gaze curiously at other animals, and, occasionally, eat them, too."

It was getting dark. "I felt my home calling. I backed away, facing the snake. Thinking about our chance meeting, I left it there. It probably continued to watch the awkward creature toppling down the hill on long, bony legs. I left with it a big chunk of my fear."

Perhaps for Benavides, a snake held the spirit of the *apukuna*.

For many of us, our first encounter with a snake was in the presence of an adult using a hoe or a shovel to kill it. Today most of us would be more inclined to hold back; a few of us would even avoid killing a venomous snake. Part of the reason is greater awareness of the ecological importance of all animals. Another possibility is a growing recognition that there is *more* to other animals than we consciously understand.

This question hovers: Do animals, other than humans, have souls?

To Bernie Krause, the answer is more experiential than intellectual. Krause, the recordist of nature sounds, told me a story about Lisbet, a graduate student from the Netherlands. When they met, she was working at a remote research site in the rainforest of Sumatra's Aceh Province, close to where the 2004 tsunami hit, the same wave that killed perhaps as many as 250,000 people in Thailand and elsewhere. Lisbet was there a few years later to study the Sunda clouded leopard, a cat weighing between twenty-six and fifty-five pounds and marked, Krause said, with "very distinct and beautiful oval-like markings on its coat that look like small clouds."

For six months, Lisbet saw only scat on the rainforest game trails. So she studied the scat, analyzing its contents to unlock the mysteries of the cat's digestion and health. But she wanted desperately to see the mysterious animal before her research grant expired in two weeks. "That night, my colleague and I arrived at the camp," continued Krause. "We joined the other researchers and guides for dinner, and Lisbet asked if we'd ever recorded the clouded leopard." He had recorded one in a zoo but never in the wild, where its vocalizations would be different. Lisbet asked Krause if she could go with him on a recording trip. The next morning, before sunrise, they hiked one of the forest trails to a promising spot two miles from camp. Krause set up his recorder and unfolded small camp stools at the intersection of what looked like several game trails. Sitting as quietly as possible, Krause recorded "the hour-long dawn chorus, then the midday soundscape."

Ten hours later, they were still sitting. Krause described what happened next:

> Just as we were about to give up and head back to camp—tired, hungry, and stiff from sitting for so long—we watched amazed as the rare clouded leopard circled right in front of us, glancing in our direction once as it moved elegantly past us in a wide circle, perhaps a twenty-foot radius. Then it treated us to another round at about the same distance. When I glanced at Lisbet, who was sitting about ten feet away, I saw tears of joy, relief, and frustration streaming down her cheeks—fearing she would frighten the stunning animal,

she didn't want to move to retrieve the camera she had already placed in her backpack. As if in a gesture of affirmation, the leopard slowly circled us one final time, and then, as mysteriously as it appeared, the creature vanished from sight into the dense understory of the forest never to be seen by either of us again. Although my recorder was rolling tape, that day, the leopard did not emit a single sound. All we could hear when we played back the recording were our gasps of joy and surprise.

Getting back to the earlier question, was this a soul passing by? Krause believed that the leopard was "spirit-like" but not a spirit. Yet both Krause and Lisbet felt as if they had been touched by it.

If souls exist, they surely feel awe. Researchers at Claremont McKenna College in Claremont, California, reviewed how humans cope with awe-induced uncertainty. They found that it moves people to be less likely to accept that what they experienced occurred at random and more likely to credit an "agent"—another person or supernatural force, including some concept of God. At the same time, the uncertainty of awe can push people to search for a scientific explanation for what occurred. Piercarlo Valdesolo, an associate professor of psychology at Claremont McKenna, argues that such an experience "generally increases this desire to explain what's in front of you. You gravitate toward whatever explanatory framework you prefer." Setting aside religious, ideological, and temporal arguments, beyond what is named or cannot be named, the essence of *relationship* is universal. When we fall in love with another person, we may do so first out of lust or a loneliness that finally breaks us open, allows entry. In the end, sometimes even in the beginning, we fall in love with the spirit of another person. A spirit separate from flesh or the intellect or even personality.

For some, the idea of a person's spirit is more acceptable than the concept of soul. We feel that spirit, it touches us, it is the pure essence of the person we love. We "fall in love outward," in the words of the poet Robinson Jeffers. In "The Tower beyond Tragedy," he includes lines to describe the sense of kinship he feels in nature: "I was the stream / Draining the mountain wood; and I the stag drinking; and I was the stars. ..." In other writing, he describes "the feeling—I will say the certainty—that the universe is one being, a single organism, one great life that includes all life and all things."

When we fall in love outward, we are made less lonely, and this is as true for our connection to other animals and all of nature as it is for our attachment to other human beings. Even when love is fleeting, say, a single moment when the paths of two creatures intersect, their spirits meet and create an essence that lingers even after death, even if only in the temporal or genetic memories of the living who have been touched by this combined spirit. If nonhuman animals are excluded from that ongoing love, then ours is a darker world.

Many people, of course, are uncomfortable with any discussion of the spiritual life of animals and human interpretation—or projection—of the spiritual domains of humans and other animals. In fact, the science of animal behavior began in the early part of the twentieth century with a focus on countering what was considered superstition about animals. Similarly, some religious institutions and individuals specifically disapprove of the notion of spiritual experiences that include other animals. But over time, the resistance has softened. Millions of Catholics, for example, celebrate the feast day of St. Francis of Assisi by taking animals, usually their pets, to churches for a ceremony called the blessing of the animals.*

In 2014, widespread media described how Pope Francis had met a little boy grieving for a dog who had died. Comforting the boy, the pope was quoted as having said, "One day, we will see our animals again in the eternity of Christ. Paradise is open to all God's creatures." Vatican traditionalists gasped. Was this a reversal of traditional Catholic theology? Debate ensued. The U.S. Humane Society was deluged with emails. The Vatican denied it happened, or at least not in that way. (Part of the quote was conflated with a reported statement by Pope Paul VI.) Media outlets, including the *New York Times*, backtracked.

But then, in a 2015 encyclical focused on global environmental challenges, *Laudato si'* (*Praise Be to You*), the pope, true to his St. Francis of Assisi namesake, seemed to endorse the idea of salvation for all animals:

---

* People for the Ethical Treatment of Animals (PETA) is generally approving of this practice, though not for all animals. Cats, the organization advises, should be left at home, along with other animals fearful of crowds. Also, PETA suggests that *all* animals be blessed, including those raised on factory farms: "The ceremony . . . raises a larger question. In our society of animal lovers, how are the vast majority of animals treated?" "Saint Francis of Assisi Day: Bless All Animals!," PETA, October 4, 2017, www.peta.org/features//saint-francis-assisi-day.

"Eternal life will be a shared experience of awe, in which each creature, resplendently transfigured, will take its rightful place and have something to give those poor men and women who will have been liberated once and for all." No creature on Earth, he concluded, is forgotten in God's sight.

Rereading that beautiful statement, I wonder what the creatures, other than "those poor men and women," will get out of the deal. Where's the reciprocity? The pope still does not say definitively that dogs and crows and toads and moles have souls. And the phrase "resplendently transfigured" raises more questions than it answers, though that may be the point. Mystery lives, awe survives.

In Fire and Smoke

In any case, a debate about animal souls—or, for that matter, the spirits of trees, rocks, and Earth itself—would be a needless puzzle to our oldest ancestors and to many who live with us now.

For two days in 1988, I traveled with Bob Shimek to high-security prisons in the Pacific Northwest. That first morning, we traveled by boat across a stretch of Puget Sound to McNeil Island Corrections Center, off Steilacoom, Washington. In the 1970s, Shimek was chosen by his elders to learn the Anishinaabe rituals, known to only a handful of people. I asked him if he was worried that these rituals would disappear. "No. Four people is enough," he said. "And I was told by my elders to pass these secrets on and that when that person [to whom the rituals should be passed down] appeared, I would know him." Shimek was the first Native American chaplain in the United States to be hired by a prison system. For years, the Anishinaabe medicine man conducted sweat lodges and pipe ceremonies for prisoners, building trust among inmates and prison officials.

In the beginning, he met resistance from the administrators because of his insistence on bringing medicinal herbs, pipes, bear claws, and drums through the gates. Several lawsuits had been filed in western states by Native American groups who sought religious freedom in prisons, but at least at that point, resistance was ebbing in the Washington Department of Corrections. One reason for the early resistance, Shimek explained, was unfamiliarity with the process, partly because Native American spiritual beliefs come from oral traditions. By some interpretations of Anishinaabe myths, Shimek's ancestors were created by divine breath. But Shimek avoided using only one word to describe this essence, because he believes fully capturing it is beyond human linguistic capability.

As we crossed the dark water, the waves began to roll. The boat docked, and we walked up a prison ramp illuminated by spotlights. "Sometimes deer come up along this beach in the early morning, and the inmates feed them through the fence," said Shimek. "This whole island is a game preserve." A long-haired, lanky man, he carried a daypack filled with herbs, rattles, and deer antlers as we entered the old prison.

Opened in 1875, McNeil Island Corrections Center once housed several famous inmates, including murderer Robert Stroud, who killed a guard there. Later he raised and sold birds at the Leavenworth penitentiary and became a recognized ornithologist known as the "Birdman of Alcatraz" (though administrators of Alcatraz Federal Penitentiary put an end to his bird work). We entered the prison through an old ornate iron gate and walked past a manicured cabbage garden. Shimek moved slowly upstairs and into the building. A guard in the front office handed Shimek a telephone, its cord wrapped around it, and another guard took us down several flights of stairs, deep beneath McNeil Island, directly below the main cell block. We were in a basement room, the "quiet room," surrounded by steel girders and heating pipes. The inmates came filing down and into the room. I heard a door clank shut somewhere, echoing. There were no guards with us.

"What's the phone for?" I asked.

"I plug it in down here. It's our lifeline. I call if anything goes wrong." He checked his wallet. "I think I lost the number." He sauntered off and disappeared for a moment.

I looked around. Some of the men appeared to be Native Americans; others did not. One young guy said, "I'm Blackfoot and Cherokee, but I was raised in LA and never knew my culture. I'm learning it, you know, from pamphlets they leave around here." A Cherokee from Tulsa told me about the first time he had been invited to sweat: "I showed up in my sweatpants. I thought we were going to run." He said that when he first came here, he was "white on the inside." But, he added, all that was changing.

Shimek returned with the phone number on a slip of paper. Another man said his Indian name was Deer and that he had rediscovered, through Shimek, what he had lost and that his aimless violence was going out of him.

He told how deer and raccoons can be seen on the other side of the fence sometimes, and how he watches them and how that takes him outside. And he described the way eagle feathers sometimes dropped from the sky onto the prison grounds. He collected them for the rituals. Someone else was talking about getting out of prison, and Shimek moved past, saying quietly, "It's a lot harder out there than it is in here."

The men formed a circle and Roger Eagle Elk from the Black Hills carefully unwrapped a wooden pipe, about a foot and a half long, and held it up. It was passed to Shimek, along with a small deer horn used to tamp down the tobacco, the cedar, and the other herbs within it. Shimek lit the pipe, held it up to the sky, to the Four Directions, and pointed it to the Fifth Direction, inside his heart. The pipe was passed, thick smoke rose to the metal rafters, and prayers were said. The men's faces became blurry and wavering in the smoke, and as the pipe was handed to me, I thought of something Shimek had said: "Unless we remember where we are from, and find our spiritual roots, then everything we have won we will lose. Then we are all in prison."

The next day, I traveled with Shimck to a second prison, the Twin Rivers Corrections Center near Monroe, Washington. As I described in *The Web of Life*, Shimek told me he spent twenty to thirty hours a week with inmates inside emotionally and physically challenging sweat lodges. Dehydration can be hard on the kidneys. I asked him how his were doing. "Fine so far," he said, grinning. "Anyway, we got some real good kidney medicine."

Surrounded by razor wire and gun towers and snowcapped mountains, he and a dozen tribal inmates built a sweat lodge in the prison yard out of willow boughs, tarpaulins, and blankets. One of the men pointed to water buckets filled with ice water. "Pour that over your head and body," he said. "And take a towel. Here, put it in the water. You'll need it. When the heat gets to be too much, hold it up to your mouth and nose. That way you won't pass out." Shimek invited me to join them. The men sat in a circle around burning coals. In thick smoke and dizzying heat, the men spoke in turns and chanted their prayers for strength, for families, for the creatures of the world. At one point, I realized they were praying for me, too.

Shimek reached into a small medicine bag made of deer hide and tossed something into the flames. The glowing antlers of a deer seemed to emerge. For seconds that might as well have been twenty million years, the deer lived.

TWENTY

The Peaceable Kingdom

Welcome to the electronic campfire.

For the 2015 Internet Cat Video Festival in St. Paul, Minnesota, some fifteen thousand people of all ages crowded into the city's new outdoor sports stadium. They came bearing picnic baskets, and on this summer evening they spread out their blankets on the ground and settled in to watch amateur cat videos on a huge screen. A friend who attended described the scene: "It was a surreal phenomenon. . . . There were people dressed up in cat costumes, everything from fake ear headbands to full-on furry suits. It was an absolute hoot."

Funny cat videos. Guilty dog videos. They're nearly as ubiquitous as pop songs. In the movie *Ghostbusters*, Dr. Peter Venkman (Bill Murray) and his team attempt to warn the city of a pending invasion of ghosts and demons, a disaster of biblical proportions: "Forty years of darkness! Earthquakes, volcanoes! . . . The dead rising from the grave! . . . Human sacrifice! Dogs and cats living together! Mass hysteria!" Arguably, "dogs and cats living together" is the most memorable phrase in that movie. Prescient, too, given all those cross-species animal friends swarming YouTube and the gift book market. Cat and turtle. Fox and badger. Dog and lion cub. Bear and tiger. Dogs and cats living together!

University of Denver professor Philip Tedeschi described the trend:

There are countless video examples of animals helping one another, responding to each other's crisis, demonstrating love and grief and connectedness and protection. All the things that we would do with members of our own families are observable with other animals. And yet in many cases we will say, "Well, because it's not human love we don't know if it's really love." And then we distance ourselves. We can then see distressed animals and be in denial about what we are really observing. Highly sentient animals engage in these behaviors that are similar to or familiar to human beings all the time, and yet in many cases we choose to deny the relevance.

Not so for Barbara Smuts, a primate researcher at the University of Michigan. She uses the word *friendship* to describe the bonds between female baboons. Why not between members of different species? On a ranch in Wyoming, Smuts witnessed what she considered friendship between her own dog, Safi, and a donkey named Wister. Safi taught Wister to pick up a stick and carry it. Wister "looked like he didn't quite know why he was walking around with a stick in his mouth," she told the *New York Times*, which reported, "The two animals also appeared to work out a common language. When Wister, several times Safi's size, accidentally kicked the dog during play, the donkey would stand very still, as if to say, 'I didn't mean it.' Safi, for her part, would jump up and nip Wister's neck, appearing to signal, 'That hurt.' Then the two would pick up playing where they had left off."

Until recently, such talk would have raised hives among animal researchers allergic to anything resembling anthropomorphism. But that may be changing. Gordon Burghardt, who first advanced the concept of critical anthropomorphism, and other scientists believe that studying such stories and videos may reveal new knowledge about animal friendships, including our own, and the human relationships with other species. One obstacle to overcome, or opportunity to seize, is the creation of a database of examples useful in establishing criteria to determine just what it means for animals of different species to be "friends." Professor emerita Barbara J. King, an anthropologist at the College of William and Mary, suggests some criteria: The "friendship" must be sustained for a certain period of time; there must be mutuality or symbiosis, with both species engaged and interacting; and there must be an accommodation of some sort taking place in the service of the relationship.

Check your email again. There may be another unexpected animal friendship video waiting for you. Dogs and cats living together. Dogs and rabbits, too. Never mind that the dog in the video who makes friends with a rabbit is the outlier; that for every new friendship, other rabbits are devoured by other dogs. These videos have less to do with existing reality than with human species loneliness and also our longing for peace in our families and the world. And so animal friendship videos are viewed, then sent by the millions as attachments of love to sons, daughters, and friends—and then projected at festivals drawing thousands.

This intense desire for connection and harmony among unlikely friends and relatives is not a new phenomenon.

> The cow will feed with the bear,
> their young will lie down together,
> and the lion will eat straw like the ox.
> The infant will play near the cobra's den,
> and the young child will put its hand
> into the viper's nest. (Isaiah 11:6–8)

This biblical verse can be interpreted as a radically different, even unnatural, compact among species and with the divine. I asked a friend, Rev. Cyndi Jones, a Lutheran minister, to decipher the verse. Her initial, cheeky reply: "A friend of mine used to say, 'The lion and the lamb will lie down together, but the lamb won't get much sleep.'" Her serious response came next: "In Eden, God created plants for the animals to eat, but after the fall of Adam and Eve, the animals started eating each other. When the new heaven comes we will reclaim the created order. Humans and all animals will be vegetarians. Therefore, the animals can lie down together. The passage talks about a new heaven and a new earth."

With or without sanction from any religion, a new arrangement between humans and other species is emerging as territorial boundaries are challenged by climate change and unchecked development. We see the incorporation of human technology into the bodies and lives of both domestic and wild animals, from identification chips in pets to animal-enhanced drones and the genetic blending of humans and other animals. In 2016, the National

Institutes of Health (NIH) moved to lift its moratorium on the scientific exploration of human-animal hybrids for the purposes of medical research. Such research, the NIH admitted, could conceivably lead to human organ farms (for instance, pigs carrying human livers or even human brains)—or who knows what—the stuff of science fiction until recently. Even the definition of life itself is mutable.

For centuries, the dominant scientific descriptor for nature has been reductionist, mechanistic, and exploitative. Our generation is poised on the brink of one future in which human genes are written into the code of chimera or of another future in which humans and other animals become closer through kindness, in generative ways already rooted in the natural code we share. Most likely the human story will evolve into a hybrid of the two contrasting scenarios. But even such a compromise will require a values shift. Farmer and poet Wendell Berry writes of the war between two ethics:

> The standard of the exploiter is efficiency; the standard of the nurturer is care. The exploiter's goal is money, profit; the nurturer's goal is health—his land's health, his own, his family's, his community's, his country's.... The exploiter typically serves an institution or organization; the nurturer serves land, household, community, place. The exploiter thinks in terms of numbers, quantities, 'hard facts'; the nurturer in terms of character, condition, quality, kind.

In a more peaceable kingdom or queendom, exploitation of nature would recede as the nurturing ethic of care grows. A nurturing ethic would depend on two concepts that happen to be the lifeblood of cultural anthropology: reciprocity and redistribution. In the academic world, interpretations of those terms can become complicated, to say the least. Among economists and political scientists, these are loaded words. But let's take them at their face value: reciprocal relationships are about give-and-take; redistribution is about sharing. Today we receive more from nature than we give, and redistribution is usually a one-way arrangement that favors our enrichment, at least in the short term. We take from other animals and, with the exception of our pets, give very little in return.

We can change this equation, beginning in our daily lives. We can consider if in our immediate relationships with other animals, we are giving as much as we get. We can create spaces that allow animals to survive and thrive, including the creation of more wildlife preserves or pollination gardens through the use of native species in our yards. We can act to create more biodiversity or support the construction of wildlife bridges or tunnels across or under highways. Colorado University professor emerita Louise Chawla describes the basis of an emerging new nature movement as "the idea that as humans we can not only make our ecological footprints as light as possible, but we can actually leave places better than when we came to them, making them places of delight." What a fine legacy, a place of delight.

The Right to Be

Our moral challenges will intensify as we recognize that our connection to other animals is unattainable through technology alone and is deeper even than biology. Descartes's concept of *bête machine*—that animals, unlike humans, are stupid machines—is outdated. Our coexistence with animals is essential to the survival of all species. Consequently, protecting our extended family is ultimately an issue of rights—the rights of human beings to a nature connection and the rights of nature itself.

Dr. Nooshin Razani is the founder of the Center for Nature and Health, which conducts research on the connection between time in nature and health and is the nation's first nature-based clinic associated with a major health provider, UCSF Benioff Children's Hospital in Oakland, California. In June 2018, the center began billing insurance companies for patient visits that include nature connection as part of the treatment. Razani argues that nature connection can mean the difference between life and death, especially in less advantaged neighborhoods. In 2017, a study published in the prestigious medical journal the *Lancet Planetary Health* suggested that people who live in green neighborhoods live longer than those with little nature nearby. The study, conducted in Canada's thirty biggest cities, considered socioeconomic and education differences as control factors. As I reported in *Sierra* magazine in 2019, The psychological, physical, and cognitive benefits of nature connection may be universal, but access to natural areas is not. "This is a social justice issue," Razani told me. Many of her patients suffer from a lack of nature access and from pollution in their immediate neighborhoods. Every day, she witnesses the profound stress that urban families experience. Some lack the seemingly basic opportunity to spend time outside—parents who feel compelled to keep their children indoors because of neighborhood crime. "It's important not to assume that people with less income value nature less," she added. "This isn't a question of their values—it's about housing, about equal access to nature.... Some people get stuck on the idea that we need to teach people how to love nature. The truth is that people whose cultures were colonized often had more true nature connection in their histories than did the colonizers."

Razani is part of the nascent global movement—made up of parents, educators, researchers, and health practitioners—that insists that universal and equitable access to nature is fundamental to our humanity as well as to the future of life on Earth. Its proponents are moving forward toward that recognition, some steps larger than others.

In Scotland in 2005, the so-called right-to-roam law went into effect. The Land Reform Act now gives everyone a right of *responsible* access on most land and inland waterways throughout Scotland. Hikers can go just about anywhere on public or private land if they treat the land and the owners of that land with respect. When the right to roam was discussed at the 2018 Nurturing Nature Play in Scotland conference, held at the Royal Botanic Garden in Edinburgh, Minister for Childcare and Early Years Maree Todd quoted a line from poet Norman MacCaig that is etched on the side of the Scottish parliament building: "Whose land is it anyway, he who owns it or he who is possessed by it?" The American author, and frequent roamer, Ken Ilgunas, makes a passionate case for the passage of a similar right-to-roam law in the United States. In the United States, such a right is unlikely to be established. But Scotland's example suggests that broadening access to nature there and in other countries is possible.

In 2012, the International Union for Conservation of Nature passed a resolution declaring that a positive connection to nature is a human right for children. All children need nature—not just the kids with parents who appreciate nature or those of a certain economic class or those whose abilities allow them uncomplicated access. This right should also be declared for adults. I am not talking here specifically of a legal right but instead of a certain moral right. And the right to connect with nature is not a right to damage nature. As with the right to roam, responsibilities come with it. In order to protect this right, to see the value of protecting it, people need to feel connected to the natural world.

And an even broader issue: the rights of nature itself. Thomas Berry believed that "everything has a right to be recognized and revered. Trees have tree rights, insects have insect rights, rivers have river rights, and mountains have mountain rights." Movement toward this thinking is picking up speed. In 2008, Ecuador changed its constitution to give nature "the right to exist, persist, maintain, and regenerate its vital cycles." In 2010, Bolivia passed the Law of the Rights of Mother Earth, giving nature rights equal to those of humans. And in 2017, New Zealand declared that the country's third-largest river, the Whanganui, has the same legal rights as a person. This made the Whanganui the first river in the world to be recognized as a living entity. The designation resulted from a 140-year campaign by Indigenous groups, including New Zealand's Maori tribes, who view the river as essential to the well-being of people and all the other lives that depend on it for survival and nurturance. The bill gave the river all the rights, duties, and liabilities that come with personhood, and the river can now be represented in court proceedings. Two guardians will act on the river's behalf: a member of the Whanganui iwi and a representative of the Crown.

To some, of course, the idea that nature has rights is ridiculous. But all life, all the plants and animals touched by a river, have a right to that river, and it has a right to exist. The idea of nature rights should be woven into our education systems and into the conservation movement itself. In recent U.S. elections, the proportion of votes cast by people who identify themselves as conservationists or environmentalists has been embarrassingly low. One reason is because to most Americans protecting nature is an abstraction. But direct care for the welfare of animals does have deep emotional resonance with most people, liberal or conservative.

Nature becomes real only when it moves from the head into the heart. A new nature movement will not succeed if fueled only by fear or an intellectual vision of an alternative future, but it will if driven by a deeply emotional, familial, and spiritual connection to other species. For this to occur, a massive cultural, even neurological, shift will be required. A fantasy, many will say. But is a faith in the habitat of the heart any more fantastical than believing we can continue to destroy the natural world without destroying ourselves?

The goal isn't a perfectly peaceful realm but one in which life is encouraged and mutualism is prized, where unlikely alliances between different animals, including people, emerge, and where wildness returns not just in distant parks but in cities, too.

If we're serious about becoming nature nurturers, we must confront our conflicting values and competing risks and benefits. The herpetologist Harry Greene is one of the most vocal proponents of Pleistocene rewilding as a way to address mass extinctions and collapsing biodiversity. As described in chapter 18, Pleistocene Park is an effort to set aside vast tracts of land for the return of wolves, mountain lions, bison, and other megafauna that once ruled the plains. Facing heavy criticism from the public and some biologists, Greene and his colleagues conducted a values survey, finding, as Greene says, "that what really bothers most biologists is that we're proposing to put something back that can *kill* us." But the revival of biodiversity demands the protection and reintroduction of the large predators. For some people, that objective seems fair enough as long as someone else takes the risk. "We want the Tanzanians to pay the price for keeping African lions on earth," Greene said, which includes not only the cost of upkeep but of lion attacks on people as well.

But let's be *really* fair, he argues. Conservation shouldn't be something other people do and pay for; it should be pursued everywhere in ways that share the costs and the dangers and delights. "I've spent most of my career trying to get people to care about snakes, even rattlesnakes," he said. "To a degree, I think I've succeeded." The key to this success is "telling the truth about snakes. It's the same way with other dangerous animals: you have to tell the truth about them" and then practice old and new methods of nurturing participation—and deeper connection and empathy with them. Answering this call will require empathetic understanding not only of other animals but of people as well.

Human behavior is ruled not so much by law or even culture as it is by spirit—and by a natural cycle that begins and ends all debates. Our arguments about hunting and fishing, and animal husbandry, and tofu made of soybeans harvested from the land where wildlife meets its end under the tilling blade; all of that confusing, overlapping, endless circling around one another with suspicion, superiority, and sometimes humility—in this debate, we might think about reframing the taking of life, when it involves providing ourselves, our families, and our communities with the food necessary for survival. We might think about this exchange as trading life. By that I mean that when we eat other beings—animals or even the plants that we now know whisper to other plants—we are trading their lives for ours. We will live, yes, but sooner or later, even as ashes, our bodies replenish the endless chain of food and desire, fruition and life, death and decay, to be risen again and again and again. Perhaps this is the ultimate meaning of reciprocity. And communion.

Having described the biological reality of life, still dominated by tooth and fang, we also know that our species has more freedom to choose than most. In ways small and large, we can move away from mindless consumption and beyond single-lifespan concerns. We do not require encouragement to trade life for life. Rather, we need a center that holds true to a philosophy of compassion and thoughtfulness. There is our spirit, and the call.

TWENTY-ONE

Learning and Teaching
in a School of Animals

In the age of connectedness, educators are among the trailblazers, especially when they emphasize nature connection as much as or more than
electronic connection. While visiting a middle school in Los Angeles, with
a student body containing a high proportion of children of movie stars
and other entertainment figures, I was introduced to Angelina, a large
bearded lizard, and her small gecko companion, Brad. Named for the
actors and onetime marital partners Angelina Jolie and Brad Pitt. One of
the students said, "Want to know what we feed them? Cockroaches and
kale." Which sounded to me like the name of a trendy Los Angeles restau-
rant. When I asked the teachers why animals were in the classroom, the
response was unanimous: because of their usefulness for teaching science
but, more important, their emotional impact on students, especially the
unruly ones. Geckos, guinea pigs, rabbits, and visiting dogs all calm the
students. "Simply their presence," said one teacher. "That's the main thing.
The students don't even have to handle the animals to be calmed."

Not everyone believes live animals belong in classrooms. But David Sobel,
a leader in nature-based learning, explains that particularly in early childhood, the primary purpose of environmental teaching is to nurture identification with nature. Among the most basic ways to do that, he advises, is through
telling stories, singing songs, and imagining what it's like to be an animal. He
writes, "And so we must begin in empathy, by becoming the animals so we can
save them." However, until recently, the notion that schools should encourage animal connection was fading. To some education leaders, live animals
were and remain irrelevant in the preparation of students as future economic

producers; to others, the practice is a form of animal exploitation. They say, correctly, that animals, especially small ones, disguise their pain or discomfort—an evolutionary adaptation to hide their vulnerability from predators. On the other hand, proponents point out that the majority of animals in classrooms are, in fact, rescue animals—abandoned dogs, wounded and rehabilitated birds, or animals too imprinted on human beings to be released into the wild. Also, the practice is highly regulated both to ensure the safety of animals and, mainly, to reduce any risk that a classroom critter might pose to students.

In recent years, Scotland has taken a different approach. At the previously mentioned Edinburgh conference on children, play, and nature connection, Henry Mathias, a former early childhood educator and now head of professional practice and standards for Scotland's Care Inspectorate, seeks to improve children's nursery schools, child protective services, and senior care facilities. Toward that end, Mathias introduced "Animal Magic" as part of a program to encourage animal connection. "I remember when it was common for schoolchildren to take classroom guinea pigs home for the weekend," Mathias said, remembering his own days as an educator. "That ritual disappeared as people worried about infection control." He would like to see that practice return. The care inspectorate's policy guidelines explicitly state that if a child who lives in a care home wants "to keep a pet, the service will try to support this to happen." Why? Because the benefits far outweigh the risks. Whether in a nursery school or an adult care home, animals "bring transformative care through empathy, and that affects everyone." Mathias described with admiration students at one early childhood school who raised chickens and collected and sold eggs. "When I visited, the children took me to a grave of a hen who had died and told me in great detail how the ex-hen had lived and what she was like."

---

* The Royal Society for the Prevention of Cruelty to Animals, Britain's largest animal welfare charity, discourages keeping or studying live animals. The Humane Society of the United States takes a slightly different approach, which includes inviting animal experts into the classroom and creating a schoolyard habitat. "If your classroom must have a live pet," it maintains, "adopt one from your local shelter or rescue." www.humanesociety.org. In the United States, the National Science Teachers Association issues these guidelines: refrain from releasing animals into a nonnative environment; don't expose animals to chemical cleaners or pesticides (a restriction one would think was already in effect for the students themselves); and, "espouse the importance of not conducting experimental procedures on animals if such procedures are likely to cause pain, induce nutritional deficiencies." National Science Teachers Association Position Statement, www.nsta.org/about/positions/animals.aspx.

This about-face in government regulatory policy became possible after Scotland's legal system began to recognize that an adverse risk had to be assessed in the context of the benefits that also come from or to an animal, species, activity, or place. This is still a radical notion to the U.S. legal and regulatory system, which remains risk averse at all costs. But if the development of compassion in children is to be considered a fundamental part of a balanced education, one way to foster it is by learning to treat all animals, including those in captivity, with respect and care (and, yes, good people will continue to disagree on what constitutes respect and care).

Animal Class

In an ideal world, schools would be on the front line of animal connection. In addition to traditional biology and ecology courses, students could learn about interspecies and intraspecies communication, including bird language (see chapter 8); reap a deeper understanding of the school's bioregion; and come to know the Betweens, the wild animals that observant students and teachers may have seen moving through their neighborhoods (see chapter 16).

With a set of moral principles woven into the curriculum, young people could learn to live in harmony with other species. Students would learn how to build biodiversity in backyards and rooftops and schoolyards by studying, among other things, how to use native plant species. Lessons might include how different cultures connect with the natural world, the impact of natural history on human history, and the stories that animals tell each other and us. In the higher grades, the fundamentals of biophilic architecture and biomimicry could be offered, as well as courses on the disruptive and positive uses of technology for animal connection, which could lead the way to potential careers related to animals. By promoting a naturally symbiotic approach to life and the future, schools would be more interesting and engaging places for learning and would build human-nature social capital in the surrounding community.

Animals, wild and domestic, can teach us, and our children, about their inherent value. They can teach us patience, how to live in the moment, interdependence with other animals and each other, humility (that we're not as special, either as a species or as individuals, as we think we are), how to listen more carefully, how to live within our means and to use only what we need to survive or thrive. Traditional school curricula, including reading, math, and science, could be built out of the life lessons that other animals teach.

During a visit to a major nature center in 2018, I met a young teacher who was clearly passionate about nature, especially wild animals. She and others gave me a tour of the center—its museum-like taxidermy collection, its aquaria, and its terraria, which included living king snakes and red-eared slider turtles and the surrounding lands through which sandhill cranes and wolves sometimes make their way. We walked down to a pond where leopard frogs launched themselves into the water as we approached. The teacher, wearing a khaki ranger shirt, said that of all the experiences offered to visitors to the nature center, catching frogs in the pond was the most popular, at least among children.

She then gave an impressive recitation of all the biological and natural systems facts that she teaches during that experience. I was curious as to whether she ever asked the students and their parents to simply sit next to the pond, to be quiet and aware until the scattered frogs began to return to the surface. She was puzzled. Why would she do that? I answered, "To sense what it is like to be a frog." At first, she did not seem to understand the suggestion. She was clearly doing the job that she had been assigned—to teach science and to meet the state educational standards—and she was doing it well. But I couldn't help but wonder how much richer the learning experience might be if she also practiced critical anthropomorphism. If she could share with the kids the experience of becoming a frog, the lesson would facilitate science learning. It might improve the scientific questions that they ask.

The habitat of the heart has not escaped David Orr, considered by many to be the father of environmental literacy and a pioneer in ecological design. Orr is professor of Environmental Studies and Politics at Oberlin College in Ohio. Though most Americans may think of sustainability in terms of energy efficiency, he understands that it is also about sustaining and growing our relationships with other living creatures and each other.

Years ago, Orr considered dropping out of the academic world. Struggling with his disenchantment, he went on a long moonlit walk to a river. On his return, he sensed he was being followed and eventually encountered a formidably large coyote, "perhaps crossed with a bit of red wolf," as he recounts in *Hope Is an Imperative*. In Orr's life, this encounter became a touchstone. It solidified the foundation for his view of the world and of himself. "I think he was simply curious about this lone, misplaced human. I had no weapon and no machine, which made me more approachable, and I think we did communicate in a fashion. The coyote was both curious and courteous. And those who do not believe that animals think have never ventured alone and vulnerable into a conversation with one on its terms and in its native habitat."

I was struck by how similar his experience was to those of so many of the people I have interviewed and to my own. In that moment, Orr was aware of the *fullness* of space between himself and the coyote, and he contrasted that realization to the educational emptiness of a society that still views nature "as a mere commodity and animals as abstractions, much as Descartes did."

Such an emptiness is the logical product of what Orr perceived to be the "separation of head, hands, and heart in the learned world." Mainstream education started "at the neck and worked up, but it dealt with only half of what remained. The other half, that part of mind where feeling, humor, poetry, and integration reside, was considered lacking in rigor by people who were often, I thought, unable to distinguish between rigor and rigor mortis." In the "rising generation" of his own students, he was witnessing how experiences in nature were increasingly "alien to the enclosed curriculum of the academy where the matters of greatest consequence have to do with grade point averages, course units, careers, routines, tenure, and *US News & World Report*'s annual ranking."

His exchange with the coyote offered Orr a small but significant reentry point. Today he is a strong voice calling for education reform with nature in mind. He spearheaded the effort to build and design the Adam Joseph Lewis Center for Environmental Studies at Oberlin, which was named one of thirty milestone buildings of the twentieth century by the U.S. Department of Energy. Its design blurs the distinction between indoors and outside, and it uses minimal energy to operate. Orr now calls for a "higher order of heroism," the development of an expanded design intelligence that recognizes the rights of children, wildness, and a deep connection to nature among all people. Orr, David Sobel, and other educators—formal and informal—are leading the way to an educational approach that broadens rather than narrows the way students perceive and eventually understand the lives of animals and all of nature. If nature-based learning—in which animals and deep animal connection play a role—is to grow, colleges of education must encourage it and teach future teachers how to take children and themselves outdoors.

Ten Ways to Love the World

Descartes may still rule Western society, but his grip is slipping. Institutions of higher learning, from Lewis and Clark College in Oregon to Wellesley College in Massachusetts and Cornell University in New York are marketing themselves as learning environments in which students devote more time studying and recreating in natural settings.

Educators of all kinds are pushing for additional natural learning environments. College students are also pushing their institutions in the same direction. Around the country, nature-based clubs are being established by students who are focused on protecting the environment and on saving themselves from the increasing pressures they face from education, parent expectations, and the uncertain economy. And, even as some elementary-through high-school districts continue to restrict or cancel field trips and recess, pioneering independent and public schools are taking the natural learning environment more seriously.

The change is occurring at a particularly fast clip among preschools. In 2017, *Education Week* reported that five years earlier, only a couple dozen nature-based preschools operated in the United States. Today there are close to 250. This trend follows Europe's lead, in which forest schools (where students may spend the majority of their school hours learning outdoors) have been relatively popular for years and are currently surging. At the same time, research relating outdoor education to academic achievement, including higher scores on standardized tests, is also growing.

Natural learning environments encourage methods that activate the senses. For example, bioacoustician Bernie Krause engages children through "active listening." He writes, "In the U.S., in particular, what's missing . . . is a recognition of the fundamental value of the biophony—the collective voice of the natural world—an axiomatic expression found in every type of habitat, at any given time of day or night and in each season. It is a narrative of place and time and an indication of the health of a habitat." He adds, "Soundscape ecology can be taught to children as young as 3 years old . . . at an age when children are more receptive to the mysteries of the animal world. When they hear the sounds that fish produce—not to mention the typical bird, amphibian and mammal voices—faces light up with wonder and astonishment. I tell my students that while a picture may be worth 1,000 words, a soundscape is worth 1,000 pictures." He asks students to listen for the true dance music all around us, in the whispering and calls of nature, in what Krause calls the "Creature Choirs."

Any education system that ignores the full use of the senses, devalues natural history, reduces biology to numbers—and, further, dismisses any discussion of the spirit shared by animals, including people—is teaching an inaccurate version of the real world. We accept as gospel that our planet is dominated by human habitat. Yet bacteria reproduce and mutate faster than we do and make up a hefty portion of our body weight. Their biomass equals or exceeds that of all humans in the world. "Individual ants are the equivalent to the neurons in your brain—each one doesn't have a lot to say but in combination they can get a lot of things done," according to Mark Moffett, an entomologist at the Smithsonian Institution in Washington, DC, who makes an excellent case that ants already control the earth, noting, "They just do it under our feet." Should our species fail, rats or pigs, with their complex social structure, or AI creatures created by us, could one day pick up the title for world domination.

At the core of incorporating more nature connection into schools or outside the school buildings is ethics education. Ideally, educators, whether in informal or formal settings, will increasingly tap the knowledge base of Indigenous people. They will offer relief from species loneliness, and help our culture move from the exploitation ethic to the nurturing ethic.

Specific to the role of other-than-human animals, here are a ten suggestions for how to promote the engagement of students from pre-K through college:

1. Encourage students and teachers to practice empathetic listening and to tell their stories about encounters and relationships with other animals. These stories can be told around campfires; on YouTube; through writing, art, and photography; and through music.
2. Move more of the educational experience beyond the walls of the classroom into the outer habitat of wild animals and plants. This stimulates the mind and the senses. Encourage young people to bond with animals, but also teach the responsibilities that come with that bond.
3. Offer courses in nature connection to all future educators in teaching colleges, emphasizing how nature experiences improve cognition and creativity. Education should offer teachers training in how to take students outdoors to learn and experience.

4. Educate all students, not only those majoring in the natural sciences, about the new research on animal emotions and intelligence, about species loneliness, and about the impact of environmental change and urbanization on animal populations, including the new mix of wild and domestic life—the Betweens.
5. Develop and practice alternatives to vivisection and the use of animal subjects in laboratory experiments at all grade levels.
6. Teach students at every grade level how to create new physical habitats for wild animals, how to care for companion animals, and how to envision and one day help create cities that nurture the human-animal bond.
7. Encourage the presence of true service animals in classrooms, as well as rescue and rehabilitated animals that are not releasable to the wild; engage students in their care.
8. Teach critical anthropomorphism as part of the scientific method, thus deepening students' understanding and observational powers of animals' and students' shared psychological and physical habitats.
9. Expose students to the spiritual, religious, and philosophical thinking regarding the human connection to other animals—and how the concepts apply not only to their connection with other animals but also with each other, and with other cultures. Respect and engage Indigenous people as part of the process, as well as representatives from other cultures.
10. Challenge students and citizens to imagine a nature-smart future as an alternative to the current dystopian trance.

To bring more animals into the educational environment, or more students into the natural environment, schools and teachers need not work alone. Visionary educators around the world have established partnerships with animal shelters, animal rescue centers, zoos and aquaria, farms and ranches. Volunteers from these institutions already bring wild animals and therapy dogs to schools. But such approaches need more public support. Herb Broda, professor emeritus at Ashland University in Ohio, is an expert on using schoolyards as teaching environments, asserting that "what we need, to get these approaches better accepted by schools, is a groundswell of public opinion. Parents need to request that animals be a part of the school experience."

The urgency to move in this direction is growing at digital speed. Two of Apple's major shareholders, California State Teachers' Retirement System and hedge fund Jana Partners, collectively own about two billion dollars in Apple shares. In January 2018, the two investors issued an open letter calling on Apple to consider how technology affects children's well-being. Of the copious research cited, these items are of particular interest: Young people may be losing some of their ability to read emotions, and their social skills may be declining as they have less time for face-to-face interaction because of their increased use of digital media. American teens who spend three or more hours a day on electronic devices are more likely to be at a higher risk for suicide than their peers who use them for less than an hour a day. Another disturbing trend: teenagers who use knives and razors to cut themselves and then display their wounds on social media.

In contrast, we know that companion animals and contact with wild animals can help young people feel *truly* connected with life. So can more general experiences in the natural world. One study demonstrated that after five days at an outdoor camp that restricts the use of digital devices, children performed far better on tests for empathy; and children who went five days without even glancing at a smartphone, television, or other digital screen did better at reading human emotions.

An Older Way of Learning

Several related trends in educational thought and practice are converging today, building on Waldorf and Montessori education. One is called "humane education." The Institute for Humane Education (IHE) defines it as a way of teaching and learning that offers a twist on the "do no harm" ethic in medicine. IHE sums the ethic up in a single coined word, *MOGO*, which is short for "most good," a quick way of thinking about the fundamental question, How can each of us, though our daily choices, work, communities, and volunteerism do the most good and the least harm to ourselves, other people, animals, and the environment?

At the University of Denver, Philip Tedeschi is an advocate of humane education. He admits that its name can be misleading. The word *humane* suggests it's all about humans. "We do need a new language for all of this," he told me. "We're finding that the same social science indicators of health and well-being apply to humans and nonhuman animals." Cruelty to animals—for example, the dog chained outdoors and freezing to death—has a direct impact on the health of anyone, not just on the perpetrator but also on those who witness or allow it. Likewise, acts of kindness to animals improve both the well-being of the kind person as well as those people in his or her social circle.

Humane education is by no means limited to classroom learning. It also has implications for city planners. Animal shelters are often placed at the edge of industrial parks. But Tedeschi and other advocates of humane education and humane communities believe that if an animal shelter is placed in a populated neighborhood instead, and programs that engage neighbors in the care of the animals are established, social isolation is lessened—for both the humans and the animals. Denver's Institute for Human-Animal Connection is currently working with police and homeless shelters to educate them about the relationship between homeless people and their dogs. "Today in Denver, almost no homeless shelters allow animals. We're hoping to change that, through design and training," said Tedeschi.

Beginning with the University of Denver, he wants colleges and universities to think of themselves as delivery points for humane education, first as examples, by becoming animal-friendly institutions with, for instance, animal-friendly dorms. "We know how stressed first-year students are, and access to companion animals can have a positive impact on their mental health and ability to learn," he said.

Wouldn't this be seen as just one more perk for students? No, he said, not if it were part of an educational program centered on the reciprocal kindness that animals deserve, including their proper care as well as understanding the special needs of different dog or cat breeds. Beyond the dorms, such a program would address the health and welfare of all animals, domestic or wild. In the dorm, the classroom, or the city, humane education about our relationships with other animals will naturally spill over into the relationships among humans.

The humane education movement has focused mainly on companion animals, but that emphasis is widening. When I mentioned my notion for Neighborhood Wildlife Watch groups, Tedeschi suggested that schools could sponsor them or partner with a city campaign to promote such groups. He could see educators joining these groups or starting their own and, through them, spreading the idea that we all live in a neighborhood of animals, and that well-being of humans and other animals is reciprocal. An additional application of humane education could be tailored for expecting parents, newborns, toddlers, and their caregivers; early-parenting classes could offer an opportunity for educators to teach soon-to-be parents about the relationship between humans, other animals, and good health.

This should be said: the nature connection movement, in all of its forms, has yet to connect equitably with diverse populations and economic groups. Though progress is being made, nature-based preschools, for example, reach mainly white, economically privileged families. For conservation, environmental education, and the nature connection movement, Indigenous people and teaching are underrepresented and underutilized. That glaring gap should be closed. One hopeful sign comes from Canada.

In 2017, the Laboratory School at the Dr. Eric Jackman Institute of Child Study at the University of Toronto developed the remarkable book *Natural Curiosity 2nd Edition*, created in collaboration with Indigenous educators. Reframing nature education, the authors report on nontraditional educators and their approaches, including a case study by University of Toronto researcher Farveh Ghafouri, who, with a classroom of kindergartners, discovers a dead squirrel in the park behind their school. According to *Natural Curiosity*, "This experience triggered a week of intense observation, examination, and questioning that touched upon children's deep interest in (and associated fears about) the nature of death."

Later, the children begged to return to the site, where they spent hours every day "examining, sketching, and pondering the mysteries of the dead squirrel." They expressed concern for the squirrel's "current well-being (despite its being dead)," and they became increasingly reluctant to leave the animal when they returned to the classroom. Tellingly, "the evident decomposition did nothing to deter their caretaking impulses." After a week, the teacher became concerned about the children's preoccupation and secretly removed the squirrel. This "triggered a flurry of questions and speculations about where it had gone." A few months afterward, when two of the children's fathers unexpectedly died, the teacher wrote to the authors that relating the tragedy of the squirrel helped these students understand death at a deeper level. To expand students' understanding of being in the world, *Natural Curiosity* suggests a general framework of Indigenous thinking. Family, intimacy, and reciprocity are at its core:

Indigenous views broaden the basis for knowledge integration to include *everything around us*, ultimately erasing the environment as a concept, immersing and connecting us in a blooming sense of place, until everything we are, every aspect of our existence, is one whole, inseparable, living system, united from within. . . .

Even the term "sustainability" fails to really capture what would be implied, since this term is often limited to looking at natural resources, that is, how we might more responsibly consume some-*thing* that is apart from us, extracted from elsewhere. We need to ask rather: what would be different if we lived with a strong sense that *water, land, all of the world around us, are relatives*? What if we *love the world* around us deeply, as our family? Our actions would then begin to reach reciprocity in how we live and move in any direction, including seven generations into the future. Rather than *contributing* to a stewardship *cause*, we would *ensure balance in all our interactions with the world around us*, through space and time.

In *Natural Curiosity,* Norah L'Espérance, who works with young children at Toronto's Laboratory School, described the evolution of her thinking this way: "The more I've learned about ecology and the story science tells us of the unfolding universe, the more my language has changed in my teaching. When I talk about the planet Earth, I no longer say, 'we are on the Earth.' Now I talk about 'the planet that we're part of.' It's a small change in words but a big shift in consciousness: we're not separate from everything else on the planet—we are actually, literally, completely a part of it."

Over time, too many of us have lost a sense of who we are in relation to both the physical world and to other living beings, human and otherwise, who share the same space. The technologies designed to connect us have fallen short. Throughout human history and prehistory, people depended on their neurological ability to make mental maps to find their way, first on landscapes and the sea, then on trails and roads and freeways. Once reliant on our own brains, we are now dependent on electronic devices. Researchers have shown that the more we use GPS units in our phones and cars, the less ability we have to create mental maps.

All students, young or old, should be given a chance to develop a deeper connection to the universe that holds them. One of their teachers should know the route there.

TWENTY-TWO

The Bear

The only way people come to truly care about animals is to know them, to immerse themselves in the flow of nature and the lives of animals—including the ones who can hurt us. Nothing stimulates awe and humility, not to mention the survival instinct, quite as much as being on the receiving end of a wild predator's fury or unfathomable mercy. The liminal space between life and death is where both vulnerability and change are most possible.

Ron Swaisgood is chief conservationist for the San Diego Zoological Society. He is also one of the biologists responsible for saving the giant panda from extinction (he and his colleagues in China figured out how to encourage the animals to mate in captivity—it's all about scent). He also spends several weeks a year as a leader at the Cocha Cashu Biological Station on the Peruvian Amazon. The locale there is considered among the most remote, pristine places left on the planet. Recently the outpost scored outdoor showers; before that, the scientists bathed in a river . . . with piranhas. Swaisgood could have died there when a cut became infected, as Cocha Cashu is days away from a fully functional hospital. Fortunately, he carries antibiotics. Talking about his work in China, he points out that people are attracted to pandas because of their flat faces, large eyes, and roly-poly shape. But they are not cuddly, at least not with humans. Their bamboo-shattering bite is among the most powerful of any carnivore. Swaisgood has never had a problem with a panda, but he does tell hair-raising stories of being stalked by African lions and being charged by a white rhino from fifty feet away before it inexplicably shuddered to a stop directly in front of him.

The liminal space between life and death is where both vulnerability and change are most possible. In 2013, when Swaisgood was fifty-one, he was diagnosed with schwannomatosis—the aggressive growth of relatively benign but painful tumors throughout his body. Because of the tumors, he lost feeling in his legs. Over many months, he taught himself to walk again. He thinks about that charging rhino almost every day. "I have some control over whether I'm taken by a lion or rhino. I don't have control over whether I get the tumors. But I do have control over how I deal with both," he said when we met for coffee one day. He mused on the power of this particular kind of animal story and the lessons it conveys:

> I've told the rhino story a hundred times or more. My boys love it: "Tell the rhino story, Dad!" So the true transformative power is more for the boys than for me. The little critters—the bacteria that almost killed me and whatever it is that causes the tumors—are more likely to get you than rhinos or jaguars or bears. But the big animals make for better stories. Near-death encounters do make the best camp-fire stories. We're wired to pay attention to those. That's why people stop and gawk at auto accidents. The morbid fascination —that's how we learn to avoid being killed. Other animals will sometimes show the same kind of fascination when another animal is killed. Maybe they're learning from someone else's mistake. The great advantage that humans have is our ability to tell stories, which can lead not just to personal change but to cultural learning and survival.

It's one thing to listen to cautionary tales; it's another to deliberately invite a tiger to dinner. To absorb predator karma, people cozy up with grizzly bears, swim with the sharks (usually in protective cages), and keep pet tigers, cheetahs, and lions—as did Tippi Hedren, star of Alfred Hitchcock's *The Birds*, whose fully maned male African lion enjoyed the run of her house alongside Hedren's young daughter, Melanie Griffith. Photos of lions hugging humans are particularly popular on YouTube and elsewhere. Why do lions hug people? Most likely not because they're filled with love, but because lion cubs do the same with each other, to express dominance.

Thrill seeking is one motivation for getting up close and personal to dangerous animals. Another is enthrallment, the feeling of being blessed and chosen for such a moment. Reciprocity is not necessarily expressed. However, this reaction also occurs when people have encounters with animals that cannot hurt them. Tia Ghose, writing for Live Science, proposes two other motivations. "That need for connection with the wild is part of human nature, but wild-animal chasing may also stem from isolation or machismo." That's true, but people who have encounters with wild predators also report another impact that can take place. It's the opposite of machismo. Humility.

Whether by design or accident, such an experience can become a triptych that a person opens and closes for the rest of her life. A few years ago, oceanographer Paul Dayton, while staying with his son in a cabin in the Big Bend area of Texas, had an experience that moved him as much as the octopus he met.

> So we're asleep on a little porch. I could hear something crunching in the gravel. I sat up under the full moon and heard something coming around the edge of the building. I thought it was a big coyote. It came around the porch and walked right up to the end of my sleeping bag. It was a big adult mountain lion. We looked at each other for fifteen seconds. Total curiosity. No twitching tail. No predator behavior. His expression was, "Oh, I didn't expect to see you there." Then he made an unfamiliar sound, as if he were saying, "See you around." Cougars don't jump; they flow. He flowed over a fence and away. And I'm thinking, "I've been looking for you all my life."

As Dayton told this story, I remembered Michael Pelton's description of the spell he fell under as a boy, when he had his first close encounter with a bear, and his admiration for Paul Shephard, who in *The Sacred Paw* writes:

> The bear strikes a chord in us of fear and caution, curiosity and fascination. In self-absorption we may fool ourselves, forgetting his otherness, and feed him in a national park as if he were a pet dog. Perhaps the impulse is the same, whether we invite the bear to share

our food or our folklore: the urge to be reunited with something lost and treasured, seen in the animal that most resembles us. It is almost as though in him we can see how great is our loss of contact with ourselves. Perhaps the bear can still serve as a pilot and messenger.

Beyond the Horizon

For three days, Ann Bancroft knew the polar bear was stalking her. She saw its tracks, how it would approach, circle far out on the ice, and watch. Sometimes it would disappear for hours, and she would feel a sense of relief.

"Normally polar bears are curious about humans but not *that* interested. They much prefer seal meat than bitter old women," she said, smiling, referring to herself and Liv Arnesen, a Norwegian adventurer who accompanied Bancroft on this particular expedition.

Charismatic, funny, and brave, Bancroft is among the best-known polar explorers. In 1986, she was the first woman in recorded history to cross the ice to the North Pole (though surely Indigenous women, not recorded, made similar treks), traveling by dogsled a thousand miles from the Northwest Territories in Canada. In 1993, Bancroft led the first all-female expedition to cross the ice to the South Pole, and in 2001 Bancroft and Arnesen became the first women to ski across Antarctica. In 2005, Bancroft and Arnesen set out to ski across the Arctic Ocean. This was the expedition when they were joined by the persistent polar bear.

Polar bears, it is worth mentioning, are considered the bears most dangerous to humans, and such encounters will increase as climate disruption drives them south. Some Indigenous people of the Arctic still hunt polar bears for food and treat even the carcass with utmost respect, in hopes that its spirit will share the news of their proper etiquette with other bears, who will then be more willing to be killed. Some believe that the spirits of humans and polar bears are interchangeable. Legends survive of polar-bear men who live in igloos, walk upright—like our friend Pedals!—and are able to talk.

Bancroft told me her story in the warm comfort of a friend's house in Minneapolis. I forgot all about that warmth as she grew increasingly animated, her eyes widening. She described in minute detail each lesson learned, each behavioral clue the bear gave her, each mistake she made. "On skis, both of us were wearing waist belts to pull the weight of the sleds, which made turning around to look back so difficult. So it took us a little while to figure out that we were being tracked by a single bear. Very unnerving," she said. "We didn't take a rifle. A lot of people challenged us on that—but in my experience, a rifle tends to stay on the sled. If you seldom see a bear, the rifle can end up buried in the equipment." But a .44 Magnum firearm (which Liv did carry) "is always on your hip." Still, having it handy doesn't guarantee it will solve the problem. Shooting a gun into the air usually doesn't scare a bear away "because the bear wouldn't know where the noise was coming from; in the Arctic, noise is diffused."

Each defensive tool has its limitation. Bear spray, which they carried, can be of questionable effectiveness in wind. They did duct-tape pen flares to bungee cords, which were attached to their jackets. "The pen flare is the first line of defense," she said. "The Magnum is the last." For some bears, a flare's explosive sound and its burst of light, shot at the ground in front of it, will do the trick. "But this bear was cagier. He was crafty, followed us at a distance. He would pull back from the flare and then reappear."

As the days went on, the bear would appear on the horizon. Bancroft would blink and the bear would be gone, like a spirit. "The pan ice—old ice—would flatten out, and then you would come to areas of rubble that were almost like boulder fields. Every time the bear would appear, it would be right after we had left the pan ice and entered another stretch of rubble ice. We were most compromised when we were passing through the rubble ice. You can't outrun them. I realized if he decided to take us, or one of us, he would probably drag us onto the pan ice so he could see his competition."

One expanse of ice was so rough that even though they knew the unseen bear was still following them, Bancroft and Arnesen were forced to remove their skis, leave them, and walk their sleds through the rubble.

"I said to Liv, 'Watch my back,' and I went back to get the skis. I'm bent over clicking my boots into the bindings, and I stand up."

The bear was three hundred feet in front of her, standing on its hind legs.

So I yelled to Liv, "Bear!" With any predator, you do not run, and in some cases, you don't even back up, because the animal will interpret this as submissive behavior, and this can trigger their chase instinct. The two of us come together, shoulder to shoulder, to look bigger. I pull out a flare and she pulls out the Magnum. The bear puts his nose down in the ski track and he looks up at us, and we're shaking. We don't want to shoot him. I fire a flare and he goes up on his hind legs again. He's close, moving toward us but not charging. I ask Liv if she is going to shoot him. She says yes. By then, I've shot two flares and am loading another two. I hear a click. It's Liv's gun. It doesn't fire. I shoot a flare at his feet. He makes a noise, not a roar but not a good noise, and he turns and runs. We stood there a half second. I was loading a flare, just shaking. Liv looked at the gun. It unfroze and she fired.

The women were cold and nervous in their parkas. Rather than turning their backs on the bear, they reloaded and followed its tracks to make sure he was gone. They saw drops of urine, so they knew they had scared him. The bear was retracing his own tracks out of the rubble field. The two explorers were fully in the rubble ice now. Aware that the bear could be behind any ice boulder, they continued to follow the tracks. "When we went back," Bancroft said, "I saw from his prints that when I had been putting my skis on, he had been sitting right there behind a boulder." The tracks also told her that the bear's gait had picked up as it moved toward her. "That really got us shaking in our boots. There was nothing more to do but to continue our strategy. From my sled, I would navigate and look for the bear 180 degrees in front of us. Liv's job was to follow me and watch 180 degrees behind us. Because you're wearing a hood, it's hard to see, and the bears are so quick and quiet."

They completed their journey. This experience is woven into Bancroft's mind and heart.

She now lives in a Minnesota farmhouse on the St. Croix River, which she shares with her partner. Sometimes a black bear passes through the property. She worries about that. "With the advent of more people and bird feeders, I am much more cautious of the black bears here than I ever was," she says. "They're so much more used to dogs and human beings now."

She keeps chickens in the yard. She describes their quirkiness and surprising individuality, how they have become essential to her emotional life. She said she grew up on a Minnesota farm feeling like the odd one, the nature girl, the one who preferred other-than-human animals to people. She loved her family, but "imagination and animals kept me engaged with the rest of the world." She spent part of her childhood in Kenya, too. She has always preferred to live at the "intersections of domestic and wild animals, the places where they remain separate but come into our sphere."

She calls the chickens and rooster her forty children.

The older I get, the more stressful and demanding my life is. But then I enter the chicken coop and sit on a bench and watch their crazy expressions and the way they interact. People think chickens are dumb, but considering they have a brain the size of your thumb, they have a lot going on. They're comical and insightful. They socialize with each other, constantly sorting out their social order, verbalizing with me and others. I try to talk to the chickens and the rooster in their language, the different tones, the clucking when a food source is discovered, a bug or seed. There's a "pay attention" sound—almost like a little whistle—they have these different sounds. Particularly when I'm with the young ones, and I'm the mother—or want to be—I duplicate those sounds. When I find a worm, I cluck them over. I haven't been totally successful with their language. Now and then I deal with them in a way that ruffles their feathers, their pecking order.

Yesterday I'm sitting in there and this young woman comes over to pick up some eggs. She has a mental disability. She sat in the coop with me. She knelt over the adolescent birds, scooped gently under their feet and brought them up on her lap. Normally a person will come down from above like a raptor would, but she knelt and held them in the gentlest way, and they stayed right on her lap.

After a while in the chicken coop, Bancroft begins to feel that all is right with the world. Time slows. She observes the hens and rooster almost as carefully as she watched the polar bear as it stalked her across the pan ice into the rubble. She feels no adrenaline rush, no worry. She watches and listens. Sometimes she sings to them.

Our Calling

Once, we were born in kinship with the ones we hunted or worshipped and the one who hunted and watched us; the wolves who came closer and eventually became our friends and workmates; the cattle and sheep and pigs that, for a time, shared our houses. Within our collective lifetime, in most of the world, the ancient patterns fell away. We struggle to fill that emptiness. Sometimes we succeed.

Like E. O. Wilson, Paul Shepard has had a profound impact on the study of the human relationship with nature. His most famous contribution is the "Pleistocene paradigm," a critique of modern, sedentary civilization. "In such a world there is no wildness, as there is no tameness," he writes. Our alienation from the rest of nature traps us in an infantile or adolescent psychological state. Our healing as a species, according to Shepard, requires us to become closer to our roots in the Pleistocene. Shepard, who died in 1996, offered little practical advice about how to get to that state of grace— not back to nature, because one cannot return to what is already inside us and always has been. Rather, we should recognize the psychological and spiritual space that we share with other animals, learn to enter it at will, and then go forward to nature. In that world, Shepard writes, the "otherness of nature becomes accessible to humans in fabulous forms of incorporation, influence, conciliation, and compromise."

People are not going to start chipping obsidian arrowheads anytime soon, at least not in large numbers, but perhaps we can advance toward the Symbiocene, the age of connectedness—encompassing reciprocity and redistribution—where wildness survives, albeit in newer forms and in unexpected places, where we live in balance with other life. Many of us can at least *feel* the possibility of that newer world. Especially during those times when our hubris recedes momentarily, when, like polar explorer Ann Bancroft, we find ourselves suspended between life and death, in a place where a still-wild god walks on four legs just beyond the horizon.

Thomas Berry reminded us that "the Earth functions at a depth beyond our capacity for active thought" and that as humans are forced to experience their damage to the Earth as damage to themselves, they may yet change course: "We probably have not had such participation in the dream of the

Earth since earlier shamanic times, but therein lies our hope for the future for ourselves and for the entire Earth community."

Our times call for the adoption of a basic principle that embraces both survival and joy. We might call this the reciprocity principle: For every moment of healing that humans receive from another creature, humans will provide an equal moment of healing for that animal and its kin. For every acre of wild habitat we take, we will preserve or create at least another acre for wildness. For every dollar we spend on classroom technology, we will spend at least another dollar creating chances for children to connect deeply with another animal, plant, or person. For every day of loneliness we endure, we'll spend a day in communion with the life around us until the loneliness passes away.

Poems are constructed not only with words but also from the spaces between the words. This is true for our relationships with other people, and it is also true for our connection to other animals. Our lives are poems. As are theirs. We write them together. In the habitat of the heart—in that whisper of recognition between two beings when time seems to stop, when space assumes a different shape—in that moment, we sense a shared soul. That is what connects the woman and the bear, the diver and the octopus, the dog and the child, the boy and the jaguar, the fisherman and the golden eagles on the shore.

Through the eyes of the people who have shared their stories, I have come to see the world differently. In their voices, I hear a refrain. Expectation still arrives with the spring, as do beautiful acts.

ACKNOWLEDGMENTS

I am deeply indebted to my wife, Kathy, who helped make this book possible at every stage and at every level, and to my sons, Matthew and Jason, who offered keen insights and support.

Thanks, too, to my immensely patient and brilliant editor and publisher, Amy Gash and Elisabeth Scharlatt, respectively, and Algonquin Books' staff, among them Craig Popelars (a.k.a. Jack London), Brunson Hoole, Anne Winslow, Kendra Poster, and Jude Grant; and, beyond Algonquin, Jim Levine, Jackie Green, Robyn Bjornsson, John Johns, Karen Landen, Larry Hinman, Leigh Fenly, and Henry Bloomstein. My deep appreciation goes to longtime friend Dean Stahl, whose editorial talent is only exceeded by his wisdom. His contributions to the book were incalculable. Thanks also to everyone at the nonprofit Children & Nature Network, which supports the great work of connecting children, families, and communities to the natural world.

And I offer my gratitude to the wildlife biologists, anthrozoologists, philosophers, ecopsychologists, animal-assisted therapists, and others who are pioneering the study of the human-animal relationship. To those I have quoted, I hope I have been true to your stories and your research and that my extrapolations and speculations reflect well on your work and lives.

NOTES

Introduction: A Mystery

3 **In her Pulitzer** Elizabeth Kolbert, *The Sixth Extinction: An Unnatural History* (New York: Henry Holt, 2014).

3 **Between 1970** M. Barrett, A. Belward, S. Bladen, T. Breeze, et al., *Living Planet Report 2018: Aiming Higher*, World Wildlife Fund, Gland, Switzerland, 2018, c402277.ssl.cf1.rackcdn.com/publications/1187/files/original/LPR2018_Full_Report_Spreads.pdf.

3 **inescapable network** Martin Luther King Jr., "Letter from a Birmingham Jail [King, Jr.]," April 16, 1963, African Studies Center, University of Pennsylvania, www.africa.upenn.edu/Articles_Gen/Letter_Birmingham.html, accessed March 22, 2019.

1. In the Family of Animals

9 **A Dutch Artist** Jan van Boeckel, "At the Heart of Art and Earth: An Exploration of Practices in Arts-Based Environmental Education" (Ph.D. diss., Aalto University, Aalto, Finland, 2014).

10 **Whoever you are** Mary Oliver, "Wild Geese," *Dream Work* (New York: Atlantic Monthly Press, 1986), 14.

2. The Aching Heart

14 **The world is** William Wordsworth, *Poems, in Two Volumes, 1807*, ed. Richard Matlak (London: Henry Frowde, 1913), 122.

15 **Epidemic may be** Jena McGregor, "This Former Surgeon General Says There's a 'Loneliness Epidemic' and Work Is Partly to Blame," *Washington Post*, October 4, 2017, www.washingtonpost.com/news/on-leadership/wp/2017/10/04/this-former-surgeon-general-says-theres-a-loneliness-epidemic-and-work-is-partly-to-blame/?utm_term=.de19f9abcd9f.

15 **A 2006 study** Miller McPherson, Lynn Smith-Lovin, and Matthew E. Brashears, "Social Isolation in America: Changes in Core Discussion Networks over Two Decades," *American Sociological Review* 71, no. 3 (2006): 353–75.

15 **In a 2010** G. Oscar Anderson, "Loneliness among Older Adults: A National Survey of Adults 45+," AARP Research, September 2010, doi.org/10.26419/res.00064.001.

15 **According to recent** Emily Schondelmyer, "Fewer Married Households and More Living Alone," U.S. Census Bureau, August 9, 2017, www.census.gov/library/stories/2017/08/more-adults-living-without-children.html;

U.S. Census Bureau, "Historical Census of Housing Tables: Living Alone," 2000, www.census.gov/data/tables/time-series/dec/coh-livealone.html; U.S. Census Bureau, "Unmarried and Single Americans Week: Sept. 17–23, 2017," U.S. Census Bureau Newsroom, August 14, 2017, Release Number CB17-TPS.62, www.census.gov/newsroom/facts-for-features/2017/single-americans-week.html; Benjamin Gurrentz, "How Much Does Economic Security Matter to Marriage Rates for Young Adults?," June 26, 2018, www.census.gov/library/stories/2018/06/millennial-marriages.html.

15 **But the** Economist Maggie Fergusson, "Loneliness Is Not Just a Problem for the Elderly," *Economist*, July 27, 2018, www.economist.com/open-future/2018/07/27/loneliness-is-not-just-a-problem-for-the-elderly?fsrc=scn/tw/te/bl/ed/.

15 **In 2017** Selby Frame, "Julianne Holt-Lunstad Probes Loneliness, Social Connections," *American Psychological Association*, October 18, 2017, www.apa.org/members/content/holt-lunstad-loneliness-social-connections.

15 **A second review** Julianne Holt-Lunstad, Timothy B. Smith, Mark Baker, and David Stephenson, "Loneliness and Social Isolation as Risk Factors for Mortality: A Meta-Analytic Review," *Perspectives on Psychological Science* 10, no. 2 (2015): 227–37, doi.org/10.1177/1745691614568352.

16 **The findings** J. M. Twenge, T. E. Joiner, M. L. Rogers, and G. N. Martin, "Increases in Depressive Symptoms, Suicide-Related Outcomes, and Suicide Rates among U.S. Adolescents after 2010 and Links to Increased New Media Screen Time, *Clinical Psychological Science* 6, no. 1 (2017): 3–17.

16 **A 2018 generational** Cigna, "Survey of 20,000 Americans Examining Behaviors Driving Loneliness in the United States," Cigna U.S. Loneliness Index, May 2018, www.multivu.com/players/English/8294451-cigna-us-loneliness-survey/docs/IndexReport_1524069371598-173525450.pdf.

16 **The term species loneliness** Michael V. McGinnis, "Myth, Nature, and the Bureaucratic Experience," *Environmental Ethics* 16, no. 4 (1994): 425–36.

16 **Nearly two decades** Michael Vincent McGinnis, "Species Loneliness: Losing Our Sense of Place in the Machine Age," *Santa Barbara Independent*, January 14, 2012, www.independent.com/news/2012/jan/14/species-loneliness/.

17 **Parks with** Guiseppe Carrus, Massimiliano Scopelliti, Raffaele Lafortezza, Giuseppe Colangelo, et al., "Go Greener, Feel Better? The Positive Effects of Biodiversity on the Well-Being of Individuals Visiting Urban and Peri-Urban Green Areas," *Landscape and Urban Planning* 134 (February 2015): 221–28.

17 **Over the past** Research and Markets, "United States Pet Population and Ownership Trends Report 2017—Focus on Dogs, Cats, and Other Pets," GlobeNewswire, July 17, 2017, globenewswire.com/news-release/2017/07/17/1047437/0/en/United-States-Pet-Population-and-Ownership-Trends-Report-2017-Focus-on-Dogs-Cats-and-Other-Pets.html.

18 **Harvard professor** "Beware the Age of Loneliness," *Economist*, November 18, 2013, www.economist.com/news/2013/11/18/beware-the-age-of-loneliness.

19 **The late Thomas Berry** Thomas Berry and Mary Evelyn Tucker, *Evening Thoughts: Reflecting on Earth as Sacred Community* (San Francisco: Sierra Club Books, 2006).

19 **Similarly, the Australian** Glenn Albrecht, "Exiting the Anthropocene and Entering the Symbiocene," Psychoterratica, August 29, 2018, glennaalbrecht.com/2015/12/17/exiting-the-anthropocene-and-entering-the-symbiocene/.

20 **In distant ancestral** John Berger, "Why Look at Animals?," *About Looking* (New York: Pantheon, 1980), 3–18.

20 **HAS spans several** For the definition of HAS, I have relied on Erica Elvove, associate director of Institute for Human-Animal Connection, University of Denver Graduate School of Social Work, Denver, CO.

21 **A research team** Kelly A. George, Kristina M. Slagle, Robyn S. Wilson, Steven J. Moeller, et al., "Changes in Attitudes toward Animals in the United States from 1978 to 2014," *Biological Conservation* 201 (September 2016): 237–42.

21 **Writer Brandon Keim** Brandon Keim, "America Is Becoming a Kinder, Gentler Place (toward Animals, Anyway)," *Conservation*, August 3, 2016, www.conservationmagazine.org/2016/08/changing-attitudes-towards-wildlife/.

3. The Mind-Altering Power of Deep Animal Connection

23 **Indigenous traditions** Ralph Waldo Emerson, *Emerson's Essays: The First and Second Series Complete* (New York: Library of America, 1983).

23 **That movement's** Ralph Waldo Emerson, "The Over-Soul," *Essays*, 1841. (Emerson later changed the title of *Essays* to *Essays: First Series*.)

23 **More recently** Barry Lopez, "A Literature of Place," *Heat* 2 (1996): 5–58.

24 **A few years ago** Martin Buber, *I and Thou*, classic ed., trans. Ronald Gregor Smith (New York: Scribner, 2000).

24 **Paraphrasing twentieth-century** Martin Buber, *I and Thou*, trans. Ronald Gregor Smith (New York: Scribner, 1958).

26 **Michelle Brenner** Michelle Brenner, "Lean into Liminality," Mediate.com, July 2018, www.mediate.com/articles/brenner-liminality.cfm.

27 **In "Why Look** John Berger, "Why Look at Animals?," *About Looking* (New York: Pantheon, 1980), 3–18.

4.The Octopus Who Stopped Time

34 **As one neurobiologist** Gabriela Quirós, "If Your Hands Could Smell, You'd Be an Octopus," Deep Look, *KQED*, April 14, 2017, www.kqed.org/science/1391513/if-your-hands-could-smell-youd-be-an-octopus.

36 **Meeting an octopus** Peter Godfrey-Smith, "The Mind of an Octopus," *Scientific American Mind* 28, no. 1 (August 2016): 62–69, doi.org/10.1038/scientificamericanmind0117-62.

36 **Later this story** Mindy Weisberger, "No, Scientists Haven't Found a 512-Year-Old Greenland Shark," Live Science, December 14, 2017, www.livescience.com/61210-shark-not-512-years-old.html.

37 **In 2018** Stephen J. Martin, Roy R. Funch, Paul R. Hanson, and Eun-Hye Yoo, "A Vast 4,000-Year-Old Spatial Pattern of Termite Mounds," *Current Biology* 28, no. 22 (2018): R1292–93.

37 **In her 1937** Rachel Louise Carson, "Undersea," *Atlantic Monthly* 78 (1937): 55–67.

37 **In *The Log*** John Steinbeck, *The Log from the* Sea of Cortez: *The Narrative Portion of the Book,* Sea of Cortez *(1941), by John Steinbeck and E. F. Ricketts* (New York: Viking Press, 1941).

39 **Joanne Vining** Joanne Vining, "The Connection to Other Animals and Caring for Nature," *Human Ecology Review* 10, no. 2 (2003): 87–99.

39 **Vining is careful** Ibid.

39 **Psychologist Abraham Maslow** Abraham H. Maslow, *Toward a Psychology of Being* (New York: Van Nostrand Reinshold, 1968).

39 **During a peak** Abraham H. Maslow, *Religion, Values, and Peak-Experiences* (Columbus: Ohio State University Press, 1964).

40 **In 2003** Dacher Keltner and Jonathan Haidt, "Approaching Awe, a Moral, Spiritual, and Aesthetic Emotion," *Cognition and Emotion* 17, no. 2 (2003): 297–314.

5. Becoming the Grasshopper

46 **University of Toronto** Patricia A. Ganea, Caitlin F. Canfield, Kadria Simons-Ghafari, and Tommy Chou, "Do Cavies Talk? The Effect of Anthropomorphic Picture Books on Children's Knowledge about Animals," *Frontiers in Psychology* 5 (October 2014), doi.org/10.3389/fpsyg.2014.00283.

46 **Aristotle, in** Aristotle, *The History of Animals,* trans. D'Arcy Wentworth Thompson (Oxford: Clarendon Press, 1910).

47 **"It prevented people** Melissa Dahl, "Maybe It's Time to Take Animal Feelings Seriously," Cut, *New York*, February 23, 2016, www.thecut.com/2016/02/the-scientific-case-for-anthropomorphism.html.

48 **As Burghardt** Jesús A. Rivas and Gordon M. Burghardt, "Understanding Sexual Size Dimorphism in Snakes: Wearing the Snakes Shoes," *Animal Behaviour* 62, no. 3 (2001): F1–6.

52 **Later he would** Harry W. Greene, "Appreciating Rattlesnakes," in "Facing the Serpent," ed. Tom Butler, special issue, *Wild Earth* 13, no. 2/3 (Summer/Fall 2003), republished by the Environment & Society Portal, Multimedia Library, www.environmentandsociety.org/node/6106.

52 **"Empathy," Greene writes** Ibid.

6. Intimacy Is All around Us

53 **When Alan Rabinowitz** "An Indomitable Beast: The Remarkable Journey of the Jaguar," radio interview, Diane Rehm Show, August 18, 2014, dianerehm.org/shows/2014-08-18/alan-rabinowitz-indomitable-beast-remarkable-journey-jaguar; Alan Rabinowitz, "A Boy's Promise," video, Brink, Weather Channel, May 7, 2015, weather.com/series/weatherfilms/brink/video/a-boys-promise-graphic-warning?isSubsequent=true.

54 **Rabinowitz (whom *Time*)** Bryan Walsh, "The Indiana Jones of Wildlife Protection," *Time*, January 10, 2008, content.time.com/health/article/0,8599,1702308,00.html.

56 **Author and scientist** Aldo Leopold, *Sand County Almanac and Sketches Here and There* (New York: Oxford University Press, 1972).

57 **Thomas Patrick Malone**   Thomas Patrick Malone and Patrick Thomas Malone, *The Art of Intimacy* (New York: Simon & Schuster, 1992).

58 **Like us, animals**   Melissa Dahl, "Maybe It's Time to Take Animal Feelings Seriously," Cut, *New York*, February 23, 2016, www.thecut.com/2016/02/ the-scientific-case-for-anthropomorphism.html.

59 **Ravens may have**   Sam Wong, "Ravens' Fear of Unseen Snoopers Hints They Have Theory of Mind," *New Scientist*, www.newscientist.com/article/2076025-ravens-fear-of-unseen-snoopers-hints-they-have-theory-of-mind/.

59 **Scrub jays hide**   Joanna M. Dally, Nathan J. Emery, Nicola S. Clayton, "Avian Theory of Mind and Counter Espionage by Food-Caching Western Scrub-Jays (*Aphelocoma californica*)," *European Journal of Developmental Psychology* 7, no. 1 (2010): 17–37.

59 **As for the domestic**   Ashley Prichard, Peter F. Cook, Mark Spivak, Raveena Chhibber, et al., "Awake FMRI Reveals Brain Regions for Novel Word Detection in Dogs," *Frontiers in Neuroscience*, October 15, 2018, doi.org/10.3389/fnins .2018.00737.

59 **A team**   Jen Wathan, Anne M. Burrows, Bridget M. Waller, and Karen McComb, "EquiFACS: The Equine Facial Action Coding System," *PloS One* 10, no. 9 (2015): doi.org/10.1371/journal.pone.0131738.

60 **Patty Born Selly**   Patty Born Selly, *Connecting Animals and Children in Early Childhood* (St. Paul, MN: Redleaf Press, 2014).

7. Earth's Oldest Language

63 **We make the assumption**   Megan Garber, "Animal Behaviorist: We'll Soon Have Devices That Let Us Talk with Our Pets," *Atlantic*, June 5, 2013, www.theatlantic.com/technology/archive/2013/06/animal-behaviorist-well-soon-have-devices-that-let-us-talk-with-our-pets/276532/.

64 **Lizards also employ**   Jorge Sáiz, R. García-Roa, J. Martín, and B. Gómara, "Fast, Sensitive, and Selective Gas Chromatography Tandem Mass Spectrometry Method for the Target Analysis of Chemical Secretions from Femoral Glands in Lizards," *Journal of Chromatography A*, 1514 (2017): 110–19.

64 **Researchers at Tel Aviv**   Yosef Prat, Mor Taub, and Yossi Yovel, "Everyday Bat Vocalizations Contain Information about Emitter, Addressee, Context, and Behavior," *Scientific Reports* 6, no. 1 (December 2016), https://www.nature .com/articles/srep39419.

64 **Using underwater microphones**   Vyacheslav A. Ryabov, "The Study of Acoustic Signals and the Supposed Dolphins' Spoken Language," *St. Petersburg Polytechnical University Journal: Physics and Mathematics* 2, no. 3 (2016): 231–39, doi.org/10.1016/j.spjpm.2016.08.004.

64 **Elephants generate**   Mark Shwartz, "Looking for Earth-Shaking Clues to Elephant Communication," *Stanford Report*, June 1, 2005, news.stanford.edu/ news/2005/june1/elephant-052505.html.

64 **The tiny coqui frog**   Helen Czerski and Patrick Aryee, "Facts about Sound, Animal Super Senses," BBC Earth, bbcearth.com/shows/animal-super-senses/ modal/facts-sound/.

64 **Then there's this** Katherine Hignett, "Once a Year, Fish Swim to Mexico for an Orgy so Loud It Can Deafen Dolphins,"*Newsweek*, December 20, 2017, www.newsweek.com/corvina-mating-call-machine-gun-deafens-dolphins-753389.

65 **However, the neural** A. Andics, A. Gábor, M. Gácsi, T. Faragó, et al., "Neural Mechanisms for Lexical Processing in Dogs" *Science* 353, no. 6303 (2016): 1030–32.

65 **A purr can** John Bradshaw, *Cat Sense: How the New Feline Science Can Make You a Better Friend to Your Pet* (New York: Basic Books, 2014); Melissa Dahl, "Your Cat Is Trying to Talk to You," Cut, *New York*, April 29, 2015, nymag.com/scienceofus/2015/04/your-cat-is-trying-to-talk-to-you.html.

65 **In coming years** Melody in Human-Cat Communication (MEOWSIC), vr.humlab.lu.se/projects/meowsic/; Sarah Knapton, "What Is Your Cat Saying? Swedish Scientists Launch Five Year Project to Find Out," *Telegraph*, March 10, 2016, www.telegraph.co.uk/news/science/science-news/12190257/What-is-your-cat-saying-Swedish-scientists-launch-five-year-project-to-find-out.html.

65 **Other domesticated** Christian Nawroth, Natalia Albuquerque, Carine Savalli, Marie-Sophie Single, et al., "Goats Prefer Positive Human Emotional Facial Expressions," *Royal Society Open Science* 5, no. 8 (2018), doi.org/10/1098/rsos.180491.

66 **In 2017** Elena M. Panova and Alexandr V. Agafonov, "A Beluga Whale Socialized with Bottlenose Dolphins Imitates Their Whistles," *Animal Cognition* 20, no. 6 (2017): 1153–60.

66 **In a 2012** Sam Ridgway, Donald Carder, Michelle Jeffries, and Mark Todd, "Spontaneous Human Speech Mimicry by a Cetacean," *Current Biology* 22, no. 20 (October 2012): PE860–61, doi.org/10.1016/j.cub.2012.08.044.

66 **According to Smithsonian.com** Charles Siebert, "The Story of One Whale Who Tried to Bridge the Linguistic Divide between Animals and Humans," Smithsonian.com, June 1, 2014, www.smithsonianmag.com/science-nature/story-one-whale-who-tried-bridge-linguistic-divide-between-animals-humans-180951437/.

66 **Con Slobodchikoff** Megan Garber, "Animal Behaviorist: We'll Soon Have Devices That Let Us Talk with Our Pets," *Atlantic*, June 5, 2013, www.theatlantic.com/technology/archive/2013/06/animal-behaviorist-well-soon-have-devices-that-let-us-talk-with-our-pets/276532/.

67 **One-celled bacteria** "Sample Records for Bacterial Cell-to-Cell Communication," Science.gov, www.science.gov/topicpages/b/bacterial+cell-to-cell+communication.

67 **In the 1999** Paul Stamets, "Earth's Natural Internet," *Whole Earth Catalog*, 1999, www.wholeearth.com/issue/2098/article/86/earth's.natural.internet.

67 **Researchers in the** Zdenka Babikova, Lucy Gilbert, Toby J. A. Bruce, et al., "Underground Signals Carried through Common Mycelial Networks Warn Neighbouring Plants of Aphid Attack," *Ecology Letters* 16, no. 7 (2013): 835–43.

68 **Suzanne Simard** Lacy Cooke, "Mother Trees Recognize Kin and Send Them 'Messages of Wisdom,'" Inhabitat, August 6, 2016, inhabitat.com/mother-trees-recognize-kin-and-send-them-messages-of-wisdom; Suzanne Simard,

"How Trees Talk to Each Other," TED, July 22, 2016, www.ted.com/
talks/suzanne_simard_how_trees_talk_to_each_other?utm_
campaign=tedspread&utm_medium=referral&utm_source=tedcomshare.

69 **A few years ago** Peter H. Kahn Jr. and Patricia H. Hasbach, eds., *Ecopsychology: Science, Totems, and the Technological Species* (Cambridge, MA: MIT Press, 2012).

69 **Hasbach picks up** Christopher Alexander, Sara Ishikawa, Murray Silverstein, Max Jacobson, et al., *A Pattern Language: Towns, Buildings, Construction*, Center for Environmental Structure Series (New York: Oxford University Press, 1977).

70 **The journal Current Biology** Emily Doolittle and Bruno Gingras, "Zoomusicology," *Current Biology* 25, no. 19 (2015), doi.org/10.1016/j.cub.2015.06.039.

70 **For example, researchers** "Thai Elephant Orchestra," Thai Elephant Conservation Center, www.thailandelephant.org/en/orchestra.html.

71 **Bernie Krause** Bernie Krause, *Wild Soundscapes: Discovering the Voice of the Natural World*, rev. ed. (New Haven, CT: Yale University Press, 2016).

72 **In 2018** Raphaela Heesen, Catherine Hobaiter, Ramon Ferrer-i-Cancho, and Stuart Semple, "Linguistic Laws in Chimpanzee Gestural Communication," *Proceedings of the 12th International Conference on the Evolution of Language* (Evolang12), 2018, doi.org/10.12775/3991-1.039.

72 **In a Royal Society** Shalene Singh-Shepherd, "Chimpanzee Gestures Follow the Same Laws as Human Languages," *Royal Society*, February 13, 2019, blogs.royalsociety.org/publishing/chimpanzee-laws-human-languages/?platform=hootsuite.

73 **As A. A. Milne** A. A. Milne, *Winnie the Pooh* (London: Methuen Publishing, 1926).

8. How to Talk with Birds

75 **For example, in 2016** M. M. Mariette and K. L. Buchanan, "Prenatal Acoustic Communication Programs Offspring for High Posthatching Temperatures in a Songbird," *Science* 353, no. 6301 (2016): 812–14.

76 **Almost every bird** Mark Mancini, "Can Different Bird Species 'Talk' with Each Other?," HowStuffWorks, January 12, 2018, animals.howstuffworks.com/birds/can-bird-species-talk-with-each-other.htm.

78 **Mind's-eye imagining** Jon Young, Ellen Haas, and Evan McGown, *Coyote's Guide to Connecting with Nature* (Shelton, WA: OWLink Media, 2010).

80 **In fact, for hunting** Jon Young and Dan Gardoqui, *What the Robin Knows: How Birds Reveal the Secrets of the Natural World* (Boston: Houghton Mifflin Harcourt, 2012).

81 **A study at the** Robert Sanders, "Two Nostrils Better Than One, Researchers Show," *UC Berkeley News*, December 18, 2006, www.berkeley.edu/news/media/releases/2006/12/18_scents.shtml.

81 **South African Anna** Michael Theys, "How to Communicate with Animals with Anna Breytenbach," *Africa Freak*, October 3, 2018, africafreak.com/how-to-communicate-with-animals-with-anna-breytenbach.

82 **Another possibility** Erika Smishek, "Mapping the Sixth Sense," *UBC Reports* 50, no. 1 (2004), www.publicaffairs.ubc.ca/ubcreports/2004/04jan08/mindsight.html.

82 **While respecting** Lea Winerman, "A 'Sixth Sense'? Or Merely Mindful Caution?," *Monitor on Psychology* 36, no. 3 (March 2005): 62.

82 **In addition, scientists** Masaki Kobayashi, D. Kikuchi, and H. Okamura, "Imaging of Ultraweak Spontaneous Photon Emission from Human Body Displaying Diurnal Rhythm," *PLoS ONE* 4, no. 7 (July 2009): e6256, doi.org/10.1371/journal.pone.0006256.

82 **Daniel Goleman** Joshua Freedman,"Neural Leadership: Daniel Goleman on Emotional and Social Intelligence," Six Seconds, February 27, 2017, www.6seconds.org/2007/02/27/the-neural-power-of-leadership-daniel-goleman-on-social-intelligence/.

83 **In Laguna, Brazil** "Dolphins Help Fishermen Catch Fish," Live Science, May 1, 2012, www.livescience.com/20027-dolphins-work-fishermen.html.

83 **In 2016, a study** Claire N. Spottiswoode, Keith S. Begg, and Colleen M. Begg, "Reciprocal Signaling in Honeyguide-Human Mutualism," *Science* 353, no. 6297 (July 2016): 353, 6297: 387–89.

83 *Science News* **called** Bruce Bower, "Humans, Birds Communicate to Collaborate," *Science News*, July 21, 2016, www.sciencenews.org/article/humans-birds-communicate-collaborate.

9. Playing Well with the Others

86 **Helen Macdonald** "What Animals Taught Me about Being Human," *New York Times Magazine*, May 2017, www.nytimes.com/2017/05/16/magazine/what-animals-taught-me-about-being-human.html?smid=fb-nytimes&smtyp=cur.

88 **In his book** Stuart L. Brown and Christopher C. Vaughan, *Play: How It Shapes the Brain, Opens the Imagination, and Invigorates the Soul* (New York: Penguin, 2009).

90 **Similarly, chimpanzees** A review of two decades of research on human brain plasticity in childhood and throughout life can be found at the website of the Center on the Developing Child at Harvard University. A recent study challenges some of that research: Helen Shen, "Does the Adult Brain Really Grow New Neurons?," *Scientific American*, March 7, 2018.

90 **In his classic** Gordon M. Burghardt, *Genesis of Animal Play: Testing the Limits* (Cambridge, MA: MIT Press, 2006).

92 **Elephants play** Vicki Fishlock, "Playful Pachyderms: Why Elephants Have a Sense of Humour," *International Fund for Animal Welfare*, November 24, 2014, www.ifaw.org/european-union/news/playful-pachyderms-why-elephants-have-sense-humour.

10. More Than Human

99 **In 2012** Peter H. Kahn Jr., Jolina H. Ruckert, and Patricia H. Hasbach, "A Nature Language," in *Ecopsychology: Science, Totems, and the Technological*

Species, ed. Peter H. Kahn Jr. and Patricia H. Hasbach (Cambridge, MA: MIT Press, 2012), 122–314.

100 **Others have used** Sandie Suchet-Pearson, Sarah Wright, Kate Lloyd, and Laklak Burarrwanga, "Caring as Country: Towards an Ontology of Co-Becoming in Natural Resource Management," *Asia Pacific Viewpoint* 54, no. 2 (2013): 185–97.

II. The Animal Lover

104 **In 2017, the Humane** "Two Hundred Dogs from South Korean Dog Meat Farm Rescued and Transported to the US, UK and Canada for Adoption," *Humane Society International*, January 11, 2017, www.hsi.org/news/press_releases/2017/01/wonju-dog-meat-rescue-011117.html.

105 **A 2017–18 survey** "The 2017–2018 APPA National Pet Owners Survey Debut: Trusted Data for Smart Business Decisions, American Pet Products Association, americanpetproducts.org/Uploads/MemServices/GPE2017_NPOS_Seminar.pdf.

105 **Cannabis (specifically CBD** R. Scott Nolen, "Veterinary Marijuana? With Pet Owners Already Using the Drug as Medicine, Veterinarians Need to Join the Debate," *Journal of American Veterinary Medical Association*, May 13, 2013, www.avma.org/News/JAVMANews/Pages/130615a.aspx.

105 **That same year** Linday Beaton, "Top Pet Food Trends on Consumers' Minds in 2017," PetfoodIndustry.com, December 7, 2016, www.petfoodindustry.com/articles/6172-top-pet-food-trends-on-consumers-minds-in-2017?v=preview.

105 **These trends are** "Pet Diets Follow Human Trends," *NZ Herald,* April 17, 2017, www.nzherald.co.nz/lifestyle/news/article.cfm?c_id=6&objectid=11836960.

107 **In 2014** Megan Kiely Mueller and Kristina Schmid Callina, "Human-Animal Interaction as a Context for Thriving and Coping in Military-Connected Youth: The Role of Pets during Deployment," *Applied Developmental Science* 18, no. 4 (2014): 214–23, www.tandfonline.com/doi/abs/10.1080/10888691.2014.955612.

107 **As Gail F. Melson** Bill Strickland, "The Benefits of Pets," *Parents*, www.parents.com/parenting/pets/kids/the-benefits-of-pets/.

109 **Sadahiko Nakajima** Sadahiko Nakajima, "Dogs and Owners Resemble Each Other in the Eye Region," *Anthrozoös* 26, no. 4 (2013): 551–56.

111 **A research psychologist** C. Zahn-Waxler, B. Hollenbeck, and M. Radke-Yarrow (1984). "The Origins of Empathy and Altruism," in *Advances in Animal Welfare Science 1985/85*, ed. M. W. Fox & L. D. Mickley (Washington, DC: Humane Society of the United States, 1984), 21–41.

112 **One dark morning** The section about Banner is adapted, in part, from an essay in Richard Louv, *The Web of Life: Weaving the Values That Sustain Us* (Newburyport, MA: Conari Press, 1996).

113 **In 2003** Wolfgang M. Schleidt and Michael D. Shalter, "Co-evolution of Humans and Canids: An Alternative View of Dog Domestication: Homo Homini Lupus?," *Evolution and Cognition* 9, no. 1 (2003): 57–72.

113 **Schleidt, in an earlier** Wolfgang M. Schleidt, "Is Humaneness Canine?," *Human Ethology Bulletin* 13, no. 4 (1998): 14.

115 **In *The Biology*** Andreas Weber, *The Biology of Wonder: Aliveness, Feeling, and the Metamorphosis of Science* (Gabriola Island, BC: New Society Publishers, 2016).

115 **In 2011** J. Allen Williams, Christopher Podeschi, Nathan Palmer, Philip Schwadel, et al., "The Human-Environment Dialog in Award-Winning Children's Picture Books," *Sociological Inquiry* 82, no. 1 (2011): 145–59.

12. Reptiles and Ambivalence

121 **Meanwhile, breeders** Christian Cotroneo, "People Are Breeding These Giant Cats to Be Just Like Dogs," Dodo, July 16, 2016, www.thedodo.com/savannah-cats-breed-1925214076.html.

13. The Boy Who Said Horse

126 **For the psychotherapist** For anecdotal evidence supporting equine therapy, see Adele von Rüst McCormick and Marlena Deborah McCormick, *Horse Sense and the Human Heart: What Horses Can Teach Us about Trust, Bonding, Creativity, and Spirituality* (Deerfield Beach, FL: Health Communications, 1997).

131 **Presently this area** Olga Oksman, "An Emotional Support Animal Is Just a Mouse Click Away," *Guardian*, July 28, 2016, www.theguardian.com/lifeandstyle/2016/jul/28/emotional-support-animal-service-pet-flying-housing.

136 **One of the few** Sarah L. Bell, Michael Westley, Rebecca Lovell, and Benedict W. Wheeler, "Everyday Green Space and Experienced Well-Being: The Significance of Wildlife Encounters," *Landscape Research* 43, no. 1 (2017): 8–19, doi.org/10.1080/13683500903042857.

137 **The original research** Stephen Kaplan, "The Restorative Benefits of Nature: Toward an Integrative Framework," *Journal of Environmental Psychology* 15, no. 3 (1995): 169–82.

138 **As ordinary as** Susanna Curtin, "Wildlife Tourism: The Intangible, Psychological Benefits of Human-Wildlife Encounters," *Current Issues in Tourism* 12 (2009): 451–74.

138 **Some of the participants** Bell, Westley, Lovell, and Wheeler, "Everyday Green Space."

139 **A 2017 review** Rebecca Purewal, R. Christley, K. Kordas, C. Joinson, et al., "Companion Animals and Child/Adolescent Development: A Systematic Review of the Evidence," *International Journal of Environmental Research and Public Health* 14, no. 3 (2017): 234.

139 **A small Tufts** D. Lenihan et al., "Benefits of Reading Assistance Dogs," Cummings School of Veterinary Medicine, Tufts University, Medford, MA, 2011.

139 **A 2010 study** Christopher G. Owen, Claire M. Nightingale, Alicja R. Rudnicka, Ulf Ekelund, et al., "Family Dog Ownership and Levels of Physical Activity in Childhood: Findings From the Child Heart and Health Study in England," *American Journal of Public Health* 100, no. 9 (2010): 1669–71.

139 **A study sponsored** "A Pet in Your Life Keeps the Doctor Away," ScienceDaily, September 29, 2009, www.sciencedaily.com/releases/2009/09/090928172532.htm.

140 **In 2012** "Service Dogs, a Rule by the Veterans Affairs Department on 09/05/2012," *Federal Register,* National Archives, September 5, 2012, www .federalregister.gov/documents/2012/09/05/2012-21784/service-dogs#h-9.

140 **Ironically, the VA** VA Web Solutions Office, "Service and Guide Dogs," U.S. Department of Veterans Affairs, Washington, DC, August 25, 2015.

140 **In 2017** Joanna L. Becker, Erica C. Rogers, and Bethany Burrows, "Animal-Assisted Social Skills Training for Children with Autism Spectrum Disorders," *Anthrozoös* 30, no. 2 (2017): 307–26.

14. The Replacements: Do We Really Need Animals?

142 **Peter H. Kahn** Peter H. Kahn, Jr., Rachel L. Severson, and Jolina H. Ruckert, "The Human Relation with Nature and Technological Nature," *Current Directions in Psychological Science* 18, no. 1 (2009): 37–42, doi.org/10.1111/ j.1467-8721.2009.01602.x.

143 **As Kahn reported** Peter H. Kahn, Jr., "Can Technology Replace Nature?," *Psychology Today,* June 13, 2011, www.psychologytoday.com/us/blog/ human-nature/201106/can-technology-replace-nature.

143 **German author** Alexander Pschera, *Animal Internet: Nature and the Digital Revolution,* trans. Elisabeth Lauffer (New York: New Vessel Press, 2016).

145 **Further, as** *Wired* Clive Thompson, "Tech Breakthroughs Are Giving Animals the Power to Speak," *Wired,* December 7, 2015, www.wired.com/ 2015/12/talking-animals/.

145 **Molecular biologist** Adriana Heguy, "If Dogs Understand Human Vocabulary What Are the Limits of Complexity in Human to Dog Communication?," Quora, August 31, 2016, www.quora.com/If-dogs-understand-human-vocabulary-what-are-the-limits-of-complexity-in-human-to-dog-communication.

145 **In one interview** "Interview with Alexander Pschera, Author of Animal Internet," New Vessel Press, April 11, 2016, newvesselpress.com/?s=Interview+ with+Alexander+Pschera/.

146 **Marine mammal behavioral** "Could We Speak the Language of Dolphins," TED, February 2013, www.ted.com/talks/denise_herzing_could_we_speak_ the_language_of_dolphins.

146 **Here on Earth** Diana Reiss, Peter Gabriel, Vint Cerf, and Neil Gershenfeld, "The Interspecies Internet? An Idea in Progress," TED, February 2013, www. ted.com/talks/the_interspecies_internet_an_idea_in_progress#t-1185692.

146 **It might sound** Jean-Loup Rault, "Pets in the Digital Age: Live, Robot, or Virtual?," *Frontiers in Veterinary Science* 2 (May 7, 2015), doi.org/10.3389/ fvets.2015.00011.

147 **The original product** "Hasbro Introduces Robot Dog to Comfort Aging Seniors, ABC Radio WTOP, October 4, 2016, wtop.com/health-fitness/2016/10/ hasbro-introduces-robot-dog-to-comfort-aging-seniors/.

148 **A Danish study** Karen Thodberg, Lisbeth U. Sørensen, Poul B. Videbech, Pia H. Poulsen, et al. "Behavioral Responses of Nursing Home Residents to Visits from a Person with a Dog, a Robot Seal or a Toy Cat," *Anthrozoös* 29, no. 1 (2016): 107–21.

148 **After comparing PARO**   Ruby Yu, E. Hui, D. Poon, A. Ng, et al. "Use
of a Therapeutic, Socially Assistive Pet Robot (PARO) in Improving Mood
and Stimulating Social Interaction and Communication for People with
Dementia: Study Protocol for a Randomized Controlled Trial," *JMIR
Research Protocols* 4, no. 2 (2015): e45, www.ncbi.nlm.nih.gov/pmc/articles/
PMC4433493/.

149 **In 2018**   Miwa Suzuki, "In Japan, Aibo Robots Get Their Own Funeral,"
Japan Times, May 1, 2018, www.japantimes.co.jp/news/2018/05/01/national/
japan-aibo-robots-get-funeral/#.XJUkc1VKiUk.

149 **In the Hunger Games**   Suzanne Collins, *The Hunger Games* (New York:
Scholastic, 2013).

149 **To film a 2017**   Esther Addley, "BBC Series Uses Robot Creatures to
Document Secret Lives of Animals," *Guardian*, December 31, 2016,
www.theguardian.com/media/2016/dec/31/
bbc-robot-creatures-spy-secret-lives-animals-wildlife-series.

150 **In the early 2000s**   Robin R. Murphy, "Marsupial and Shape-Shifting Robots
for Urban Search and Rescue," *IEEE Intelligent Systems* 15, no. 2 (2000):
14–19.

150 **Other institutions have**   April Glaser, "Robots Copy Their Coolest Moves
from Animals," *Recode*, May 28, 2017, www.recode.net/2017/5/28/15702270/
robots-imitate-animals-movement-snakebot-cheetah-rhex.

151 **When AI is combined**   Elizabeth Pennisi, "Robotic Stingray Powered by
Light-Activated Muscle Cells," *Science*, July 7, 2016, www.sciencemag.org/
news/2016/07/robotic-stingray-powered-light-activated-muscle-cells.

151 **Larry Hinman, founder**   His books include Lawrence M. Hinman, *Ethics:
A Pluralistic Approach to Moral Theory*, 5th ed. (Boston: Wadsworth, 2013).

153 **And, according to**   Hanna L. Tuomisto and M. Joost Teixeira De Mattos,
"Environmental Impacts of Cultured Meat Production," *Environmental Science
and Technology* 45, no. 14 (2011): 6117–23.

155 **In the 1970s**   Masahiro Mori, "The Uncanny Valley: The Original Essay
by Masahiro Mori," trans. Karl F. MacDorman and Norri Kageki, *IEEE
Spectrum*, June 12, 2012, spectrum.ieee.org/automaton/robotics/humanoids/
the-uncanny-valley.

156 **A year before**   Bob Randall, in the film *The Land Owns Us*, Global Oneness
Project, 2009, www.globalonenessproject.org/library/articles/land-owns-us.
The video can be viewed here: www.youtube.com/watch?v=w0sWIVR1hXw
&feature=youtu.be.

15. New Ways to Live Together

166 **The poet Rainer Maria Rilke**   Rainer Maria Rilke, *Rilke on Love and Other
Difficulties: Translations and Considerations*, reissue ed., trans. John J. L. Mood
(New York, W. W. Norton, 1994).

168 **Among the people**   Joanne Silberner, "What Is Climate Change Doing
to Our Mental Health?," Grist, July 31, 2014, grist.org/climate-energy/
what-is-climate-change-doing-to-our-mental-health/.

16. The Betweens

176 **There's always a bear**   Roslyn Frank, "Paul Shepard's 'Bear Essay': On Environmental Ethics, Deep Ecology and Our Need for the Other-Than-Human Animals, with a Preface and Commentary by Roslyn M. Frank," *Academia*, 2006, www.academia.edu/29619795/Paul_Shepards_Bear_Essay_On_Environmental_Ethics_Deep_Ecology_and_Our_Need_for_the_Other-than-Human_Animals.

178 **This brings to mind**   Oliver Milman, "Pedals the Bear, Known for Walking on Hind Legs, Apparently Killed by Hunters," *Guardian*, October 18, 2016, www.theguardian.com/us-news/2016/oct/18/pedals-upright-bear-appears-killed-new-jersey-hunting-season.

178 **In 2016**   Veronica Pacini-Ketchabaw and Fikile Nxumalo, "Unruly Raccoons and Troubled Educators: Nature/Culture Divides in a Childcare Centre," *Environmental Humanities* 7, no. 1 (2016): 151–68, doi.org/10.1215/22011919-3616380.

180 **These cohabitating children**   Donna J. Haraway, *When Species Meet* (Minneapolis: Minnesota University Press, 2007).

182 **And now, the Cook**   Stanley D. Gehrt, "Urban Coyote Ecology and Management," Cook County, Illinois, Coyote Project, Bulletin 29, November 2006, www.animalalliance.ca/wp-content/uploads/2016/01/gehrt_UrbanCoyoteManagement.pdf.

184 **To keep everyone**   "How to Avoid Conflicts with Coyotes," Urban Coyote Research, Cook County Urban Coyote Research Project, 2019, urbancoyoteresearch.com/coyote-info/how-avoid-conflicts-coyotes.

186 **Bears, raccoons, and coyotes**   Brandon Keim, "How City Living Is Reshaping the Brains and Behavior of Urban Animals," *Wired*, August 22, 2013, www.wired.com/2013/08/urban-animal-brain-behavior-evolution/.

186 **For example, the brains**   Emilie C. Snell-Rood and Naomi Wick, "Anthropogenic Environments Exert Variable Selection on Cranial Capacity in Mammals," *Proceedings of the Royal Society B: Biological Sciences* 280, no. 1769 (October 2013), doi.org/10.1098/rspb.2013.1384.

187 **Russian biologists bred**   Lyudmila Trut, Irina Oskina, and Anastasiya Kharlamova, "Animal Evolution during Domestication: the Domesticated Fox as a Model," *BioEssays* 31, no. 3 (2009): 349–60.

187 **Normally you think**   Brian Hare, Victoria Wobber, and Richard Wrangham, "The Self-Domestication Hypothesis: Evolution of Bonobo Psychology Is Due to Selection against Aggression,"*Animal Behaviour* 83, no. 3 (2012): 573–85.

187 **Researchers in Tanzania**   Kaitlyn M. Gaynor, Cheryl E. Hojnowski, Neil H. Carter, and Justin S. Brashares, "The Influence of Human Disturbance on Wildlife Nocturnality," *Science* 360, no. 6394 (2018): 1232–35.

17. Welcome to Symbiocene City

191 **In Angers**   "Activities: Lac De Maine Theme Park—A Protected Environment," Parc De Loisirs Du Lac De Maine, www.lacdemaine.fr/en/the-lac-de-maine-theme-park-angers-n-activities-in-protected-environment-p15.html.

191 **Daniel Raven-Ellison** Hannah Fearn, "Welcome to the UK's Latest National Park... London," *Guardian*, April 28, 2015, www.theguardian.com/ sustainable-business/2015/apr/28/rebranding-london-as-an-urban-park-city- to-reconnect-with-nature.

194 **The Nature Conservancy reports** Justine E. Hausheer, "Species on the Move: Mapping Barriers for Wildlife in a Warming World," *Cool Green Science*, June 29, 2016, blog.nature.org/science/2016/06/29/ species-on-the-move-mapping-barriers-for-wildlife-in-a-warming-world/.

195 **In fact, in** "How City-Dwelling Leopards Improve Human Health," *National Geographic*, March 9, 2018, news.nationalgeographic.com/2018/03/ mumbai-leopards-sanjay-gandhi-national-park-stray-dogs-rabies-spd/.

196 **Mother Nature Network's** Laura Moss, "Commuting Critters: Animals That Ride Public Transportation," Mother Nature Network, June 5, 2017, www.mnn.com/green-tech/transportation/stories/ commuting-critters-animals-that-ride-public-transportation.

196 **Seattle, not to be** Lindsay Cohen,"Seattle Dog's Rush Hour Ride: On the Bus, by Herself, Weekly," KOMO, komonews.com/news/local/ seattle-dogs-rush-hour-ride-on-the-bus-by-herself-weekly-11-21-2015.

197 **Animal rescue organizations** Eric McLamb, "Real Ecology: Born in the Streets: The Global Impact of Feral Cats," *Ecology Global Network*, August 27, 2013, www.ecology.com/2013/08/27/global-impact-feral-cats/.

197 **Along with free-range** John Woinarski, Brett Murphy, Leigh-Ann Woolley, Sarah Legge, et al., "For Whom the Bell Tolls: Cats Kill More than a Million Australian Birds Every Day," Conversation, November 29, 2018, theconversation.com/for-whom-the-bell-tolls-cats-kill-more-than-a-million- australian-birds-every-day-85084.

199 **"While the elephants** Orion McCarthy, "8 Creative Ways to Reduce Human-Wildlife Conflict," *Conserve*, December 4, 2015, howtoconserve. org/2015/12/04/human-wildlife-conflict/.

201 **As described by** Ronald M. Atlas and Stanley Maloy, *One Health: People, Animals, and the Environment* (Washington, DC: ASM Press, 2014).

201 **In 2013** Barbara Natterson-Horowitz and Kathryn Bowers, *Zoobiquity* (New York: Alfred A. Knopf, 2012).

201 **For example, the CDC** "Lead Poisoning Investigation in Northern Nigeria," One Health, Centers for Disease Control and Prevention, October 25, 2016, www.cdc.gov/onehealth/in-action/lead-poisoning.html.

201 **The agency also** "Poisoned Sea Otters in California: Mystery in California," One Health, Centers for Disease Control and Prevention, April 12, 2017, www. cdc.gov/onehealth/in-action/poisoned-sea-otters.html.

202 **Also, the West Nile** "West Nile Virus," Centers for Disease Control and Prevention, www.cdc.gov/westnile/dead-birds/.

204 **As Bob Randall** *The Land Owns Us*, Global Oneness Project, 2009, www.globalonenessproject.org/library/articles/land-owns-us. The video can be viewed here: www.youtube.com/watch?v=w0sWIVR1hXw&feature =youtu.be.

18. The New Noahs

208 **What's next**   Joanne Vining, "The Connection to Other Animals and Caring for Nature," *Human Ecology Review* 10 (December 1, 2003), www.researchgate .net/publication/228463530_The_Connection_to_Other_Animals_and_ Caring_for_Nature.

208 **At the San Diego**   Roger Showley, "$30M Record Gift Will Jumpstart a New Children's Zoo, Opening in 2021," *San Diego Union-Tribune*, January 13, 2018, www.sandiegouniontribune.com/business/growth-development/sd-fi-childrenszoo-20180110-story.html.

213 **And then there's**   Michael Larsen, "Zealandia: The World's First Fully-fenced Urban Ecosanctuary," AA Traveller, November 28, 2016, www.aa.co.nz/ travel/must-dos/zealandia-the-worlds-first-fully-fenced-urban-ecosanctuary/. See also Zealandia's official website, www.visitzealandia.com/.

215 **An estimated one thousand**   Jessica Aldred, "More than 1,000 Species Have Been Moved Due to Human Impact," *Guardian*, April 20, 2016, www.theguardian.com/environment/2016/apr/20/more-than-1000-species-have-been-moved-due-to-human-impact.

216 **Imagine the effects**   Sean Gerrity, "Interview: An Abundance of Rarity, Prairies and Beyond," *American Prairie Reserve*, February 28, 2013, www.americanprairie.org/news-blog/interview-abundance-rarity-prairies-and-beyond.

216 **Across the Pacific**   Ross Andersen, "Welcome to Pleistocene Park," *Atlantic*, April 2017, www.theatlantic.com/magazine/archive/2017/04/ pleistocene-park/517779/.

216 **Currently the park**   Michael Irving, "Welcome to Pleistocene Park: The mammoth plan to recreate an ice age ecosystem in Siberia," New Atlas, April 20, 2018, newatlas.com/pleistocene-park-mammoth-ecosystem/54257/.

217 **The park team**   Mindy Weisberger, "Russian Scientists Hope to Restore Ice Age Steppe with 'Pleistocene Park.' Will It Work?," Live Science, December 20, 2018, www.livescience.com/64340-pleistocene-park-progress.html.

217 **One expression**   Sarah Bezan, "Regenesis Aesthetics: Visualizing the Woolly Mammoth in De-Extinction Science," Leeds Animal Studies Network, January 30, 2019, leedsanimalstudiesnetwork.wordpress.com/2019/01/30/ lasn-seminar-13-feb-dr-sarah-bezan-regenesis-aesthetics-visualizing-the-woolly-mammoth-in-de-extinction-science; Sarah Pruitt, "Are Scientists on the Verge of Resurrecting the Woolly Mammoth?," January 22, 2019, www.history.com/news/wooly-mammoth-resurrection-cloning-genesis.

217 **Dinerstein views such**   Eric Dinerstein, David Olson, Anup Joshi, Carly Vynne, et al., "An Ecoregion-Based Approach to Protecting Half the Terrestrial Realm," *Bioscience* 67, no. 6 (2017): 534–45.

218 **He reports that**   Edward O. Wilson, *Half-Earth: Our Planet's Fight for Life* (New York: Liveright, 2017).

219 **Kim Stanley Robinson**   Kim Stanley Robinson, "Empty Half the Earth of Its Humans. It's the Only Way to Save the Planet," *Guardian*, March 20, 2018, www.theguardian.com/cities/2018/mar/20/save-the-planet-half-earth-kim-stanley-robinson.

19. Dreaming Animals

225 **What you call** Ovide Mercredi, speech delivered at the Wildlife Society 22nd Annual Conference, Winnipeg, 2015.

226 **This openness** Willett Kempton, James S. Boster, and Jennifer A. Hartley, *Envnironmental Value in American Culture* (Cambridge, MA: MIT Press, 1997).

229 **Jay Griffiths's book** Jay Griffiths, *Kith: The Riddle of the Childscape* (London: Penguin Books, 2014).

230 **Christopher Moreman** Christopher M. Moreman, "On the Relationship between Birds and Spirits of the Dead," *Society & Animals* 22, no. 5 (2014): 481–502.

233 **In *Ravensong*** Catherine Feher-Elston, *Ravensong: A Natural and Fabulous History of Ravens and Crows* (Flagstaff, AZ: Northland, 1991).

233 **Lawrence Kilham** Interview quoted in ibid. Kilham's classic book on crows and ravens is Lawrence Kilham, *The American Crow and the Common Raven* (College Station: Texas A&M University Press, 1989).

234 **A local crow** Feher-Elston, *Ravensong*.

239 **Researchers at Claremont** Piercarlo Valdesolo and Jesse Graham,"Awe, Uncertainty, and Agency Detection," *Psychological Science* 25, no. 1 (2013): 170–78.

239 **We "fall in love** Robinson Jeffers, "The Tower beyond Tragedy," "*Tamar" and Other Poems* (Peter G. Boyle, 1924).

239 **In other writing** Robinson Jeffers, *Themes in My Poems*, limited ed. (San Francisco: Book Club of California, 1956).

240 **In 2014** Rick Gladstone, "Dogs in Heaven? Pope Francis Leaves Pearly Gates Open," *New York Times*, December 11, 2014, www.nytimes.com/2014/12/12/world/europe/dogs-in-heaven-pope-leaves-pearly-gate-open.html?module=Search&mabReward=relbias:r,%7B%221%22:%22RI:6%22%7D&_r=1&assetType=nyt_now.

240 **But then** Pope Francis, *Laudato si'*, Encyclical Letter of the Holy Father, Francis, on Care for Our Common Home, May 24, 2015, Libreria Editrice Vaticana, w2.vatican.va/content/francesco/en/encyclicals/documents/papa-francesco_20150524_enciclica-laudato-si.html; Philip Almond, "Endorsing the Salvation of Animals, Pope Warns of Earth's End," Conversation, July 3, 2015, theconversation.com/endorsing-the-salvation-of-animals-pope-warns-of-earths-end-43715.

243 **The next day** Richard Louv, *The Web of Life: Weaving the Values That Sustain Us* (Berkeley, CA: Conari Press, 1996).

20. The Peaceable Kingdom

244 **For the 2015** "Internet Cat Video Festival 2015," Walker Art Center, August 12, 2015, St. Paul, MN, walkerart.org/calendar/2015/internet-cat-video-festival-2015.

244 **In the movie *Ghostbusters*** For the full rhetorical impact, see the *Ghostbusters* clip on YouTube, www.youtube.com/watch?v=O3ZOKDmorj0.

245 **Not so for** Erica Goode, "Learning from Animal Friendships," *New York Times*, January 26, 2015, www.nytimes.com/2015/01/27/science/so-happy-together.html.

245 **Professor emerita Barbara** Ibid.

245 **Farmer and poet** Wendell Berry, *The Unsettling of America: Culture & Agriculture* (Berkeley, CA: Counterpoint, 2015).

248 **Dr. Nooshin Razani** Richard Louv, "Outdoors for All," *Sierra*, May 7, 2019.

249 **The American author** Ken Ilgunas, *This Land Is Our Land: How We Lost the Right to Roam and How to Take It Back* (New York: Plume, 2018).

250 **Thomas Berry believed** Thomas Berry, *The Great Work: Our Way into the Future* (New York: Bell Tower, 2000).

21. Learning and Teaching in a School of Animals

253 **But David Sobel** David Sobel, *Beyond Ecophobia: Reclaiming the Heart in Nature Education* (Great Barrington, MA: Orion Society, 2013).

254 **The care inspectorate's** "Animal Magic: The Benefits of Being Around and Caring for Animals Across Care Settings," Care Inspectorate, 2018, hub. careinspectorate.com/media/761407/animal-magic.pdf.

256 **Years ago, Orr** David W. Orr and Fritjof Capra, *Hope Is an Imperative: The Essential David Orr* (Washington, DC: Island Press, 2011).

258 **In 2017** Julie Depenbrock, "At 'Nature Preschools,' Classes Are Outdoors," *Education Week*, January 17, 2017, www.edweek.org/ew/articles/2017/01/18/ at-nature-preschools-classes-are-outdoors.html.

258 **Natural learning environments** Wild Sanctuary, www.wildsanctuary .com/; interviews with the author.

259 **Bacteria reproduce** Tia Ghose, "What Species Rules Earth? The Answer May Surprise You," Live Science, July 18, 2014, www.livescience.com/46866- planet-apes-next-dominant-species.html.

261 **In January 2018** Barry Rosenstein and Anne Sheehan, "Open Letter from JANA Partners And CALSTRS to Apple Inc," January 6, 2018, reprinted by Sacred Heart, Greenwich, Greenwich, CT, schoolpress.cshgreenwich.org/ cshmsparents/2018/01/15/open-letter-from-jana-partners-and-calstrs-to- apple-inc/.

261 **One study demonstrated** Yalda T. Uhls, Minas Michikyan, Jordan Morris, Debra Garcia, et al., "Five Days at Outdoor Education Camp without Screens Improves Preteen Skills with Nonverbal Emotion Cues," *Computers in Human Behavior* 39 (2014): 387–92.

263 **In 2017** Doug Anderson, Lorraine Chiarotto, and Julie Comay, *Natural Curiosity: A Resource for Educators—Considering Indigenous Perspectives in Children's Environmental Inquiry*, 2nd ed. (Toronto: Ontario Institute for Studies in Education, 2017).

264 **In *Natural Curiosity*** Ibid.

22. The Bear

267 **Tia Ghose, writing** Tia Ghose, "Hugging Lions? Why Humans Are Drawn to Wild Animals," Live Science, February 5, 2014, www.livescience.com/43120-why-humans-seek-wild-animals.html.

267 **As Dayton told** Paul Shepard and Barry Sanders, *The Sacred Paw: The Bear in Nature, Myth, and Literature* (New York: Arkana, 1992).

267 **The bear strikes** Ibid.

268 **Polar bears, it is** "Indigenous People and Polar Bears," Polar Bears International, polarbearsinternational.org/polar-bears/indigenous-people-polar-bears/.

268 **Some Indigenous people** "Indigenous People & Polar Bears," Polar Bears International, polarbearsinternational.org/polar-bears/indigenous-people-polar-bears/; "What Is Climate Change?," polarbearsinternational.org/climate-change/what-is-climate-change/.

272 **His most famous** Paul Shepard, *Coming Home to the Pleistocene* (Washington, DC: Island Press, 1998).

272 **Thomas Berry reminded** Ervin Laszlo and Allan Combs, eds., *Thomas Berry: Dreamer of the Earth: The Spiritual Ecology of the Father of Environmentalism* (Rochester, VT: Inner Traditions, 2011).

273 **We probably have not had** Thomas Berry, *The Great Work: Our Way into the Future* (New York: Bell Tower, 2000).

SUGGESTED READING

Abram, David. *Becoming Animal: An Earthly Cosmology*. New York: Pantheon Books, 2010.

Ackerman, Diane. *The Human Age: The World Shaped by Us*. New York: W. W. Norton, 2014.

Akomolafe, Bayo. *These Wilds beyond Our Fences: Letters to My Daughter on Humanity's Search for Home*. Berkeley, CA: North Atlantic Books, 2017.

Albrecht, Glenn. *Earth Emotions: New Words for a New World*. Ithaca, NY: Cornell University Press, 2019.

Anderson, Doug, Lorraine Chiarotto, and Julie Comay. *Natural Curiosity: A Resource for Educators—Considering Indigenous Perspectives in Children's Environmental Inquiry, 2nd Edition*. Toronto: Ontario Institute for Studies in Education, 2017.

Arvay, Clemens G. *The Healing Code of Nature: Discovering the New Science of Eco-Psychosomatics*. Boulder, CO: Sounds True, 2018.

Bailey, Elisabeth Tova. *The Sound of a Wild Snail Eating*. Chapel Hill, NC: Algonquin Books, 2016.

Bekoff, Marc. *Rewilding Our Hearts: Building Pathways of Compassion and Coexistence*. Novato, CA: New World Library, 2014.

Bekoff, Marc, and Jessica Pierce. *Unleashing Your Dog: A Field Guide to Giving Your Canine Companion the Best Life Possible*. Novato, CA: New World Library, 2019.

Berger, John. *About Looking*. New York: Pantheon Books, 1980.

Berry, Thomas. *The Dream of the Earth*. Berkeley, CA: Counterpoint Press, 2015.

———. *The Great Work: Our Way into the Future*. New York: Bell Tower, 2000.

Brown, Stuart L., and Christopher C. Vaughan. *Play: How It Shapes the Brain, Opens the Imagination, and Invigorates the Soul*. New York: Avery, 2010.

Buber, Martin. *I and Thou*. New York: Scribner, 1958.

Burghardt, Gordon M. *Genesis of Animal Play: Testing the Limits*. Cambridge, MA: MIT Press, 2006.

Carson, Rachel. *Under the Sea-Wind*. New York: Penguin Books, 1996.

Casey, Susan. *Voices in the Ocean: A Journey into the Wild and Haunting World of Dolphins*. New York: Doubleday, 2015.

Cerulli, Tovar. *The Mindful Carnivore: A Vegetarian's Hunt for Sustenance*. New York: Pegasus Books, 2012.

Childs, Craig. *The Animal Dialogues: Uncommon Encounters in the Wild.* New York: Back Bay Books, 2007.

Dinerstein, Eric. *Kingdom of Rarities.* Washington, DC: Island Press, 2013.

——. *Return of the Unicorns: The Natural History and Conservation of the Greater One-Horned Rhinoceros.* New York: Columbia University Press, 2016.

Feher-Elston, Catherine. *Ravensong: A Natural and Fabulous History of Ravens and Crows.* Flagstaff, AZ: Northland, 1991.

Fraser, Caroline. *Rewilding the World: Dispatches from the Conservation Revolution.* New York: Metropolitan Books, 2009.

Godfrey-Smith, Peter. *Other Minds: The Octopus, the Sea, and the Deep Origins of Consciousness.* New York: Farrar, Straus & Giroux, 2016.

Grandin, Temple, and Catherine Johnson. *Animals Make Us Human: Creating the Best Life for Animals.* Boston: Houghton Mifflin Harcourt, 2009.

Greene, Harry Walter, and Michael Fogden. *Snakes: The Evolution of Mystery in Nature.* Berkeley: University of California Press, 1997.

Griffiths, Jay. *A Country Called Childhood: Children and the Exuberant World.* Berkeley, CA: Counterpoint, 2015 (also published in the United Kingdom under the title *Kith: The Riddle of the Childscape* [London: Penguin Books, 2014]).

——. *Wild.* London: Penguin, 2008.

Kahn, Peter H., Jr. *Technological Nature: Adaptation and the Future of Human Life.* Cambridge, MA: MIT Press, 2011.

Kahn, Peter H., Jr., and Patricia H. Hasbach. *Ecopsychology Science, Totems, and the Technological Species.* Cambridge, MA: MIT Press, 2012.

Kolbert, Elizabeth. *The Sixth Extinction: an Unnatural History.* New York: Henry Holt and Company, 2014.

Krause, Bernie. *Wild Soundscapes: Discovering the Voice of the Natural World.* New Haven, CT: Yale University Press, 2016.

Leopold, Aldo. *Sand County Almanac and Sketches Here and There.* Oxford: Oxford University Press, 1972.

Long, William J. *How Animals Talk: And Other Pleasant Studies of Birds and Beasts.* Rochester, VT: Bear, 2005.

Louv, Jason. *John Dee and the Empire of Angels: Enochian Magick and the Occult Roots of the Modern World.* Rochester, VT: Inner Traditions, 2018.

Malone, Thomas Patrick, and Patrick Thomas Malone. *The Art of Intimacy.* New York: Simon & Schuster, 1992.

Maslow, Abraham H. *Toward a Psychology of Being.* New York: Van Nostrand Reinhold, 1968.

McConnell, Patricia. *The Other End of the Leash: Why We Do What We Do around Dogs.* New York: Random House, 2002.

McGinnis, Michael Vincent. *Science and Sensibility: Negotiating an Ecology of Place.* Oakland: University of California Press, 2016.

Mercredi, Ovide. *My Silent Dream*. Winnipeg: Aboriginal Issues Press, 2015.

Mercredi, Ovide, and Mary Ellen Turpel. *In the Rapids: Navigating the Future of First Nations*. New York: Penguin, 1994.

Monbiot, George. *Feral: Searching for Enchantment on the Frontiers of Rewilding*. London: Penguin, 2013.

Natterson-Horowitz, Barbara, and Kathryn Bowers. *Zoobiquity*. New York: Alfred A. Knopf, 2012.

O'Dell, Scott. *Island of the Blue Dolphins*. New York: Dell, 1960.

Orr, David W., and Fritjof Capra. *Hope Is an Imperative: The Essential David Orr*. Washington, DC: Island Press, 2011.

Plotkin, Bill. *Soulcraft: Crossing into the Mysteries of Nature and Psyche*. Novato, CA: New World Library, 2003.

Pschera, Alexander. *Animal Internet: Nature and the Digital Revolution*. Translated by Elisabeth Lauffer. New York: New Vessel Press, 2016.

Ross, Andrew. *Bird on Fire: Lessons from the World's Least Sustainable City*. Oxford: Oxford University Press, 2013.

Safina, Carl. *Beyond Words: What Animals Think and Feel*. London: Souvenir Press, 2018.

Schoen, Allen M. *Kindred Spirits: How the Remarkable Bond between Humans and Animals Can Change the Way We Live*. New York: Broadway Books, 2001.

Selly, Patty Born. *Connecting Animals and Children in Early Childhood*. St. Paul, MN: Redleaf Press, 2014.

Serpell, James. *In the Company of Animals: A Study of Human-Animal Relationships*. Cambridge: Cambridge University Press, 2014.

Shepard, Paul. *Coming Home to the Pleistocene*. Edited by Florence R. Shepard. Washington, DC: Island Press, 2013.

———. *The Others: How Animals Made Us Human*. Washington, DC: Island Press, 1997.

Shepard, Paul, and Barry Sanders. *The Sacred Paw: The Bear in Nature, Myth, and Literature*. New York: Arkana, 1992.

Shipman, Pat. *The Animal Connection: A New Perspective on What Makes Us Human*. New York: W. W. Norton, 2011.

Stamets, Paul. *Mycelium Running: How Mushrooms Can Help Save the World*. Emeryville, CA: Ten Speed Press, 2005.

Steinbeck, John. *The Log from the* Sea of Cortez: *The Narrative Portion of the Book,* Sea of Cortez *(1941), by John Steinbeck and E. F. Ricketts*. New York: Penguin Books, 1986.

Sterba, Jim. *Nature Wars: The Incredible Story of How Wildlife Comebacks Turned Backyards into Battlegrounds*. New York: Crown, 2013.

Stuckey, Priscilla. *Kissed by a Fox: And Other Stories of Friendship in Nature*. Berkeley, CA: Counterpoint, 2012.

Swimme, Brian, and Thomas Berry. *The Universe Story from the Primordial Flaring Forth to the Ecozoic Era.* San Francisco: HarperSanFrancisco, 1992.

Tedeschi, Philip. *Transforming Trauma: Resilience and Healing through Our Connections with Animals.* West Lafayette, IN: Purdue University Press, 2019.

Toben, Carolyn W. *Recovering a Sense of the Sacred: Conversations with Thomas Berry.* Whitsett, NC: Timberlake Earth Sanctuary Press, 2012.

Weber, Andreas. *The Biology of Wonder: Aliveness, Feeling, and the Metamorphosis of Science.* Gabriola Island, BC: New Society Publishers, 2016.

Williams, Marta. *Learning Their Language: Intuitive Communication with Animals and Nature.* Novato, CA: New World Library, 2003.

Wilson, Edward O. *Half-Earth: Our Planet's Fight for Life.* New York: Liveright, 2017.

Young, Jon, and Dan Gardoqui. *What the Robin Knows: How Birds Reveal the Secrets of the Natural World.* Wilmington, NC: Mariner Books, 2012.

Young, Jon, Ellen Haas, and Evan McGown. *Coyote's Guide to Connecting with Nature.* Shelton, WA: OWLink Media, 2010.

Online Resources

For a list of journals devoted to human-animal studies, see Animals & Society Institute, www.animalsandsociety.org/human-animal-studies/human-animal-studies-journals/.

For a list of academic programs related to human-animal studies, see Animals & Society Institute, www.animalsandsociety.org/human-animal-studies/degree-programs/.

For more on human development and the natural world, see the Children & Nature Network Research Library, www.childrenandnature.org/learn/research/.

For information on organizations helping wild and domesticated animals, and other connection resources, visit www.richardlouv.com.

INDEX